Schooling in the ASEAN Region

PRIMARY AND SECONDARY EDUCATION IN INDONESIA, MALAYSIA, THE PHILIPPINES, SINGAPORE, AND THAILAND

Schooling in the ASEAN Region

PRIMARY AND SECONDARY EDUCATION IN INDONESIA,
MALAYSIA, THE PHILIPPINES, SINGAPORE, AND THAILAND

Edited by

T. NEVILLE POSTLETHWAITE
University of Hamburg

and

R. MURRAY THOMAS
University of California, Santa Barbara

PERGAMON PRESS
OXFORD • NEW YORK • TORONTO • SYDNEY • PARIS • FRANKFURT

UK	Pergamon Press Ltd., Headington Hill Hall, Oxford OX3 0BW, England
USA	Pergamon Press Inc., Maxwell House, Fairview Park, Elmsford, New York 10523, USA
CANADA	Pergamon of Canada, Suite 104, 150 Consumers Road, Willowdale, Ontario M2J 1P9, Canada
AUSTRALIA	Pergamon Press (Aust.) Pty. Ltd., P.O. Box 544, Potts Point, NSW 2011, Australia
FRANCE	Pergamon Press SARL, 24 rue des Ecoles, 75240 Paris, Cedex 05, France
FEDERAL REPUBLIC OF GERMANY	Pergamon Press GmbH, 6242 Kronberg-Taunus, Hammerweg 6, Federal Republic of Germany

First edition 1980

British Library Cataloguing in Publication Data

Schooling in the ASEAN region.
1. Education, Elementary — Asia, Southeastern
2. Comparative education
3. Education, Secondary — Asia, Southeastern
I. Postlethwaite, T Neville
II. Thomas, R Murray
372.9'59   LA1059.S6   79-41357

ISBN 0-08-024289-8

Printed in Great Britain by A. Wheaton & Co. Ltd, Exeter

Contents

Preface   xi

List of Illustrations   ix

1   Ways to View Schooling in ASEAN Countries
by R. Murray Thomas and T. Neville Postlethwaite

The Aims of Schooling   3

The Structure and Process of Schooling   14

Cooperative Educational Ventures in the ASEAN Region   42

References   45

2   Indonesia
by Soedijarto, Lexy Moleong, A. Suryadi, Darlis Machmud,
F. Pangemanan, A. F. Tangyong, N. Nasoetion, and R. Murray Thomas

Out of Diversity – One People, One Country, One Language   49

The Government and Its Development Plans   53

Governance of the Islands – The Historical Background   57

The Evolution of Schooling in Indonesia   59

Formal Schooling in the 1970s – Problems and Solutions   69

Nonformal Education   80

The Research and Development Center   83

Improving Administrative Efficiency   86

Improving the Supply of Teachers   89

Future Problems and Prospects   92

References   95

Contents

3   Malaysia
by Arfah A. Aziz and Chew Tow Yow

The Country's Geography and Ethnic Groups	98
The Education System	105
Present School Structure and Enrollment	110
Administrative Structure	118
Curriculum	125
Examinations	132
Teacher Education	135
Problems and Priorities	140
References	143

4   The Philippines
by Josefina R. Cortes

The Islands and the People	146
The Economy and Education	148
Governance of the Philippines, Past and Present	150
The Historical Roots of Today's Schools	151
The Formal School System Today	158
Roles for Nonformal Education	160
The Administrative Structure of Schooling	162
Trends in Curriculum Development	164
Evaluating, Promoting, and Certifying Students	168
Supplying Teachers for the Schools	169
The Future of Schooling in the Philippines – Plans and Problems	172
Conclusion	177
References	177

5 Singapore
by R. Murray Thomas, Goh Kim Leong, and R. W. Mosbergen

Raffles and British Colonialism	184
The Origins of the Education System	187
The Modern School System (1959–1979) – Goals and Structure	195
The Contributions of Nonformal Education	209
Administrative Efficiency	211
Approaches to Curriculum Development	213
Teacher Education	214
Problems and Prospects for the Future	216
References	220

6 Thailand
by Chalio Buripakdi and Pratern Mahakhan

Land of the Free	224
The Education System	230
Present School Structure and Enrollment	236
Administrative Structure	244
Curriculum	251
Examinations	256
Teacher Preparation	257
Problems and Priorities	259
Conclusion	270
References	271

7 The Future
by T. Neville Postlethwaite and R. Murray Thomas

Expanding Elementary and Secondary Education	274
Qualitative Improvement of Education	278
Achieving a More Effective Structure for Education	284

Contents

Increasing Administrative Efficiency   305

Improving the Teacher-Supply System   311

Intercountry Cooperation   317

Postscript   320

References   321

Index   323

List of Illustrations

Maps

1	The ASEAN Region	xvii
2	Indonesia	47
3	Malaysia	97
4	The Philippines	144
5	Singapore	180
6	Thailand	222

Figures

2.1 Trends in import–export balance 1969–1976 — 55

2.2 Primary and secondary school system – 1970s — 68

2.3 Hierarchy of policy-making and administrative authority in Indonesian education — 87

3.1 Organization chart of formal system of education — 111

Preface

THE FOCUS of this volume is on the current condition and background of primary and secondary education in the countries that form the Association for Southeast Asian Nations (ASEAN) — Indonesia, Malaysia, the Philippines, Singapore, and Thailand. Our chief concern is to provide a description of present-day schooling in each nation separately. However, we are interested as well in cooperative efforts of the five ASEAN governments to pursue goals they hold in common.

The first of the seven chapters offers an overview of the main themes found in the next five chapters that treat each ASEAN country independently. The final chapter summarizes key points from the preceding five and offers estimates about what conditions may be expected in the years ahead for elementary and secondary schooling in the ASEAN region.

This book is actually a reaction to a complaint. The complaint has been that there is no concise yet relatively comprehensive and systematic description of education in the ASEAN countries.

By *relatively comprehensive* we mean a description not only of the formal elementary and secondary schools but also of nonformal education efforts and such support systems as the administrative and teacher-education structures. The term *comprehensive* encompasses as well the historical antecedents of present-day schools and the political-economic setting in which the education system operates. Other books about education in the region, such as Wong's *Teacher Education in ASEAN,* are useful but not comprehensive in the above sense.

By *systematic* we mean that the educational efforts of one country are described according to the same scheme as that applied to the others. Journal articles and books about education in Asian nations have suffered from the lack of a common system. In the same issue of a journal, an author writing about one country has focused on different aspects of education than those featured by authors writing about other countries. (*Asian Profile,* 1977.) As a result, it has been impossible to compare the various nations across the same dimensions. So to meet this complaint about unsystematic descriptions, the authors of the present volume have all based their descriptions on the same scheme. Thus, the effects on education of a nation's geography, religions, and ethnic patterns are described for each of the five societies. Likewise, information on the administrative organization, numbers of schools, rates of literacy, the holding power of schools, current innovative programs, and the like are provided for each country.

In sum *Schooling in the ASEAN Region* has been structured as the sort of compressed overview that appears to be sought by university students of international and comparative education and by personnel in foreign-aid agencies that deal with ASEAN nations.

The descriptive framework on which the five country chapters have been constructed reflects a series of convictions held by the editors about ASEAN countries. Although an examination of the country chapters will reveal the nature of these convictions, it may be useful for readers to be apprised of three of them beforehand.

First is the obvious observation that the high population growth rate in the four largest ASEAN nations (Singapore excepted) poses some of the countries' most serious educational problems. While educators have their hands more than full in trying to furnish enough facilities to educate today's population, the nations' high birth rates coupled with lowering death rates bring each year ever-increasing numbers of children to the school door. Educational planners are thus forced into the frustrating role of pursuing a retreating horizon. Consider, for instance, Indonesia, with an estimated population in 1980 of 145 million and likely to reach 200 million by 1992. The goal of Indonesia's educational planners has been to provide enough facilities to accommodate 85 percent of the school-age population by 1980. Reaching this goal can be difficult indeed. But how much greater the task will be to accommodate 100 percent — or even 75 percent — of school-age children by the year 2000. In effect, population growth is a crucial factor in ASEAN nations' educational progress.

A second conviction is that even successful attempts to furnish large quantities of schooling – education for everyone – may do nothing to improve the relevance or quality of education. A nation's socioeconomic development plan is hardly helped by a work force of graduates schooled in things irrelevant to the development program's requirements. And even if the curriculum is geared to the needs of socioeconomic development, national progress is unlikely to result if teaching methods in the schools and nonformal programs are so ineffective that students fail to learn what they are expected to master. In the 1950s and 1960s the major emphasis in ASEAN countries was on increasing the quantity of education – getting more students into schools or nonformal programs. However, in the 1970s more attention was centered on improving the quality of education. Examples of projects emphasizing quality are included in the five country chapters, Chapters 2 through 6.

A third conviction is that political events in Southeast Asia will continue to exert a strong influence on educational affairs. Over the past decade-and-a-half the five ASEAN members have nervously monitored the social turmoil and war in the neighboring countries of Vietnam, Laos, and Cambodia. Thailand, in particular, has been affected by the Indochina conflicts, since there have been periodic penetrations into Thai northern territories from across the borders that surround the nation's northern sector. Not only has the conduct of schools been influenced by armed intrusions, but the matter of maintaining national unity and the fidelity of the northern provinces to the central Thai government has posed problems for teaching political doctrine in the schools. In Indonesia, the attempted coup in late 1965 precipitated internal battles that resulted in the replacement of the Sukarno government, the outlawing of the Indonesian Communist Party, and the disruption of education for nearly a year. In Malaysia, the racial riots of 1969 strongly affected the direction and pace of development of the school system. And we are convinced that education in ASEAN countries in the future will be no less affected by political events in the region.

As a final prefatory note, we identify the affiliations of the authors of *Schooling in the ASEAN Region.* In keeping with the book's international character, the authors represent international diversity. The first and last chapters have been written by the two editors. T. Neville Postlethwaite, an Englishman with a Swedish doctorate, is professor of education at the University of Hamburg and chairman of the Department of Comparative Education. He is also chairman of the International Association for the Evaluation of Educational Achievement. R. Murray Thomas is a University of California professor of education with three decades of educational experience in the Pacific Islands and Southeast Asia. He directs the program in International Education at the University of California's Santa Barbara campus.

The two editors met five years ago in Indonesia while serving as consultants to the Indonesian Ministry of Education. The fact that they found themselves so frequently asked to furnish information about the Indonesian educational system to foreigners from multilateral and bilateral aid agencies was a further impetus to their motivation for organizing such a book as this.

The senior author of Chapter 2 on Indonesia is Soedijarto, chief of the curriculum-development division of the Center for Research and Development of the Indonesian Ministry of Education and Culture. In addition to his Indonesian academic degrees, he holds an M.A. in International Education from the University of California, Santa Barbara. His coauthors are all specialists in the Center for Research and Development. Lexy Moleong is head of the section on curriculum development for teacher education and higher education, and he holds an M.A. from Stanford University in the U.S.A. A. Suryadi is on the research staff of the Educational Innovation and Technology division of the Center, specializing in community education. Darlis Machmud, whose Indonesian degrees are in the field of philosophy, is on the curriculum-development staff, with principal responsibility in the areas of social studies and philosophy. F. Pangemanan is an experienced teacher serving as a senior staff member in curriculum development for elementary schools. A. F. Tangyong heads the section on curriculum research for elementary schools, special education, and preschool education. In addition to Indonesian degrees, he holds an M.A. from Teachers College, Columbia University, in educational administration and another from Stanford University in curriculum development and its economic implications. Noehi Nasoetion directs the division of educational research, as well as the national evaluation team for the Development-School Project described in Chapter 2. He holds an M.A. from Stanford.

The senior author of Chapter 3 on Malaysia is Dr Arfah A. Aziz, assistant director and head of the evaluation and research unit of the Malaysian

Ministry of Education's Curriculum Development Centre. In addition to Malaysian degrees, she has a M.Ed. from Canada (Toronto) and a doctorate from the University of California at Berkeley. Her coauthor, Chew Tow Yow of the Ministry of Education staff, is currently completing doctoral studies at the University of Malaya in Kuala Lumpur. He was formerly deputy director of the Curriculum Development Centre and now is principal officer in the teacher-training division of the Ministry.

Dr Josefina R. Cortes, who prepared Chapter 4 on the Philippines, is a professor of educational administration at the University of the Philippines in Quezon City. She earned a doctorate at Stanford University and now teaches courses in educational planning, administration, research methods, and the relationship of education to national development. She has had extensive experience as a planner and evaluator of research and development projects in the fields of education and of manpower production.

The coauthors of Chapter 4 include two officials of the Singapore education system. Goh Kim Leong heads the Planning and Review Division, while R. W. Mosbergen is the deputy director in charge of academic affairs in the Institute of Education. Mr Goh also served as secretary of the Educational Study Team which, under the direction of Deputy Prime Minister Goh Keng Swee, in 1979 issued the influential *Goh Report,* assessing conditions and proposing reforms in the Singapore education system.

The senior author for Chapter 6 on Thailand is Dr Chalio Buripakdi, director of the doctoral program in development education at Srinakharinwirot University, Bangkok. His doctorate is from Stanford. Dr Buripakdi's fellow author is Dr Pratern Mahakhan, a member of the Education Association of Thailand and of the faculty of education at Srinakharinwirot University.

These, then, are the writers who have collaborated to present the view of elementary and secondary education found in the following pages.

As a final note, we wish to express our appreciation to four individuals who aided in this work. Goh Keng Swee, Minister of Education in Singapore, was particularly helpful in providing recent information about educational developments under his Ministry's authority. Dr J. F. H. Villiers, Director of the Far East and Pacific Department of the British Council, offered useful suggestions about several of the chapters when they were in manuscript form. John Coles of the British Council office in Thailand supplied information about the preservice training of Thai teachers. And Ingrid Ruopp at the University of Hamburg typed several of the chapters.

T. NEVILLE POSTLETHWAITE

R. MURRAY THOMAS

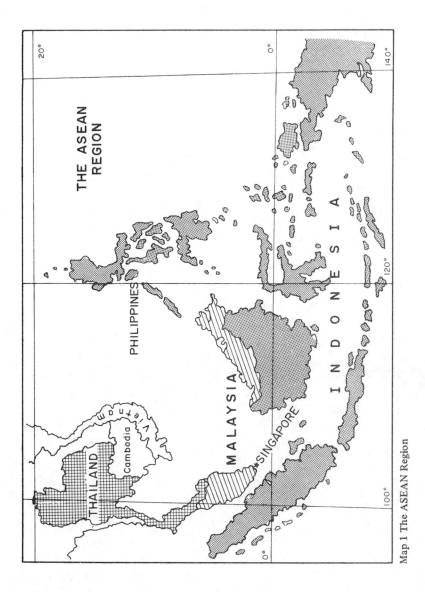

Map 1 The ASEAN Region

xvii

Mardika iku jarwanya; nora mung
lepasing pangreh; nging uga kuwat
kuwasa amandiri priyangga.

Freedom means not only liberation
from others' commands, but also
the ability to rule oneself
successfully.
                    JAVANESE PROVERB

1

Ways to View Schooling in
ASEAN Countries

R. Murray Thomas and T. Neville Postlethwaite

A MAJOR feature of international affairs since World War II has been the
effort of colonized countries to win political freedom and to pursue
economic and social prosperity under their own power. Four Southeast
Asian nations which have been engaged in this effort are Indonesia (formerly
a Dutch colony), Malaysia and Singapore (formerly British), and the
Philippines (first Spanish, then U.S. American). These four have been
joined in their pursuit of prosperity by Thailand, which avoided colonial
status during the 19th and early 20th centuries, but like the others was
occupied by Japanese troops during World War II. Today Thailand qualifies with its Southeast Asian neighbors as a developing country in terms
of industrialization and social welfare.

The typical strategy adopted by such countries to achieve their ambitions has been that of devising five-year or eight-year national-development
programs intended to marshal the nation's resources for planned growth.
Each such program includes important educational components coordinated
with the plan's political, economic, and social-welfare aspects. Thus, one

1

way to view schooling in a nation is to see it in terms of the national-growth program. This national-development view is one of the perspectives assumed in the following pages.

A second perspective, linked closely to the first, is the historical view. In each of the countries we study, there are certain characteristics of schools that may not appear to make sense under present conditions. However, they do make sense when set against their historical background. In each country, traditions from the past have given the education system a direction and impetus not readily altered, so such traditions continue to influence the patterns of schooling today, whether or not these patterns seem most reasonable in terms of national progress. Therefore, in Chapters 2 through 6, historical antecedents of education in the five nations have been included to help clarify events of the present.

Another modern-day characteristic of developing nations is their frequent banding together in regional coalitions to pursue projects of mutual benefit. One such coalition is ASEAN, the Association of Southeast Asian Nations, formed August 8, 1967, to promote, among other things:

> . . . active collaboration and mutual assistance on matters of common interest in the economic, social, cultural, technical, scientific and administrative fields; (and) to provide assistance to each other in the form of training and research facilities in the educational, professional, technical, and administrative spheres. (Solidum, 1974, p. 243.)

As a result, the ASEAN pact includes educational program plans. However, of more significance in the field of education has been SEAMEO, a special collaborative body entitled the Southeast Asian Ministers of Education Organization. This regional view of educational cooperation provides a third perspective from which we shall inspect basic schooling in the five countries.

The foregoing trio of interrelated viewpoints can be summarized as three basic questions. The national-development perspective is future-oriented and asks, "What are we aiming to become, and how can we achieve our aim?" The historical perspective is past-oriented and asks, "How have past events affected what we are now?" The ASEAN perspective is regional-oriented and asks, "What is our place in the Southeast Asian community and how can we profitably cooperate with our neighbors in achieving common aims?"

To assist readers in comparing educational developments in one nation with developments in the others, the authors of the five country chapters, 2 through 6, have organized their presentations around the same series of topics. Our purpose in this opening chapter is to prepare the way for the country chapters by introducing the topics and by suggesting the significance each topic holds from the three perspectives described above.

The contents of each country chapter are organized in terms of such topics as demographic and socio-political factors influencing schooling, historical backgrounds of education, and the present-day form and size of elementary and secondary educational efforts. However, readers will discover that the chapters contain as well the material for answering questions that fall under two major headings: (1) the aims of schooling and (2) the structure and process of schooling. To identify aims, we can answer a four-part question: For whom is schooling to be furnished, of what types, in what amounts, and why? To understand the structure and process, we can find answers to a five-part question: Under what administrative organization is schooling offered, where, by whom, with what methodology, and why?

Our search for answers to these queries is expedited when we first identify common factors that influence aims and structure no matter which country is being discussed at the time. It is to these factors we now turn.

The Aims of Schooling

An initial fact to recognize is that educational aims typically derive from more than one source in society, and these sources may not have identical motives. What economic planners want secondary schools to accomplish may not be exactly what students want to get from a secondary education. What national political leaders want the schools to do may not be what the leaders of religious minorities want. In effect, schools do not serve a single master. An understanding of which masters are being served helps explain to us why a given nation provides the particular types and amounts of schooling found there. Thus, the school system as it exists usually represents some form of compromise among competing expectations from society. To illustrate this compromise as found in ASEAN societies, let us consider some typical expectations from two

3

viewpoints, that of national-development planners and that of the general populace. The first we shall call *political-economic planning* and the second *social demand.*

POLITICAL-ECONOMIC PLANNING AIMS

In the typical five-year national-growth plan, schools are expected to help achieve manpower, citizenship, and social-welfare goals.

The schools' manpower-production assignment is established in two steps. First, economic planners predict the kinds and numbers of workers needed to staff the development of the economic system envisioned for the coming years. Then the planners propose which of these needed workers the schools should be responsible for producing and which workers should gain their needed skills through nonformal educational channels. In this manner, the schools and nonformal educational agencies acquire their manpower-production assignments. So far Singapore has been the ASEAN society that has been able to make this approach work most effectively.

The citizenship assignment in its most basic form requires the schools to equip students with common communication skills and a strong sense of allegiance to the national government. Over the past two decades all five of the ASEAN governments have faced serious problems in this realm of national unity. Economic progress and the improvement of social welfare become difficult in a divided society in which citizens dissipate their energies by wrangling among themselves. Systematic development can be expected only in a nation that is experiencing a modicum of peace. Therefore, the schools are expected to prepare students with common communication skills, such as a national language, and with primary allegiance to the nation rather than to a particular ethnic, religious, or social-class segment of the society.

Although all five ASEAN countries have faced a national-unity problem, the form of the problem has been somewhat different in one nation than in another. Malaysia has faced two sorts of unity difficulties. First is the problem of molding the large proportions of Malay and Chinese citizens and the smaller proportion of Indian citizens into a cohesive political unit. Second is the problem of engendering a sense of nationhood among the people of peninsular Malaysia and those of the north

4

coast of the island of Borneo. One method of encouraging unity has been to require that only the Malay language be used as the basic instructional medium in schools. Singapore has sought to achieve political unity among its multicultural population (Chinese, Indians, Malays, and others) by requiring pupils to master two languages — English and one other. Indonesia's motto of "Unity in Diversity" (*Bhinneka Tunggal Ika*) reflects the government's attempt to fashion a sense of nationhood among 145 million citizens living on nearly 1,000 islands and composing more than 300 ethnic groups speaking as many languages and dialects. Like Malaysia, Indonesia has required that the national Indonesian language (a variant of Malay, as is the Malaysian national tongue) be used as the medium of instruction in schools. The Philippines, as another nation of islands, has faced ethnic and language diversity as well, though not so great as that of Indonesia. But perhaps more prominent in the Philippines have been divisions along religious lines, with the Moslem minority in the southern islands feeling less integrated into the national fold than do Christians who make up the majority in the rest of the country. Filipino leaders, like their neighbors, have adopted a national language (Tagalog, now called Pilipino) as the unifying medium for teaching in the schools. In Thailand, tribes in the northern mountains have posed some concern for the central government, since they have continued to follow their own language and customs rather than identifying with national Thai culture. Efforts in Thailand to integrate such minority groups into the national society have been similar to those in the other ASEAN countries, with emphasis on learning the Thai language and identifying one's fate with that of the nation.

The citizenship goal has been pursued not only by teaching a national language in the schools but also by devising nationalistic-focused social-studies curricula. As in countries in other parts of the world, the social studies in the ASEAN regions have included a heavy fare of ethnocentric history. Such history features exploits of patriots of the past, battle victories, cultural contributions, and the glories of ancient empires that encompassed the territory the nation now covers. This factor, though not discussed in detail in Chapters 2–6, is implied in the national plans and curricula of the nations' schools.

So far we have inspected the first two national-development assignments of the schools, those of manpower production and of citizenship training. Both can be seen as what the people are expected to do for their nation — to enter occupations required by the new economy and to support the political system. The third assignment — promoting social welfare — can be seen from the opposite perspective. Social welfare is what the people want the country to do for them.

For purposes of analysis, it is useful to divide social welfare into three categories: universal welfare, subgroup welfare, and personal welfare. For example, the school serves universal desires through instruction in health and safety practices, since all citizens wish to be energetic and free from disease and injury. Next, the school serves subgroup desires in a given ethnic region by instruction in the regional language's literature, in cultural traditions and history, and in the arts. Furthermore, each ASEAN country provides opportunities for religious instruction in the chosen faith of the pupil's family. Finally, the school serves individual desires and aptitudes by offering increasing amounts of educational and vocational guidance that is intended to fit the student's interests and skills into a reasonable career plan for the future. Personal needs are also met through varied curriculum choices and through special schooling for the handicapped and the gifted.

The perfect national-development plan would be one in which the three assignments to the schools complemented each other harmoniously. No conflict would exist between what people desire and what the country requires in terms of manpower and political unity. However, no country's plan approaches this perfection. There is always some degree of mismatch. Some of the reasons educational planners face difficulties in achieving a better coordination of these elements are recognized when we analyze the social-demand side in more detail.

SOCIAL-DEMAND AIMS

As suggested above, the term *social demand* identifies those things sought by the people in a society. For the field of education, the direction and strength of social demand are revealed by such indicators as the number of school applicants and dropouts for various types of schools, the sorts of private schools people establish on their own initiative, and the educational requests and complaints the government receives.

Ways to View Schooling in ASEAN Countries

We have noted that serious problems arise when what the people want for themselves conflicts with what development-planners think is best for the nation. This does not mean that the people necessarily disagree with the planners' analysis of what will make the country prosper. Indeed, the populace often supports the national plan on the level of theory. But people come to like the plan less when they realize the implications it holds for their own lives.

To illustrate, let us consider the relationship among manpower production, levels of schooling, and the prestige of occupations in two ASEAN societies, Singapore and Indonesia.

Singapore has achieved an enviable record of enrolling all children in school and in keeping most of them there for several years. For instance, of all children who enter the first grade of the primary school, 95 percent complete the sixth grade. Of those who enter secondary school, virtually all complete the third year and 95 percent complete the fourth. This holding power of Singapore schools contrasts sharply with the record of schools in Thailand, where only 19 percent of children who enter primary school ever reach grade six, and only 19 percent who enter secondary school are still attending five years later. (*Education Building Facilities in the Asian Region,* 1976, pp. 117, 133.) Because of the high retention of pupils in school in Singapore, the country has succeeded rather well in preparing the manpower to staff the upper echelons of the commercial, manufacturing, and government enterprises on which this city-state depends for its survival. However, Singapore now faces problems of filling the lower levels of the economic structure with willing workers. Students who complete secondary schooling nearly all wish to enter high-prestige occupations, ones they feel are equal to their educational level. Too few are interested in laboring with their hands. So while the public agrees that the nation needs workers at all levels of the job structure, when people face the question of who will fill which jobs, they nearly all want the higher-prestige positions. They expect others of their country-men to take the manual-labor jobs.

Indonesia is similar to many other developing nations in its attempt to modernize the economic system. Such modernization requires a major increase in the number of people trained for high-level and middle-level technical and management jobs. The school system is expected to contribute to this effort by graduating large numbers of top-level professionals

7

from the universities and even greater numbers of middle-level personnel from the nation's high schools. Not only are the numbers of graduates to be increased, but a far larger proportion are to come from science, technical, and business programs than from the humanities and social sciences. However, this plan has come into continual conflict with social demand. People's attitudes about which occupations carry the greatest prestige and reward have influenced the output of schools in two main ways.

First, most families that are sufficiently ambitious to urge their children to complete secondary school do not want to stop at that level. They want the youths to continue into college, although oftentimes more for the sake of the college diploma than for love of the knowledge that such a diploma is expected to represent. As a result, too few secondary-school graduates, upon finishing high school, are interested in entering middle-level technical and management positions. Instead, they want to go on to "something better".

Second, the classical curricula in the humanities, social sciences, and advanced sciences continue to carry more prestige, as they did in the past, than do technical or business curricula. A vocational school simply does not attract the quantity or quality of applicants that are attracted by a traditional academic institution. This fact is illustrated by enrollment figures from the 1960s when Indonesia's eight-year national development program was in effect. In 1959 the proportion of college students in the humanities and social sciences had been 53 percent, while the remaining 47 percent were in science, technical, and vocational programs. The government's eight-year economic-development plan called for increasing the proportion of science-technical-vocational students to 68 percent. However, by 1967 the ratio not only had failed to move in the desired direction, it had shifted in the opposite direction. In that year there were 64 percent of public-university students in social-science and humanities courses and 36 percent in the exact sciences and vocational studies. This does not mean that the government's plan failed entirely. Indeed, the absolute numbers of students in science and vocational studies rose by 246 percent between 1959 and 1967, so the plan did provide the economy with more of the kinds of people it needed. However, during the same period students in the humanities and social sciences rose by 390 percent, and at least part of this increase was a result of social demand. (Thomas, 1973, pp. 193, 196–197.)

Ways to View Schooling in ASEAN Countries

Observers of educational problems in developing nations have often remarked about the unfortunate social consequences of the continued popularity of classical academic curricula in these countries along with a lack of popularity of vocational studies. Some critics have implied that they cannot understand why residents of developing regions continue to support so-called "dysfunctional" classical schools inherited from the Europeans who held these territories as colonies until the mid-1900s. However, closer inspection of the developing societies shows that classical schools may be dysfunctional in terms of national economic growth and manpower planning, but they continue to be highly functional in terms of personal-social prestige. In the former Dutch colony of Indonesia, a degree in law or political science is still prestigious and can lead to improved social position for a youth who earns it. Thus, even though the choice of the level and type of schooling on the part of a large segment of the populace may not be the most functional from the viewpoint of national manpower planning, it is functional from the viewpoint of the ambitious individual citizen. An official in the Ministry of Education may help formulate a manpower plan that calls for large numbers of vocational-school graduates at the secondary level. However, he is likely to enroll his own sons and daughters in classical, college-preparatory courses, because he wants them to enjoy the prestige that a university education, even in the humanities, can be expected to bring. Hence, factors of tradition and personal ambition contribute to the conflict between the aims of schooling from the viewpoint of national-development planning and the aims from the viewpoint of social demand.

Not only does social demand cause difficulties for achieving manpower goals but also for pursuing national unity. Each ASEAN society is composed of subgroups which define themselves by their geographic location or ethnic origin or religious affiliation. Many times, members of these groups feel stronger allegiance toward their group than toward the nation as a whole. In Malaysia, many citizens still identify themselves primarily as Malay, Chinese, or Indian and only secondarily as Malaysian. The same is true in Singapore. In the Philippines, the primary group identification may be reflected in millions of citizens who speak Cebuano, Iloko, or Pampango as their mother tongues and make only infrequent and less fluent use of the national language of Pilipino. In Thailand, northern mountain tribes display similar primary identification with their tribe rather than the nation. Some Indonesians see themselves chiefly as Ambonese Christians, Balinese Hindus, or Achenese Moslems and secondarily as Indonesians. The demands of these subgroups on the national government is for attention to their subgroup needs. They will support a national political and economic plan only if it does not sacrifice regional economic progress and a measure of local political control. They will encourage the growth of a national language, only if it does not threaten the deterioration of their regional language and literature. They will cooperate with the national religious policy, only if it does not diminish the number and quality of adherents of their own faith. Thus, national-development planners can devise a successful plan only if they are sensitive to the power of such subgroups and if they accommodate the demands of the more powerful groups in the social-welfare portion of the development program. The nature of schooling in ASEAN countries cannot be understood without our recognizing the force of regional, ethnic, and religious demands.

Finally, an over-arching stimulus behind social demand has been people's seeing the school as a vehicle for conveying them to higher levels of the social-class structure. Prior to World War II, all ASEAN peoples had lived for centuries under feudal and colonial social systems. Feudal domains were ruled by princes, sultans, rajas, or chieftains. These royal families and their aristocratic cohorts enjoyed prestige, privilege, and comfort in far greater measure than was available to the peasantry. In colonized regions, top-level power and privilege were the province of the white overseers from Europe and America. These overseers typically exercised control of the society through the medium of feudal princes willing to participate in colonial rule. And as was true under indigenous feudal governments, the peasants and laborers who made up the bulk of the population received a far smaller share of privilege and worldly goods than did the colonialists or the indigenous aristocracy.

One of the advantages the upper social classes accorded themselves in feudal and colonial times was the opportunity for schooling, particularly for the favored sort of education of the day. The type of education most favored during a particular era was determined by the sorts of knowledge and skill admired by those currently in power. In the princely courts of Indonesia six to fifteen centuries ago, it was Buddhist—Hindu religious lore imported from India. Members of the aristocracy were tutored in religious mysteries, a sort of learning that helped aristocrats maintain their distance from and superiority over the common people. In Malaysia, one to six centuries ago the favored schooling was in Islamic traditions, Moslem law, and the Arabic language. In 19th century Thailand, King Rama IV, in admiration of the learning from Western Europe, imported an English woman, Mrs Anna Leonowens, to instruct him and members of his court in Western culture and politics. And in all ASEAN societies in the 20th century, schooling of a European variety became highly valued, for that was the schooling of the colonial masters and of children from the native aristocracy. In addition, Western schooling led to the certificates required for a valued position in the colonial civil service and in commercial enterprises. Such an education also enabled the graduate to grasp significant political and economic theories (democracy, socialism, communism) and to unravel the puzzles of Western technology (mechanical and chemical engineering, agriculture and animal husbandry, modern medicine).

At the end of World War II, native leaders of colonized peoples in Asia and Africa successfully declared for independence, thereby raising the hopes of the masses that they would at last receive privileges they had been denied under both the indigenous feudal systems and the colonial governments. A chance for schooling was one of those privileges. Schooling was a symbol of a better life ahead, an opportunity to climb to higher levels in the social structure. The governments of the new republics were now expected to satisfy this freshly whetted appetite for the coveted certificates and degrees. Like other fledgling nations around the world, ASEAN governments recognized this expectation by including a commitment to universal schooling in their constitutions and education laws.

While all governments have pledged themselves to equal opportunities for all citizens, no nation has been entirely successful in producing the conditions that make equal educational opportunities a reality. With few exceptions, children require several conditions if they are to attend school regularly and progress satisfactorily. First, they need enough money to pay fees that cover the cost of books, of a proper building, and of well trained, dedicated teachers. If the school is not within walking distance, they also need transportation. Or if they must live away from home, they need food and lodging. In addition, the most successful students are usually ones who have the psychological support of a family

11

that respects the school's purposes, encourages regular attendance, and monitors students' work on home assignments. Therefore, the more fully a government pays school costs and enforces compulsory attendance laws, the more likely schooling can serve as a vehicle to carry lower-class children into upper strata of the social structure. Conversely, the less adequate the public financing of education, the less likely youths from the lower class will move to positions higher in the social system and the more likely children of the upper classes will get the same favored opportunities for education that obtained for the aristocracy in feudal and colonial times.

Therefore, the aims of schooling in a society are reflected somewhat in the types and amount of support accorded to schools by the government and private bodies. If a government claims to furnish equal opportunities to all citizens for schooling — a sort of schooling that permits each individual to rise or decline in the social structure by virtue of his talent and diligence — then this claim is not the true aim of the government if officials divide the national budget in ways that give favored chances to some social-class or regional or ethnic groups at the expense of others.

In brief, one perspective from which to view the aims of schooling is that of the social class structure and of opportunities for vertical social mobility. People at lower levels of the class system often want to use schooling as a method for rising in the system. At the same time, those at the top tend to reserve favored schooling opportunities for their own children so their children's position in the upper strata will not be threatened by bright, ambitious youths from the lower levels. In each of the ASEAN countries, this struggle between egalitarian ideals and traditional favored treatment for an elite continues to be reflected in educational opportunities. The most conspicuous evidence of such a struggle in recent years has been the practice in Malaysia of affording favored opportunities to Malays by means of scholarships and special school-admission quotas intended to correct what has been considered an imbalance of privilege and welfare from the past — an imbalance which ostensibly found Malaysians of Chinese and Indian heritage enjoying undue economic and social advantages. (*Third Malaysia Plan 1976–1980*, 1976, pp. 399–404.)

The struggle between egalitarianism and favoritism has also been apparent in Indonesia, where officials over the past decade have manipulated the assessment of school fees in ways which they felt might place some of the burden of school finance directly on the parents, yet still ensure that all children receive equal chances for primary schooling. For example, in 1974 a schedule of school fees for all levels of the education system was set according to parents' apparent ability to pay. But because children from poor families were being denied a chance for schooling under this system, in 1977 the government eliminated all fees for the primary grades. The government was able to carry through such a plan in 1977 because sales of petroleum to foreign nations produced revenues sufficient to make up the funds lost by eliminating fees for the lowest grades. So we note that the ability of a government to fulfill its educational commitments – to make its stated aims a reality – is obviously influenced by its financial condition at the time.

THE EFFECT OF INTERNATIONAL STANDARDS

Up to this point we have discussed ways a nation's internal political-economic plans and the people's demands can influence the aims of schooling. Another factor affecting aims in the ASEAN countries has been the set of standards of modernization to which informed people throughout the world usually subscribe. One such standard is the rate of literacy of a nation. The higher the percentage of people who can read and write, the greater the nation's prestige. Another standard is the percentage of school-age children who actually attend school. A third is the number of years of compulsory schooling. A fourth is the percentage of youths who graduate from secondary school. A fifth is the proportion of the population who have attended college. Nations that rank high on these measures are often accorded greater acclaim within the community of nations than are countries that do not.

To formalize their dedication to such international standards of maturity, the ASEAN governments on several occasions have allied themselves with other countries in publicly adopting certain of the standards as part of their educational aims. For example, all five ASEAN countries were signatories to the Karachi Plan, which called for universal schooling through the seventh grade. In the 1970s the ASEAN governments, through the medium of SEAMEO (Southeast Asian Ministers of Education Organization), continued to influence each other's schooling aims by means of joint conferences and cooperative projects.

The Structure and Process of Schooling

In the chapters that focus on individual ASEAN countries, a large amount of space is devoted to describing structure and process, that is, to answering the question: Under what administrative organization is schooling offered, where, by whom, with what methodology, and why?

For each nation the authors furnish two levels of description. One level centers on the visible features of the school system, such as administrative organization, types and numbers of pupils and schools, methods of finance, kinds of curricula, the examination and promotion system, forms of teacher preparation, and the like. The second level centers on background factors that have helped determine the particular features of the school system. To clarify the nature of such factors, in the following paragraphs we identify five of the most prominent ones and illustrate their influence with examples from the ASEAN nations. The five are (1) population size and distribution, (2) the subgroup characteristics of ethnic origin, religious affiliation, and social-class membership, (3) the composition of the nation's work force, (4) the financial support for schools, and (5) the current political system of the nation.

POPULATION SIZE AND DISTRIBUTION

The ASEAN countries are alike in their commitment to universal elementary schooling. However, they differ greatly in the magnitude of the task of carrying out this commitment. And much of the reason for the difference is found in the ways the five nations vary in size and geographical characteristics.

The largest ASEAN country in terms of area and number of people is Indonesia, whose 145 million residents make it the fifth most populous nation in the world. The fact that this population is spread over 931 of the archipelago's 13,667 islands, stretching more than 4,800 kilometers (3,000 miles) across the ocean, makes the administration of schooling from the capital city of Jakarta extremely difficult. Java and its small companion island of Madura represent less than 7 percent of the nation's land area, but they contain about 65 percent of the population or nearly 95 million people. In contrast, Irian Jaya (Western New Guinea) has 22 percent of the land but less than 1 percent of the people. This makes

Java, with over 1100 people per square kilometer (1700 per square mile), one of the most crowded large land areas on earth, and Irian Jaya, with around 5 per square kilometer, among the sparsest.

The smallest ASEAN nation is Singapore, a strictly urban commercial and industrial seaport at the southern tip of the Malay Peninsula. It is a city-state covering only 597 square kilometers, less than one-thousandth the size of Indonesia. Its population was about 2.4 million in 1980, a density of 2,513 people per square kilometer, with nearly half of them housed in public high-rise apartment complexes. Singapore's small size and concentrated population make its schools the most convenient to administer of any in the ASEAN region.

The Philippine Islands' task of providing and supervising schools is similar in nature to Indonesia's, though on a far smaller scale, since the Philippines have only 16 percent of the land area of Indonesia. The area is made up almost entirely of 45 larger islands on which an estimated 47.5 million people lived in 1980.

Although Malaysia's land area is only 13 percent greater than the Philippines', the problems of educational administration are rather different because Malaysia is not an island nation but rather a country of two large land areas separated by 400 miles of the China Sea. The western sector, consisting of the Malay Peninsula jutting south from the Asian mainland, makes up 40 percent of the total land and traditionally has been the more developed politically and economically. The largest number of schools and those with the best facilities and best prepared staffs are in West Malaysia. The eastern sector, covering the northern coast of the island of Borneo (Kalimantan), has been relatively neglected until recently. One of the vexing problems facing Malaysia's educational planners has been that of melding East and West into a cohesive educational enterprise in which equal opportunities are provided for residents of both sectors.

Thailand, extending 1,000 miles (1,600 kilometers) from north to south, is a kingdom 50 percent larger than Malaysia, making it the second largest of the ASEAN countries, slightly more than a quarter the size of Indonesia. It consists of a major land mass surrounded by Burma, Laos, and Cambodia, plus a narrow finger of peninsular territory stretching south to Malaysia. The population of an estimated 47 million in 1980 is located mostly in the great central plains north of the coastal capital

15

of Bangkok, the plains that have been called the rice bowl of Asia. Thai educationists in recent years have faced not only the problem of furnishing adequate schooling services for the central plains, northern mountains, and southern peninsula, but of promoting political unity and educational progress while war has been waged just beyond the entire southeastern and northeastern borders. Furthermore, Thai society and thus the educational establishment were strongly affected by the presence of large foreign military forces, primarily American, that were engaged in the Vietnam war from the late 1950s to the mid-1970s. Thailand served as a staging area for military operations, and the influence of the foreigners has left a mark on the education system in terms of styles of life and educational procedures.

In summary, the geography of ASEAN nations and the distribution and size of populations have helped determine the type and magnitude of problems in furnishing schools, in preparing teachers and locating them where they are needed, and in supervising schools and renovating curriculum practices.

Another important dimension of geography and population has been the urban-rural distribution of people, particularly in the migration of large numbers of young people to the cities. Each of the ASEAN countries, except Singapore, continues to experience what has been called an urban-rural problem. The problem has several aspects, with education involved as both a cause and an effect of the problem. Several forces have motivated villagers, particularly the young, to leave the country for life in the city. High birth rates in agricultural areas are one cause, since each new generation brings more family members to share the available land. This means that with succeeding generations farm plots become smaller and there are too many people to work the land, causing unemployment and underemployment. Thus, youths who have heard of job opportunities in the cities move to the urban areas to find work. Another cause has been the publicized glamor and modernity of the cities. The latest movies, dances, and songs are found in the cities along with amusement parks, night life, and goods to purchase. Youths see the city as up-to-date, pointing the direction to the future, while regarding the village as old fashioned, passé. The structure of the school system also encourages the flow of the most apt rural youths to the city. Bright pupils in village primary schools cannot usually progress higher in the academic system unless they move to a town which has a junior-secondary school. And graduates of small-town junior-secondary schools cannot move further in the system unless they go to a larger town that operates a senior-secondary school. To attend college or a specialized trade school, the senior-secondary graduate usually must move to a city. Once in the city the student finds a concentration of other students with interests and talents similar to his own. He also finds the sorts of cultural facilities (museums, theaters, clubs, bookshops) and job openings for which he has been suited by his advanced education. Hence, the prospect of returning to a rural setting devoid of these attractions usually does not appeal to the youth, and he stays in the city.

Urbanization causes a variety of educational problems. If people move to cities faster than development planners can provide suitable housing and school facilities to meet their needs, slums multiply rapidly. Unemployment, poverty, and delinquency abound. It is then difficult for educational planners to find sites for schools to serve the slum children, to find teachers willing to work in such areas, and to equip the schools in a manner they would like. It is also difficult to find graduates of teacher-education programs to take positions in remote rural areas, so rural youths have a disadvantage in obtaining proper schooling. Consequently, in all the ASEAN countries except Singapore, which has no rural areas, the differences between city and country life and the migration to cities present educational planners with serious challenges.

We conclude, therefore, that the nature of education in ASEAN countries cannot be understood if we neglect to consider geographic and demographic factors.

SUBGROUP CHARACTERISTICS: ETHNIC ORIGIN, RELIGIOUS AFFILIATION, SOCIAL-CLASS MEMBERSHIP

The ethnic, religious, and social-class diversity of all ASEAN societies has been one of the most significant factors in determining the nature of education in the region. Although these three varieties of subgroups are oftentimes interrelated, it is convenient for the sake of analysis to consider each separately.

Schooling in the ASEAN Region

Ethnic Origin

The two chief causes of the patterns of ethnic diversity found in Southeast Asia have been population isolation and migration. By population isolation we mean that such physical barriers as seas or high mountains have prevented easy interaction between peoples so that tribal groups have evolved their own cultures — their own languages, artistic endeavors, modes of governance, objects of respect, occupational styles, and the like. By migration patterns we mean the movement of large numbers of one ethnic group into a territory already occupied by other ethnic strains. Sometimes that movement is by official design, as when the British colonial government brought laborers from China and India to work in the plantations of the Malay Peninsula, so that today a large proportion of both Malaysian and Singapore citizens are of Chinese and Indian heritage. In other cases, the migration is at the individual initiative of the migrants, who may move in small numbers into an area, then increase as friends and relatives back in the country of origin are encouraged by the first migrants to follow. Such migration by personal initiative accounts for the Chinese residents of Thailand, Indonesia, and the Philippines as well as the small Arab strains in Indonesia and Malaysia.

The greatest ethnic variety is found in Indonesia, as a result of the mountainous–island character of the geography and the wide territory over which the nation is spread. More than 300 different indigenous ethnic strains have been identified throughout the islands, each speaking its own distinct language or dialect and displaying social patterns that are often in striking contrast to those of Indonesians living on other islands. Some of these groups are very large, such as the Javanese who number perhaps 60 million or more and the Sundanese (in West Java) who number from 20 to 30 million. Other groups are small, counted in the thousands.

In the Philippines, are found over 40 distinct ethnic groups that speak nearly 90 dialects. The two largest language groups, those speaking Tagalog and Cebuano, each contains about nine million members or almost half the Philippine population.

As noted above, the populations of Malaysia and Singapore display an ethnic pattern resulting from British colonial labor-importation policies. In Malaysia, 55 percent of the citizenry are either of Malay stock or of tribal groups of North Borneo. Another 34 percent are of Chinese extrac-

18

tion and 11 percent Indian. Singapore, while made up of the same three general ethnic types, is dominantly Chinese. That is, 76 percent of the citizens are of Chinese stock, 15 percent of Malay, 7 percent of Indian, and the remaining 2 percent of other ethnic strains.

The ethnic mix of Thailand is predominantly of Thai and Thai–Lao subgroups who make up 80 percent of the population. The most significant minority group is that of Chinese or a Chinese–Thai mixture, who represent about 10 percent of the people. The remaining 10 percent of the population consists mostly of a Thai–Malay mixture, Vietnamese, Cambodians, Indians, and Pakistanis.

Before considering the educational implications of these ASEAN ethnic patterns, we shall review briefly the religious composition of the five nations, since ethnic and religious influences on the schools have much in common.

Religious Affiliation

The profile of religious affiliation is markedly different from one ASEAN country to another.

The Philippines is primarily Christian, Thailand mostly Buddhist, Indonesia mostly Moslem, and Malaysia and Singapore a more even mixture of several faiths. But even in the countries that are predominantly of one religion, there are minority religious groups. Furthermore, within the dominant religions there are factions which represent a measure of diversity. For example, Indonesians are identified as 88 percent Moslems. In certain sections of the nation, such as the Aceh region of North Sumatra and the Sundanese region of West Java, this is a deep-seated dedication to traditional Islamic doctrine. But in Central and East Java it is often a veneer laid over earlier mystical *abangan* philosophy. Besides the large proportion of Moslems in Indonesia, there are also Christians (7 percent), Hindus (2 percent), and Buddhist–Confucianists (2 percent), along with other sects (2 percent).

The Indonesian government maintains a religious-freedom policy which involves no adoption of an official state religion. However, in Malaysia the state religion is Islam, though only half of the population is Moslem. The rest of the population is divided among Buddhists (25.5 percent), Hindus (7.4 percent), Christians (5.3 percent), and others (11.7 percent).

19

Schooling in the ASEAN Region

In the Philippines, nearly 85 percent of the people are Roman Catholics, a residue of Spanish colonial control for nearly 350 years before the United States took the islands from Spain in 1898. Another 8 percent are Protestant Christians, and about 4 percent are Moslems.

Thailand's population is overwhelmingly Buddhist (94 percent), with the remainder made up of Taoists, Moslems, Christians, and Hindus.

The principal religious groups in Singapore are Buddhists, Taoists, Moslems, Christians, and Hindus.

Ethnic and Religious Influences on Education

When different ethnic or religious traditions meet in a society, one of three things occurs over the following years to elements of the traditions. Either one subculture will eliminate the other in the competition so only one of the original traditions remains, or else elements of the two traditions merge to form a new syncretic culture, or the two traditions continue to exist in parallel to form what has been called a *plural society*. Oftentimes this third form, two cultures proceeding intact and parallel, is actually a temporary state that eventually resolves into one of the first two forms — elimination of one or integration of the two into an amalgam that represents a compromise culture.

The process of cultural adjustment can become very complex because some elements of one of the confronting traditions may be eliminated, others may be retained and become dominant, some may merge to form a new combination, while still others live on in parallel accommodation. For instance, in the present-day Malaysian language the basic words and syntax are the original Malay. However, the language is printed in roman letters brought by the British colonialists. The spelling system is one negotiated over the past decade with Indonesia so that the two nations, whose languages have the same Malay base, now have the same orthography. And when the entire vocabulary of Malaysian is reviewed, it is found to contain borrowings from Sanskrit, Arabic, English, Chinese, and other tongues.

When two religions or ethnic cultures meet, the tendency is for the adherents of each religion or culture to want their own tradition to dominate, to be the winner. There are several reasons for this ethnocentricity, which is particularly prominent among the older generation. First, a person's identity — his knowledge and feelings about who he is — is bound up in religious convictions, language, occupational pursuits, folklore and proverbial knowledge, and artistic expressions. Having to adopt new ways and give up old ones can damage the secure feeling of identity for many people, so they resist adopting a new culture. Second, changing one's ways requires extra energy and risk. Learning a new language, giving up old religious practices, learning to use new implements or machines, viewing art works for which one lacks the background knowledge causes confusion and strain and the risk of making mistakes. In short, older people are frequently "too set in their ways" to readily adopt a new culture. Third, just as fighting a battle on your own territory gives you the advantage of familiarity over your opponents, so communicating with strangers in your own language, with your own laws and customs, and with your own tools puts you at an advantage. In the competition for the good things of life — prestige, power, freedom from undue tension — it is usually easier to operate with the cultural skills you have already mastered.

We conclude, then, that people are willing to change their religion or ethnic subculture only if it promises substantially to promote their welfare. In some cases, the obvious advantages of the others' culture are sufficient to effect its willing adoption. For instance, in Indonesia two or three centuries ago the superiority of printing books with movable type on paper over writing on palm leaves with a stylus was sufficiently apparent to eliminate the production of palm-leaf learning materials. The advantages of television over newspapers and word-of-mouth as a medium of entertainment, news dissemination, and instruction have made it a rapidly adopted technology throughout the ASEAN region in less than two decades.

In other cases, people do not adopt new cultural elements willingly but because they are forced to do so. If they do not adopt the elements, unpleasant sanctions will be invoked against them. For example, after the attempted coup of 1965 in Indonesia, anti-Chinese sentiments on the part of the dominant indigenous Indonesian cultural groups increased, because the government on mainland China was seen as a sponsor behind the coup. As a result, Chinese residents in Indonesia were forced to close Chinese-language schools, and they were encouraged to adopt Indonesian names so they would display greater integration into the dominant cultural stream. Faced with these social pressures and threats of sanctions, many Indonesian Chinese did indeed change their names. Many others went back to China.

As a further example, the Malaysian government after racial riots in 1969 accelerated its policy of Malayanizing society, a policy that involved having a common content syllabus in all schools and the national language (Malaysian) as the main medium of instruction in primary schools and as the sole medium at secondary and tertiary levels. The common syllabus was seen as a unifying factor for all children at the primary level, whether they received instruction in Malaysian, Chinese, or Tamil. Adopting Malaysian as the medium of instruction at secondary and tertiary levels may have been one factor which caused some qualified citizens of Chinese or Tamil heritage to emigrate to other countries, since they felt their future in Malaysia was not secure.

In contrast, Singapore has sought to maintain a parallel-accommodation tack by its bilingual policy – requiring each youth to become fluent in two languages: (1) English as a medium of intergroup and international communication and (2) one other language as a means of maintaining one's own cultural identity and communicating within one's traditional subculture.

Much of the concern of educational policy makers in all five ASEAN countries is with solving the problems posed by ethnic and religious diversity. Details of many such problems and their historical roots are described for the separate countries in Chapters 2 through 6. In the following paragraphs, as a preview to those detailed treatments, we shall consider a few of the educational implications of ethnic and religious matters.

Educational planners can view ethnic and religious differences either as a welcome opportunity or, as is far more often the case, as a troublesome problem.

Diversity, from a positive perspective, offers educators the chance to enrich students' lives with cultures other than their own. Students can enjoy the literature, art, drama, dances, and games of other ethnic traditions. They can learn the philosophical and ceremonial meanings of other religions. They can learn segments, at least, of other languages and thus expand the range of people with whom they communicate. This positive view of diversity has to some degree affected educational offerings in each ASEAN country. For example, the cultural division of the Indonesian Ministry of Education sponsors classes in representative dances and drama from a variety of the nation's ethnic regions. Collections of songs from different regions are published for use in the schools. And historical accounts, such as books about the Indonesian Revolution against Dutch colonialism (1945–1949), cite the exploits of heroes of different ethnic backgrounds.

Therefore, attempts have been made by ASEAN educators to take advantage of cultural disparities in the society to broaden students' perspectives in a positive way. However, despite some measure of such positive influence, ethnic and religious diversity are far more commonly seen by educational planners as a source of difficulties. The difficulties are of several kinds.

One obvious problem is that of language instruction and of supplying textbooks. In Singapore, with its bilingual policy, school books are needed in English, Chinese, Tamil, and Malay. Malaysia has sought to simplify the textbook problem by its relatively recent shift to instruction in the national Malaysian language at the primary level, so that all schools which previously had used English as an instructional medium now use Malaysian. However, primary schools that continue to offer instruction in Chinese and Tamil still face the problem of furnishing text materials in those languages as well as in Malaysian. Children who attend primary, secondary, or tertiary schools in which Malaysian is the medium can face some language difficulties, if the tongue spoken in their homes is Chinese, Tamil, or English. But such difficulties are regarded by authorities as temporary and soon overcome.

The Indonesian government has adopted a policy of offering instruction in the lower-primary grades in regional languages, then shifting instruction gradually into the national language in the upper-elementary grades. This means that textbooks in regional languages are needed for the lower grades, placing an additional burden on a textbook publishing industry that has had trouble with the needs for books in one language, a burden increased by the variety of languages in use. A further problem in both Indonesia and the Philippines is that even when texts are published in the major regional tongues, children from smaller ethnic groups that have their own dialects never have the opportunity to study books in their own language. They start the lower grades in a strange language, the regional tongue, and then must shift in the upper grades into another strange tongue, the national language. This is further complicated in the Philippines where the bilingual policy allows the use of English and Pilipino as languages of instruction in the schools.

Ethnic differences also cause problems for the training and placement of teachers in ASEAN countries. Teachers from one ethnic group often are uncomfortable or unwelcome, if assigned to a school in the region of a different group. Not only are the customs and language strange to them, but they may feel isolated socially, particularly in small, close-knit communities. And if the religion of the community is different from their own, the isolation or rejection is doubly serious.

Religious differences present difficulties of religious instruction in the schools. For a country like Thailand the matter of furnishing children instruction in the religion of their family's choice is not a serious problem, for nearly all Thais are Buddhists. But in certain sections of Indonesia, particularly in the larger cities, time is set aside each week for religious education, with children having the right to be instructed in their own faith (Moslem, Protestant Christian, Catholic, Bali-Hindu, Buddhist). When only a few children in a class or in a school are of a minor faith, it is often impossible to furnish a suitable instructor for them.

Difficulties also arise in determining the proper contents of certain textbooks and courses of study, particularly those in history and the social studies. For instance, in historical accounts of the waves of immigration into a region – as in Malaysia and Singapore – or of conflicts between one religious group and another – as between Moslem and Christian in the Philippines – the blame for the difficulties of past eras is often placed more on one of the groups than another, either by direct account or by implication. Such placing of blame frequently distresses students of the ethnic or religious group held at fault, so that conflicts arise between both the students of the two cultural groups and their parents.

The ethnic group most frequently pictured in an unfavorable light in ASEAN countries, more often by implication than outright accusation, has been the Chinese. This has been true in all ASEAN nations except Singapore, where Chinese dominate both in numbers and in political strength. In the Philippines, Thailand, Malaysia, and Indonesia, the Chinese residents have for many decades held a strong position economically.

In addition, they have tended to congregate in the cities, have valued education, and have urged their children to succeed in school and progress as far as possible up the education ladder. Except for Singapore and Malaysia, the proportions of Chinese in the populations of the ASEAN nations have been small — 10 percent in Thailand, 5 percent in Indonesia, under 1 percent in the Philippines. Malaysia is about 35 percent Chinese and Singapore 75 percent. But because of their advantageous position at the top of the economic and educational structures, the Chinese have been envied, and steps have been taken in several of the nations in recent decades to limit their access to education. The Malaysian policy has been forthright — offering favored opportunities to Malays so as to increase the percentage of Malays in schools, particularly in secondary and tertiary institutions. In the nation's Third Five-Year Development Plan, under the topic "Racial Balance and Education", the authors comment on the improvement of the enrollments of Malays in schools during the Second Plan, 1970—1975, and propose that during the Third Plan period, "continuing efforts will be made to increase enrolments among the Malays and other indigenous people in areas where they are in short supply. . . ." (*Third Malaysia Plan 1976—1980*, 1976, pp. 399, 404.) The policy in Indonesia has not been so forthright. However, informal quotas have existed for at least two decades in higher education institutions to restrict the percentage of Chinese entering state universities.

Such formal or informal favoritism of one group over another results in political consequences that may disrupt the peaceful operation of the society. When the Singapore government in the early 1960s ordered the English language to be taught in traditional Chinese-language school and set examinations for entrance to the university exclusively in English, public demonstrations and boycotts of the examinations ensued.

Appointments of officials in the educational system are also influenced by group affiliations. Political organizations established along ethnic or religious lines often seek to ensure that their group is favorably represented in the officialdom of education — in the central ministry, in the school inspectorate, and among headmasters. When its own adherents are in key administrative posts, the political organization can better ensure favorable — or at least fair — treatment of their viewpoint and of their constituents. This competition for appointments can contribute to inefficiency in the educational system when appointments are founded more on a candidate's political sponsorship than his professional competence.

The foregoing examples thus illustrate ways that ethnic and religious diversity in the ASEAN countries affect the conduct of education.

Social-Class Influences on Education

In our earlier discussion of social demand, we observed that prior to World War II most of the peoples of Southeast Asia lived in feudal and colonial social orders. From the viewpoint of social-class structure, these societies were essentially closed to vertical movement. It was extremely difficult, and usually impossible, for a person to rise to a social stratum above the one of his origin. A variety of forces contributed to the continuance of these closed class systems.

First, the ruling elites imposed regulations and enforced customs that kept the social order intact, that kept everyone in his assigned place. For example, colonial authorities restricted entrance to the better schools and to top government posts to exclude the middle and lower classes and certain ethnic groups. In addition, the indigenous aristocracies passed family titles down to succeeding generations, with each title attached to the bearer's name to signify his status to all who met him.

A second force was the set of subculture characteristics that marked a person's class level. The more closed a stratification system is, the more it encourages the development of separate subcultures at the different class levels. A person acquires the cultural characteristics of his level so that he reveals the stratum of his origin by his speech, mode of dress, manners, occupation, choice of friends, forms of recreation, and housing facilities. The more open a class system, the less likely a person will acquire distinguishing characteristics that suggest he has come from a particular social stratum.

Schools can serve as strong forces either to maintain a closed class system or to open up the system so youths can rise or decline in the structure on the basis of talent and diligence rather than solely on the basis of their family origins. Prior to World War II the schools in ASEAN nations helped maintain closed social classes by supporting a schooling structure that paralleled the social-class pattern. Such a structure is illustrated by the schools in Indonesia under the Dutch East Indies government.

In the elementary-school system of the Netherlands Indies the top stratum was occupied by European primary schools (*European lagere scholen*), taught entirely in Dutch and using a curriculum and text materials imported from Holland. The great majority of pupils in these schools were from white European or Eurasian (Dutch-Indonesian) families. A small number of children from the Indonesian aristocracy and families of high government employees were also admitted along with children of the wealthiest, most influential Chinese. On the second layer down in the structure were other Western-oriented schools taught mainly in Dutch but designed for particular Asian ethnic groups — one variety for the upper classes of the native Indonesian population (*Hollands-Inlanse scholen*), another for Chinese (*Hollands-Chinese scholen*), and a third for Arabs. Still farther down the ladder were three layers of lower-strata schools intended for indigenous commoners. The lowest of these was the three-year village primary school taught in the native dialect. However, there were not nearly enough village schools to enroll the majority of children of school age, so many children went without any formal education or else they attended private Moslem schools that offered a fare that was entirely religious. While the Dutch-language institutions at the top of the structure received government funds and supervision, the village schools were left up to the native princes to finance and oversee, so village schools were generally poor and inadequately supervised. The Moslem schools were essentially neglected by the government. In effect, the school system was a mirror of the social-class structure and served to maintain the structure intact by giving favored opportunities to the ruling elite, fewer opportunities to the middle-class Indonesians needed for operating the economic system, and very meager opportunities to the peasantry. The school system also served to maintain the subculture characteristics of each class level by separating the children from the different classes. A lower-class child of talent and ambition had no chance to mix on a continuing basis with children of upper classes so as to learn their manner of speech and dress, their interests, and their occupational skills. (Hutasoit, 1954, p. 36.)

After World War II, Southeast Asians pressed for self rule, supporting their plea either by armed revolution, as in Indonesia, or by peaceful demands, as in Singapore, Malaysia, and the Philippines. Linked to the demands for self rule were ambitions to break down the old-time social-class barriers. Such ambitions were rooted in the political doctrines of democracy, socialism, and communism which had been introduced from the West and which leaders among the indigenous peoples had learned about in colonial schools. The communists felt they should and could produce a completely classless society, with no citizen receiving any more privilege or status than any other. Other activists, philosophically under the banners of socialism or capitalistic-democracy, did not aspire to eliminate social classes entirely but at least hoped to open the closed systems to easy vertical mobility. They wanted a system in which everyone would have a fair start, then could rise or decline in the class structure on the basis of personal talent and diligence rather than family origin. In the process, they planned to decrease the great gaps they had observed between the rich and poor in the feudal and colonial societies.

In all ASEAN societies, education has been seen as a key tool for opening the social-class structures to vertical movement and for reducing the disparity between rich and poor. All five governments are officially dedicated to furnishing compulsory, universal primary schooling, ranging at least from grades one through six. In addition, they are committed, either by outright declaration or by implication, to some form of post-primary education for most or all youths sometime in the future.

Over the past three decades, great strides toward the goal of universal elementary education have been made in all ASEAN nations. In the Philippines, primary-school enrollment increased 53 percent between 1948 and 1965 (from 3.8 to 5.8 million), was 91 percent over the 1948 figure by 1974 (to 7.3 million), and was expected to reach 10 million by 1980 (a gain of 163 percent over 1948). (*The Philippines,* 1976, p. 304.)

Indonesia's elementary-school enrollment of nearly five million in 1950 had risen 100 percent by 1964 and another 30 percent by 1975. (*Pendidikan di Indonesia,* 1976, p. 54.)

In Thailand, in 1960 there were 3.9 million children in primary schools. By 1970 enrollment had increased 42 percent to 5.6 million and had grown another 34 percent to 6.9 million by 1977. (*Population Dynamics and Educational Development,* 1976, p. 77, Ministry of Education, Thailand, 1977.)

Malaysia's primary-school pupils increased by 27 percent between 1966 and 1976 (from 1.5 million to 1.9 million).

Singapore, in contrast to its four larger neighbors, did not increase elementary-school enrollments over the 1960s and 1970s because virtually 100 percent of primary-school-age children were already attending school by the early 1960s. Then, as a result of Singapore's successful population-control program of the 1960s and 1970s, the number of school-age children actually had decreased between 1966 and 1976 (from 368,846 to 316,265), still representing 100 percent enrollment. Thus, primary-grade attendance figures are not an accurate index of Singapore's progress over the past two decades in providing a fair educational start for children from all social-class strata. For such an index, we can turn to secondary-school enrollments, which rose 35 percent between 1966 and 1976. In other words, Singapore was making even greater progress than its neighbors toward the goal of equal educational opportunities for all youth. (*Yearbook of Statistics, Singapore,* 1977, p. 191.)

In view of these enrollment gains, we might imagine that the prospects are bright for all the ASEAN nations soon achieving the ideal of a sound educational foundation for all children of all social classes. But with the exception of Singapore, the prospects are actually in doubt, for high population growth rates in the other four nations have brought larger waves of children to the educational planners' doorstep each year while planners have been trying to make up for the shortage of schools to accommodate last year's crop of children. The financial and planning burden placed on a society with a high growth rate is enormous. In both Indonesia and Malaysia, 45 percent of the population is under age 15, so that nearly half the citizenry are in economically nonproductive age groups, and a large proportion of these children need schooling opportunities if they are to have a fair chance to succeed in the world that political idealists have promised them. Even if a nation has the financial support to provide the desired school facilities and staff, developing societies are not well equipped to prepare high-quality teachers, administrators, and teaching materials at the rate required. When a great quantity of learners must be cared for immediately, quality usually suffers.

The problem is not simply one of getting all six- or seven-year-olds into classrooms. Of almost equal importance is the task of keeping them in school long enough to ensure a good educational foundation. And the holding power of schools in the ASEAN region, particularly in the rural areas, has often been rather poor. For instance, Thailand has had one of the best records in Asia for providing places for entering primary-school children, but of the pupils who entered grade one in 1964, only 21 percent had completed grade five by the end of the decade. And by 1975 only three percent had reached grade twelve of the upper-secondary school. (*Educational Building and Facilities in the Asian Region*, 1976, p. 133.) Thus, the holding power of schools in most ASEAN nations needs improvement.

We noted earlier that in feudal and colonial times, the upper social classes not only received more education but better education. Efforts in the ASEAN nations since World War II to provide the same quality of schooling for all children, no matter what their socioeconomic status, have met with some measure of success. For example, after Indonesians won their independence, they eliminated the stratified primary-school system of Dutch times and replaced it with a single curriculum for all primary pupils and a common set of textbooks. Similar steps have been taken in the other four countries. However, the problem of ensuring uniform quality from one school or one region to another has not been adequately solved. Schools in all ASEAN nations vary in quality of their staffs, their facilities, and the richness of the pupils' home environments. The economic and intellectual elites of each nation can and do provide more favorable schooling today for their own children than is available to the average or poorer families. This matter of furnishing quality schooling for all children continues to be one of the primary challenges facing educational planners in the ASEAN region. If they fail to meet the challenge adequately, ASEAN social structures will not open further to permit vertical movement between class levels, and the traditional barriers between levels will become more formidable.

THE STRUCTURE OF THE WORK FORCE

In each ASEAN country's national-development plan, the most important responsibility of the education system, other than to promote national unity, has been to produce suitable manpower for the work force. A key component of each plan has been an assessment of manpower needs and a subsequent program for meeting these needs.

The manpower-production plans have been designed to meet two requirements. The first has been to provide the correct number of properly trained workers at the time and place they are needed to meet the nation's economic-development schedule. The second has been to ensure that every able-bodied citizen has a suitable job. In other words, the plan should ensure full employment, which means there will be neither unemployment nor underemployment. (In the ASEAN region, as in other parts of the world, a nation's production/consumption balance is disturbed not only by unemployment but also by widespread underemployment. This condition is common in agricultural areas made up of small land holdings, with a large family trying to live off each holding. In such cases, all adults in the families are listed as employed in farm work, yet no one spends much time over the course of the year in actual agricultural activity.)

Identifying general steps of manpower planning is simple in principle. The process consists of (1) assessing the numbers, types, and quality of workers in the existing economic structure, (2) envisioning the sort of economic structure desired at a specified future date, (3) computing the numbers, types, and quality of workers needed to staff the envisioned economic establishment, then (4) setting up programs to produce the desired work force. Although identifying these general steps is simple, specifying the components within each step and carrying them out efficiently has proven very difficult, particularly in the largest of the ASEAN countries.

The complexity of identifying and of implementing the proper role for the education system in manpower production can perhaps be appreciated if we inspect the sorts of tasks educational planners have faced in ASEAN national-development programs.

The first step — establishing the numbers of each type of worker in the existing labor force — is a difficult job in itself for nations with widely dispersed populations and very modest skills in survey research. The second step — furnishing a realistic estimate of the number of each type of worker needed at specified future times and places — is even more difficult, for it requires accurate speculation about a variety of factors that are incompletely understood. Such factors include (1) the amount of income to be expected from the nation's exports on the world market, income needed to finance manpower programs, (2) the construction rate of facilities for expanded industries that will employ the workers, (3) the availability of such infrastructure items as transportation and communication facilities to move supplies and products in the evolving economic system, (4) the rate at which each sort of worker should be recruited and trained, (5) the willingness of suitably trained workers to take jobs in the locations where they are needed, and (6) the extent to which training for one type of employment serves also as training for another type.

But even more complex is the educators' assignment of determining who should be trained, when, where, and how, and of then carrying out this decision efficiently. This is not simply a matter of learning how many of each sort of worker are needed and then trying to set up enough specialized schools to produce those numbers. If the planning job is to be done well, it requires a good knowledge of the existing dynamics of vocational training in the society. The wisest approach is to examine present training systems and take advantage of their strong points before determining what new schools are needed or what changes should be made in the existing schools. For example, in Malaysia there has been no systematic schooling for motorcycle or motor-scooter repairmen, yet there is a widespread and apparently efficient network of repair shops throughout the country. Training for this vocation is furnished by means of an informal apprenticeship arrangement, with interested young men frequenting the repair shops and learning the trade from the existing repairmen. Under such circumstances, it would be wasteful to set up special curricula or schools for training an expanded corps of motorcycle mechanics for the future. Thus, educational planners need to understand the existing routes taken by workers into their jobs and to adjust new plans to the estimated efficiency of these routes for meeting future needs. If more or better mechanics are needed in the future, then improving the operation of the apprenticeship system might well be a better solution than setting up special classes in vocational schools.

The matter of improving agricultural practices so as to achieve higher yields from crops or to diversify the crops of a particular region is a concern of planners in all ASEAN countries except Singapore. To achieve these goals, several of the nations have sought to increase the amount of agricultural training in the schools. For example, in its national-development plans for the 1970s, the Indonesian Ministry of Education provided for agricultural training in the upper grades of the primary school, because many pupils did not continue school after Grade 5 or 6. Planners hoped to equip such children with skills they could apply as farm workers upon leaving the primary school. However, a variety of questions have worried the educators. In cultures which traditionally have accorded much respect to elders, are parents who farm likely to accept newer ideas about farming from their children who have attended only elementary school? How much can elementary-school teachers who have been studying in a teacher-training school in a city influence the farming practices of children and their parents whose whole life has been farming? That is, are not the upper-elementary-grade pupils more expert at farming practices than their teachers? Is it not better to invest in nonformal training programs for parents, through agricultural-extension services, and then have parents teach their children on-the-job, than to teach pupils better farming practices in school and expect them to alter their parents' farming techniques? These questions that concern vocational educators in the area of agriculture are similar to ones posed about the best vocational-training techniques for such occupations as fishing, furniture making, general carpentry, metal work, and the like.

Establishing sound teacher-training programs for vocational education has been particularly difficult in developing countries, especially in the industrial and business-practice skills which are in such short supply in these nations. First, it has been difficult to recruit the more apt pupils into vocational-teacher programs. The brightest students usually prefer to enroll in the more prestigious curriculum streams that lead to professions and managerial positions or government employment rather than vocational courses or teacher training. Second, an efficiently trained teacher of business practices or of electronics or auto mechanics can usually make far more money working in a business office, electronics plant, or auto repair shop than teaching in a vocational school. Therefore, even when an education system is able to graduate capable vocational teachers, a large proportion of such teachers often enter the business or industrial world rather than the classroom.

The task of producing a modern work force is further complicated by the cost of equipment for programs training machinists, electronic technicians, business-machine operators, welders, printers, mechanics, draftsmen, sheet-metal workers, and the like. Most equipment for such training facilities must be imported and kept in good repair. Thus a country not only needs the funds to import the required equipment but must have at hand spare parts, supplies, and personnel trained in maintaining and

33

repairing the equipment. These requirements have been difficult to meet in most of the ASEAN nations, particularly outside of the nations' largest cities.

One solution to the equipment problem has been to train students on-the-job through a combined work-and-study program or an apprentice-. ship system. In a typical work-and-study plan the students spend part of the day or part of the week in school classes learning foundation skills, such as mathematics or accounting practices, and on theory, such as the nature of electrical circuits. The rest of the day or week they spend in a business office, factory, or shop gaining practical experience. However, if this system is to operate effectively, it requires careful coordination between school and shop. The program fails if the machinist in the shop or the electrical repairman does not allow the student to use the tools himself, but requires the student simply to watch or to serve as a janitor. The program also can fail if the machinist or repairman lacks the patience or instructional skills to turn the student into an apt and enthusiastic worker during the training period. And in some ASEAN nations, efficient operation of planned work-and-study programs has not been achieved very successfully.

Once a vocational-training system has been established, its operation requires constant monitoring so that adjustments can be made as conditions warrant. For instance, if too few students enroll in a vocational school whose graduates are badly needed for the socioeconomic development plan, special incentives such as scholarships may be required to recruit the needed students. Or if too many new vocational secondary schools are erected so that the job market cannot absorb graduates at the rate they are produced, then some of the vocational schools may need to change their curricula to graduate other types of students who can find jobs. If graduates of certain programs are unwilling to move to locations where jobs need filling, some of the programs may need to be relocated into areas short of job applicants. If students prepared to work in small business ventures are unable to find employment, the curriculum of the programs in which they are enrolled may need to be changed so students learn means of setting up their own businesses. In effect, constant feedback of information to the directors of the manpower-production system is necessary if adjustments in the system are to be made. The larger ASEAN nations, in particular, have had difficulty maintaining an efficient monitoring program.

Thus, one of the major challenges before educational planners has been that of efficiently carrying out their assignment in manpower production.

FINANCING EDUCATION

Perhaps the most obvious factors influencing the quantity and quality of education are the society's ability and its willingness to pay for schooling. Ability to pay is reflected in such economic indices as gross national product and per capita income. Willingness to pay is revealed by such indicators as the percent of public budgets devoted to the support of educational institutions. Combined ability and willingness is shown by the percent of people of different ages receiving education, the proportion of schooling costs borne by the government as compared to that borne by individual citizens, and the amount of education available to people who would like to have it.

The manpower-production plan is not the only determinant of how money is spent. Rather, the pattern of expenditures is a kind of compromise intended to satisfy a number of competing forces, including general social demand and the pressures of special interest groups in addition to the manpower-production scheme. Consider, for example, the economy of the typical ASEAN nation (Singapore excepted) that has been based almost exclusively on agriculture and the export of such raw materials as latex, tin, lumber, crude oil, and rice. In their present-day national-growth plans, each of the nations is seeking to develop its manufacturing sector so as to reduce dependence on imported finished goods — textiles, automobiles, electronics equipment, plastic goods, and the like. They are also endeavoring to build up such basic industries as steel, electric power, aluminum, and petroleum while continuing to develop their original agricultural sector toward greater efficiency. This shift toward more basic industry and the manufacture of domestic goods requires the training of more workers at a higher level of skill in a formal educational setting (such as in a school or nonformal program) than has been traditionally true of farm or plantation laborers. To produce such skilled workers for industry and business offices, economic planners often desire more to invest in secondary-level vocational schools than to spend the nation's limited funds on expanding primary schools so everyone would complete four to six years of basic schooling – reading, writing, computing, geography, history, and some natural science. From the viewpoint of economic development, most of the agricultural laborers or those who will work in lumbering, mining, and fishing can learn their trade on the job and do not even need to be literate. However, this option of setting aside for the present the general primary-education program for the masses in favor of more intensive secondary schooling for a selected minority entering the manufacturing and business sector is not really available to economic planners. Social demand will not allow it. For purposes of national unity and political stability, the masses must feel they, too, are having a chance for an education, a chance for the prestige and upward social mobility that schooling seems to promise. Therefore, in allocating funds for schools, economic planners do not have a free hand to invest in the sorts of education they think will bring the quickest economic gains.

Not only are expenditures affected by general social demand but also by the pressures of special interest groups. As noted earlier, pressures from the Malay ethnic group in Malaysia have influenced the government to furnish special opportunities for schooling to Malays, opportunities that have required the use of large sums of money to build special institutions, such as the Mara colleges and Universiti Kebangsaan, and provide scholarships for Malays to study both within the country and abroad.

Not only is the expenditure of funds a complex matter in ASEAN educational systems, but the sources of finance of education in all five nations is complicated as well. In fact, financing schooling is often so involved that it is impossible to determine clearly how much is being spent on education. Let us consider some of the factors contributing to this complexity.

The most obvious source of information about how much is spent on education is the national budget. Using this source, we learn that in the mid-1970s the largest portion of a national budget devoted to education was in Malaysia (21 percent), slightly less in Thailand (19 percent), still less in the Philippines (15 percent, down from 29 percent a decade earlier), and 13 percent in Singapore. When these amounts are expressed as numbers of United States dollar per capita devoted to education, we discover that Singapore devoted $73 per citizen of public funds for education, Malaysia

$32, Thailand $7, and the Philippines $6. (Cheetham and Hawkins, 1976, p. 286; *Yearbook of Statistics, Singapore,* 1977, p. 163.) However, when we analyze the sources of income for schools more closely, we find the national budget figures to be very inadequate. For example, in the Philippines the elementary-school system is funded almost entirely out of the national budget. However, secondary schools are supported either by local authorities, whose funds do not appear in the national budget, or by private organizations, many of them affiliated with religious orders. More than half of the country's secondary-school students attended private schools in the 1970s. (Cheetham and Hawkins, 1976, p. 288.) And even Singapore's rather impressive per capita expenditure fails to reflect the true amount devoted to education, since industrial groups in Singapore contribute substantially to vocational education out of their own funds.

In Indonesia, the funding picture is even more complicated. The budget for the Ministry of Education fails to reflect a major portion of public educational expenditures since elementary-school teachers' salaries are paid by the Ministry of Internal Affairs, and publicly supported Islamic schools are funded by the Ministry of Religion. Furthermore, during the economically difficult 1960s and early 1970s in Indonesia, both private and public schools took the initiative to charge parents extra fees not authorized by the government. In the mid-1970s the government regularized the schedule for parents' fees in elementary schools so the system might be standardized by region and more equitable. Then in the late 1970s all fees for the lower primary grades were eliminated, and the government made up the loss of revenue with extra funds to the schools. However, the practice of charging special fees had become so ingrained that in some schools headmasters and teachers continued the practice despite government regulations forbidding it. Consequently, determining the cost of schooling in Indonesia, as in the other ASEAN countries, is not yet a precise art. The factors affecting the financing picture are still too variable.

Despite the foregoing difficulties in achieving precision, some basic information about financing education in the ASEAN countries and about the effects of funding policies is available. These matters are touched upon in the chapters focusing on the separate nations.

THE CURRENT POLITICAL SYSTEM

Before sketching each ASEAN government's structure, we should mention several generalizations from the field of political science that underlie the relationship between politics and education reflected in Chapters 2 through 6.

The first generalization is that political systems are designed to sustain and perpetuate themselves. No political system, even one instituted by violence, intentionally encourages its own replacement or destruction. Indeed, there is perhaps no government less interested in facing a revolution than one which has itself gained power through revolution.

Second, a political system allows dissent only to a degree that does not threaten the system's survival. When freedom to speak, to assemble, to demonstrate, to publish, or to bear arms is seen as a threat to either the system or those in power, such freedoms are curtailed.

Third, educational institutions sponsored by, or permitted to operate within, a political system are expected to support it. People in control of government view schools as instruments for perpetuating and strengthening the existing government, not as instruments for fomenting criticism or for encouraging the replacement of the present political structure. Educators who appear unduly successful in criticizing the existing government and in advocating a different political structure are usually discredited or suppressed.

Fourth, a nation's constitution and its laws are intended to describe the components of the political system, its benefits (rights) and obligations (responsibilities) for people in the system, and how the whole scheme is supposed to operate. In other words, the legal documents define the game and its rules. For purposes of analysis, we can identify two sorts of political dissent that can arise within or be generated by the education system. The first type is not directed at the political structure itself but at people in it who are accused of not playing by the rules. In other words, government officials are charged with corruption or inefficiency. The critics in this instance can be considered patriots, for they support the present system and base their attacks on its tenets. They are the guardians of the faith. The second type is directed at changing the system itself. Dissenters of this variety are not simply demanding more honesty and efficiency in operating the government, nor are they only asking that the players at the top of the hierarchy be replaced by better ones. Rather, they are advocating a new game which requires a different structure and different rules, and in most cases, different players at the top. From the viewpoint of the existing system, this second sort of critic is not a patriot but a subversive.

Over the past two decades, each ASEAN government has faced both kinds of dissent. As an example of the first kind, university and secondary-school students in the ASEAN countries have on occasion assailed public officials for deviating from either the spirit or the letter of the law − for failing to play by the rules. To support their charges, students have cited principles learned in their civics, citizenship, or social-studies classes. In effect, an educational program that efficiently teaches the nation's political system and engenders strong allegiance to it may be expected to generate this type of dissent. And though this variety of criticism may be undesired by those in office, it can be considered good for the system since it is founded on the system's own rules and is aimed at perpetuating them.

The most prominent example of the second kind of dissent, aimed at replacing the extant political system, has been that produced by advocates of Communism in the five ASEAN nations. In Singapore and Malaya, the Communist challenge came from the Barisan Sosialis political party formed in 1961. In addition, since shortly after World War II the Malayan (and later Malaysian) government has struggled to rid the northern-most province that borders on Thailand of Communist forces. Over the 1950−1965 period, the Indonesian Communist Party regularly gained strength and appeared to be fashioning the nation's political structure more and more. Then an attempted coup d'etat in late 1965, attributed to the Communists, precipitated a violent reaction on the part of the Indonesian army, Moslems, and students. Within a few months the Communist Party was outlawed and the present Suharto government installed. Thailand has increasingly felt the pressure of Communism as Laos, Cambodia, and Vietnam along the Thai northeastern and southeastern borders have adopted Communist political systems. The Philippines has also faced pressures from within its own citizenry to install a Communist form of government. However, none of these attempts has been successful, so the five ASEAN governments are as yet strongly anti-Communist.

In like manner, the educational institutions of all five countries are anti-Communist as well, since they are intended by political leaders and their faithful constituents to sustain the existing political systems and to discourage the adoption of competing systems. The schools' citizenship programs and their social-science curricula should be interpreted from this vantage point. The programs either omit the discussion of competing political systems or else cast them in an unfavorable light. In view of the political history of the ASEAN countries over the past four decades, this state of affairs is hardly surprising. As implied earlier, when a government's position seems secure, educators are more often allowed to describe and even praise competing forms of government. But when the existing government's position feels precarious — as has been true periodically for each of the ASEAN countries — educators are discouraged or even proscribed from depicting alternative political systems in a favorable manner. The treatment of political matters in schools of the ASEAN region usually has been carefully monitored. Likewise, the appointment of people to positions in the education system depends partially on how loyal they are to the existing political system. The appointment of dissidents is generally discouraged.

Though the ASEAN nations do not have an identical government structure, each has some form of representative government in which the people are entitled to elect all, or at least a majority, of their representatives. The Indonesian government is headed by a president who is appointed to office by the People's Deliberative Council, consisting of 920 individuals, of which two-thirds are elected by the people through the medium of political parties. The remaining one-third are appointed by the government to represent segments of the society for which political parties do not speak, such as the military and diverse geographical regions. Over the past three decades elections have been held whenever the government has deemed the internal stability of the nation sufficient to ensure that the elections will be conducted properly and peacefully.

The Malaysian government is an elective constitutional monarchy. The supreme head of state, called the Yang Di Pertuan Agong, and his deputy head, the Timbalan Yang Di Pertuan Agong, are elected for five-year terms by the nine hereditary Malay rulers from among their own group. The nation's Conference of Rulers consists of the nine hereditary rulers plus the Yang Di Pertuan Negara of Sabah and the governors of Malacca, Penang, and Sarawak. However, the actual executive power is held by the Cabinet, headed by the Prime Minister who is the leader of the political party that has won the most seats in a parliamentary election. Since gaining independence on July 4, 1946, the Republic of the Philippines has had a government modeled after that of the United States, a government headed by an elected president with a strong executive branch balanced by a bicameral congress. Voter participation in elections has been high. A two-party system has evolved with candidates from each party frequently holding high office. (Cheetham and Hawkins, 1976, p. 8.)

Singapore technically is a republic organized like the British parliamentary democracy. However, its original two-party system disappeared in 1966 when members of the opposition who made up a small minority of the elected members of parliament resigned in objection to the dominance of the People's Action Party which had first won effective control of the government in 1959. Since 1966 the city-state has been governed by the PAP unopposed, with Lee Kuan Yew as prime minister, a post he has held over the 20 years since the party first gained power. The government has been described as a "bureaucratic state".

> The Prime Minister and his cabinet formulate policy, direct its implementation, and hold the bureaucracy accountable for loyal, honest, and efficient administration. Parliament exercises little effective authority. (Skolnik, 1976, p. 10.)

Thailand's government is a constitutional monarchy led by King Bhumibol Adlyadej, Rama IX, who came to the throne in June 1946 after the Japanese occupation of World War II ended. Since that time a number of revolutions and reformations of the government have taken place, but none affected the institution of the monarchy nor influenced the established bureaucracy in any major way. As Burpakdi and Mahakhan observe later in Chapter 6, "What has been taking place is a struggle for a workable system of democratic government that fits the Thai personality. Thais have been experimenting for nearly 47 years and are prepared to wait a little longer for success." A notable feature of Thai education is the prominent place given to teaching loyalty to the crown and respect for the royal family and for the king as a Buddhist leader.

In view of the foregoing discussion, the question now may be asked, "How is the relationship of politics to schools treated later in the separate country chapters?" The answer is that little direct mention of the relationship is made, but at many points in each country description readers will find it possible to draw inferences about connections between politics and education. For example, political implications lie in the nation's stated educational aims, in the role of education in national-development programs, in the ethnic and religious patterns of educational opportunity, in the segments of the school system that receive the most financial support, and in social-class differentials in educational facilities and opportunities.

From the standpoint of political affiliation, Chapters 2 through 6 clearly represent a view of schooling that supports instead of finding fault with the policies of the governments now in power. Such a favorable rather than critical perspective is to be expected, since the authors of the country chapters, with one exception, are either officials in the nations' ministries of education or are professors in public universities. In other words, the authors are insiders, members of the established bureaucracy. As such, they are well qualified to give an accurate description of the nature of schooling in their countries. They could not reasonably be expected to assail the political system which the schools support nor to spend much effort on exposing weaknesses or inefficiencies in the operation of the educational systems they represent.

CONCLUSION

In this second section of Chapter 1 we have identified some of the ways that education in the ASEAN nations is influenced by such factors as geography and the distribution of the population, ethnic and religious affiliation, social-class patterns, the nature of the existing and future work forces, the financing of education, and the political system of the nation. Each of these factors receives consideration in the five country chapters.

As the final section of Chapter 1, we turn now to the nature of educational cooperation among the ASEAN members.

Cooperative Educational Ventures in the ASEAN Region

Most cooperative educational projects carried out by the ASEAN countries are sponsored by the Southeast Asian Ministers of Education

Organization (SEAMEO). When this coalition of Southeast Asian educational leaders was originally formed in 1965, South Vietnam, Cambodia, and Laos were also members. But when the former French Indo-China territories came under Communist control in the early and middle 1970s, they became "non-contributing" partners in SEAMEO, leaving the organization actually composed of only the five members of ASEAN.

The work of SEAMEO has been conducted through the medium of six research and development centers, each situated in a different location. Three of the centers have been concerned chiefly with tertiary education and research. These are the centers for Graduate Study and Research in Agriculture (SEARCA at Los Banos in the Philippines), for Research Training and Postgraduate Study in Tropical Biology (BIOTROP at Bogor in Indonesia), and for Tropical Medicine (CCB TROPMED or Central Coordinating Board for Tropical Medicine in Bangkok, Thailand). The other three regional centers have more direct bearing on elementary and secondary education. They are the centers for Education in Science and Mathematics (RECSAM at Penang, Malaysia), for Language Education (RELC in Singapore), and for Educational Innovation and Technology (INNOTECH, originally in Saigon, then temporarily in Singapore, and now in Manila, the Philippines).

The RECSAM facility in Malaysia carries out a variety of activities aimed at improving the teaching of science and mathematics in all ASEAN countries. Through research into science teaching, the center has developed new courses of study, reading materials for pupils, and audio-visual teaching materials that are suited particularly to the needs of educators in ASEAN countries. The center serves also as a clearing house of information on science and mathematics teaching to keep member nations up-to-date with advances in the field. Short-term courses and workshops for science and mathematics educators from the member nations are sponsored by the center to train educators in such skills as evaluation, creating science-teaching equipment, training teachers, and the like.

The Regional Language Centre in Singapore sponsors activities in the realm of language instruction that parallel the science-and-mathematics projects of RECSAM. The center collects and distributes information on improved methods of English instruction, trains teacher-educators and supervisors from the member nations, offers consultant services to solve specific problems faced by institutions in the ASEAN region, and supports

43

scholars who are focusing on problems of teaching English in the region.

As its name suggests, the Innovation and Technology Center (INNOTECH) in the Philippines sponsors research and development programs that encourage departures from the traditional educational practices of the ASEAN countries, particularly departures featuring advanced educational technology. An illustration of a typical INNOTECH project is the nonformal-education experiment conducted in the Philippines and in Indonesia since 1973. The purpose of the project has been to develop alternatives to the traditional primary school for offering villagers elementary education. In the Philippines the program has gone under the acronym IMPACT (Instructional Management by Parents, Community, and Teachers) and in Indonesia under the name PAMONG, an Indonesian translation of the Philippines title. Through a brief description of the Indonesian plan, we can demonstrate how a typical INNOTECH project evolves.

The PAMONG program has been designed to provide the equivalent of an elementary-school education for two sorts of people, those who did not have an opportunity to attend a six-year elementary school and those who dropped out of school before finishing. In this nonformal-learning plan a tutor spends his time each week among four "learning posts", with each post located in one of the neighborhoods (*kampungs*) that make up a village community. Whenever the tutor arrives once or twice a week at the post (which is a room in someone's home, a part of a shop, or a village meeting center), students from the neighborhood meet with the tutor to get help with self-instructional (programmed-learning) modules.

One of the key activities in the project has been the development of the self-instructional materials. Another activity, developed in regular classrooms of the Central Java region where the project has been conducted, has been peer teaching. In this portion of the plan, sixth-grade pupils have tutored first graders, and fifth-grade pupils have tutored second graders. Hence, children in the lowest grades, lacking the reading skills needed to profit from the programmed reading texts, still could learn with the help of the older students.

The initial PAMONG development steps were completed in Central Java in the late 1970s so that beginning in 1979—1980 the project was scheduled for transfer to the islands of Bali and Kalimantan with far larger numbers of students. Throughout the program SEAMEO officials have coordinated activities with the Philippines version of nonformal elementary education, have provided foreign experts in the area of preparing instructional materials, and have obtained funding from such bodies as the U.S. State Department's Agency for International Development.

Although SEAMEO has been the most prominent sponsor of intercountry educational cooperation, projects have also been carried out in ASEAN nations under the auspices of such international organizations as UNESCO and UNICEF. In addition, pairs of ASEAN countries in bilateral arrangements have pursued joint projects, such as the Indonesian-Malaysian activities focusing on producing a uniform spelling system for the two countries' Malay-based national languages.

In summary, over the past decade and a half, cooperative educational ventures in the ASEAN region have increased in number and quality, and further growth in joint efforts are expected in the future.

Conclusion

As explained earlier, the purpose of Chapter 1 has been to provide readers with a set of expectations or viewpoints that may help them profit more from the following chapters that consider the five ASEAN country's education systems in detail. The general scheme of each country chapter is the same. Readers are first introduced to demographic, economic, political, and historical factors that influence the form and conduct of elementary and secondary schooling. Then the educational system itself is described against its historical background. Finally, problems and prospects for the future are outlined. The book's final chapter once again draws the ASEAN countries together as a group and outlines educational issues they are expected to face during the last two decades of the 20th century.

References

CHEETHAM, R. J. and HAWKINS, E. (1976) *The Philippines, Priorities and Prospects for Development,* IBRD and World Bank, Washington, D.C.

Schooling in the ASEAN Region

Education Building Facilities in the Asian Region (1976) Bulletin 17, UNESCO Regional Office in Asia, Bangkok.

SKOLNIK, RICHARD L. (1976) *The Nation-wide Learning System of Singapore,* Institute of Southeast Asian Studies, Singapore.

SOLIDUM, ESTRELLA D. (1974) *Toward a Southeast Asian Community,* University of Philippines Press, Quezon City.

Third Malaysia Plan 1976–1980 (1976) Government Press, Kuala Lumpur.

THOMAS, R. MURRAY (1973) *A Chronicle of Indonesian Higher Education,* Chopmen, Singapore.

Yearbook of Statistics, Singapore 1976/1977 (1977) Department of Statistics, Singapore.

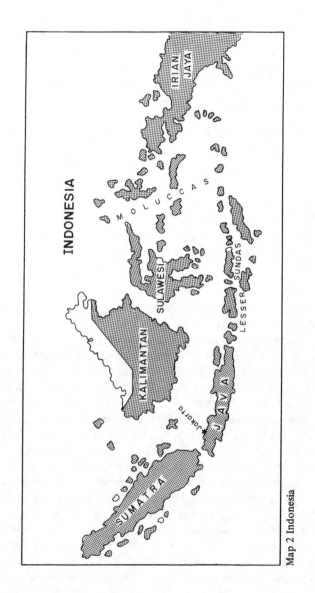

Map 2 Indonesia

Satu bangsa, satu negara,
satu bahasa.

One people, one country,
one language.
INDONESIAN YOUTH PLEDGE

2

Indonesia

Soedijarto, Lexy Moleong, A. Suryadi, Darlis Machmud, F. Pangemanan,
A. F. Tangyong, N. Nasoetion, and R. Murray Thomas

AS A LAND and as a society, Indonesia is by far the largest and displays
by far the greatest diversities of all the ASEAN countries. It has the
largest number of islands and the greatest land and sea area. It is the
richest in natural resources. It has the most ethnic groups and tribes,
types of villages, regional social structures, languages and dialects. It
exhibits the widest diversity of art forms – in drama, dance, music,
carving, painting, and textiles.

Because of its size and diversities, Indonesia also has the largest educational system with the most complex problems to be solved. In order to
depict the nature of these problems and the solutions applied to them,
we shall first consider the physical and social environment in which
the educational system operates – the distribution of people throughout
the islands, ethnic and religious affiliations, the political and economic
structures, and the historical antecedents of the present-day political
establishment. Then we shall inspect the nation's formal and nonformal
educational efforts, including the administrative structure, curricula and
examinations, and the modes of teacher preparation. The chapter closes
with a review of problems and prospects for the years ahead.

Out of Diversity — One People, One Country, One Language

The extent and shape of Indonesia today resulted from Dutch colonial forces winning control over more and more islands in the archipelago between the early 17th and early 20th centuries to form the Netherlands East Indies. But in 1942 the Japanese military ousted the Dutch and controlled the territory until the close of World War II in late 1945, when the Dutch returned to reclaim their former colony. The island peoples, however, declared their independence on August 17, 1945, then fought the Dutch over the next four years to win uncontested self-rule at the close of 1949.

Inspection of a map of Indonesia shows what may appear to be illogical borders on two of the world's largest islands — Borneo (called Kalimantan by Indonesians) and New Guinea (known as Irian Jaya). The logic, however, is that of colonialism. The parts of Borneo and New Guinea held by the Dutch before World War II became the property of the Republic of Indonesia. Most of North Borneo that belonged to the British Empire became the eastern portion of Malaysia in 1963 when Malaysia was constituted as a nation. Eastern New Guinea, also formerly a British possession, is today the independent Republic of Papua New Guinea.

The land area of the Republic of Indonesia consists of 13,667 islands, only 931 of which are inhabited. The islands spread across the seas for 5,110 kilometers (3,194 miles) east to west and 1,888 kilometers (1,180 miles) north to south. The width is greater than that of the United States. The islands straddle the equator, so the entire nation is in the tropical zone, with the heaviest rainfall in the west, diminishing gradually toward the east. There is an east-wind, dry-monsoon season from June through September and a wet-monsoon season December through March.

These geographic and climatic conditions pose several problems for the educational leaders who direct the nation's centralized education system from headquarters in the capital city of Jakarta on the northwest coast of Java. Communication and transportation are particularly difficult. The inner regions of Kalimantan contain dense forests and swamps, with few roads available, so that remote schools cannot easily be furnished with textbooks, curriculum guidebooks, inservice education for the staff, or directives about new regulations. Mountain areas of Sumatra and Irian Jaya are also difficult to enter. Access to many of

49

the smaller islands is gained in a most circuitous manner — it requires taking a ship to a large island in the region, chartering a boat to a medium-sized island, then boarding a smaller boat which travels once every three or four months to the small island that is the object of the trip. The trip can take as long as five or six months. Therefore, schools in such locations not only receive supplies and directives late — or not at all — but statistical reports on enrollments in remote schools arrive back at the central Ministry of Education in Jakarta long after the data were gathered, if at all. Such delays and unreliability in communicating make precise educational planning at the central level especially difficult, since good planning and the efficient execution of plans clearly require the prompt flow of accurate messages throughout the system.

The tropical heat and humidity hasten the deterioration of equipment, particularly of typewriters, mimeograph machines, tape recorders, radios, and television receivers that are increasingly being imported during efforts to modernize the education system.

Indonesia's geography of widely distributed, mountainous islands also causes staffing problems. Apt young teachers who have attended teacher-education institutions in cities are often unwilling to take teaching jobs in remote areas, particularly if the customs and language of the areas differ from their own. Supervisors and school inspectors seldom if ever reach certain schools, and staff members from isolated districts are seldom able to attend upgrading workshops or enter advanced-degree courses in colleges.

To overcome such problems caused by geography, Indonesia in recent years has expanded both sea and air service by means of small power boats and small planes to formerly out-of-the-way spots. Teams of inservice educators have traveled by four-wheel-drive vehicles or power boats to reach distant schools. However, geography continues to be a major obstacle to the efficient administration of education throughout the Republic.

Population size and distribution are additional major factors in the conduct of schooling. Indonesia's population of about 145 million by 1980 was exceeded only by the populations of China, India, the Soviet Union, and the United States. The annual 2.7 percent growth rate, if continued, will bring the population to over 200 million by 1992. In view of such a prospect, the task of Indonesian educational planners is immense. The magnitude of their goal to furnish universal elementary schooling and large amounts of secondary education is even more impressive when we consider the population by age and sex as of 1975. Of the total 127 million people that year, 46 percent were below age 15, which is the age group known as the nonproductive segment of the population, since the children who compose the group cannot be expected to contribute ideas and energies productively to the nation's economic system. Furthermore, a large number in this group are of schooling age and therefore are customers for the services of the nation's educational system. For instance, 28 percent of the entire population falls in this 5–14 age bracket, and another 11 percent is in the 15–19 category.

In terms of rural-urban distribution, the population is overwhelmingly rural. At the time of the latest complete census (1971), only 11 percent of the people lived in cities of 100,000 or larger. However, as in most nations, internal migration in Indonesia is from rural to urban areas. As the years pass, cities must assume an increasing proportion of the task of education.

The populace is composed of dozens of ethnic or tribal groups, each with its own pattern of customs and its own language or dialect. The largest is made up of perhaps 80 million or more Javanese, who occupy central and eastern Java and who speak the socially-stratified Javanese language. By "socially stratified" we mean that a different vocabulary is used in a person's speaking to people of his same social-class level than is used in speaking to ones of superior or inferior status. Other tribal groups range in size from perhaps 25 or 30 million Sundanese in West Java to clusters in Central Kalimantan (Borneo) and Irian Jaya (New Guinea) of a few hundred or few thousand each.

In nations of such ethnic diversity a serious problem for national political leaders and educators alike is that of establishing a national language that promotes unity among all citizens and a feeling of nationhood and allegiance to the government. Typically a country's varied language groups fail to agree on which tongue everyone should learn in common. But Indonesia is the exception. During Dutch colonial times a conference of youths from widely separated sections of the East-Indies colony convened in 1928 and declared that they would in the future be regarded as one people united as a single country with one language (*satu bangsa, satu negara, satu bahasa*). The one language would be called *Indonesian language* (*bahasa Indonesia*), a variant of the Malay tongue which was spoken already as a lingua franca throughout the port cities of the archipelago. However, the use of this language did not become widespread as the instrument of official communication until the Japanese captured the islands in early 1942. Japanese military leaders outlawed further use of the Dutch language for official and educational purposes and substituted Malay-Indonesian until the time the Indonesian populace would learn Japanese. Following World War II, when the Japanese returned to their homeland, the newly declared Indonesian Republic adopted the Indonesian version of Malay as the unifying language of its peoples. And since that time the Indonesian language has been enthusiastically adopted by all tribal groups as the national language. While the local dialect may be used as the medium of instruction in schools during the first three primary grades, thereafter Indonesian is the medium of instruction in all schools through the university. In short, there is no resistance to learning the national tongue. The educational problems in relation to languages are limited to such technical matters as achieving a proper transition from the local dialect to the national language in the primary grades and producing textbooks in both Indonesian and, where it is economically feasible, the local dialect for the lower grades.

Perhaps the most serious educational problem in the realm of language has been that of maintaining local dialects and perpetuating tribal literature at the same time that school instruction is in the national language. With limited funds and limited personnel, the educational system faces the doubly burdensome task of establishing universal literacy in the Indonesian language and preventing the loss of regional languages and folklore by including these as subjects in the curriculum.

Religious diversity is a further factor which educational planners must consider. Indonesia has the largest Moslem population of any country in the world. In the 1971 census the percentages of each religious denomination were 87.5 Moslem, 7.4 Christian (Catholics and Protestants), nearly 2 percent Hindu, nearly 1 percent Buddhist, and the remaining 2 percent Confucian and other sects. The government has a policy of freedom-of-choice in religion, with religious instruction required in both public and private schools at all levels of the education system. Prior to 1966, it was possible for parents who did not subscribe to a religion to excuse their children from the hour or so of religious instruction provided each week. However, this option, supported by the Indonesian Communist

Party among others, was altered after the Party was outlawed in 1966, so that each student is now required to participate in religious education as offered by an advocate of the student's faith who specializes in religious instruction. The five faiths for which curriculum guidebooks have been published are Islam, Catholicism, Christian Protestantism, Hinduism (in the Balinese version), and Buddhism. These are the ones that officially can be taught during school hours. Others cannot.

The charge that educational planners bear in regard to the marked variations in ethnic, language, religious, and social-class characteristics is reflected in the national motto, "Unity in Diversity" (*Bhinneka Tunggal Ika*). Their assignment is to mount an educational program that promotes allegiance to the nation as a unit and at the same time protects the ethnic, language, and religious identity of the separate groups that compose the whole.

The Government and its Development Plans

The main force behind intentional changes in the education system over the past dozen years has been the series of five-year national-development plans formulated by the government to achieve the "just and prosperous society" to which the populace aspires. The development plans represent a marked departure from the socioeconomic-growth strategy followed prior to 1966. In the pre-1966 era the government was led by President Sukarno, who had held office since the Republic was first formed in August 1945. Under Sukarno the nation in the late 1950s and early 1960s increasingly reduced the role of foreign investment in Indonesia, charging that European and American imperialists were largely responsible for exploiting Indonesia in the past, so Indonesia would make its own way economically. At this same time the Indonesian Communist Party gained strength in the country's political realm, and the government depended increasingly on mainland China for its political support abroad. After an attempted Communist coup was defeated in late 1965 all this changed. The Communist Party was dispersed, Sukarno was replaced by General Suharto as president, and economic planning was assigned to economists at the University of Indonesia whose academic preparation had a strong American and European bent.

An earlier eight-year development plan under Sukarno (1961–1968) was a dismal failure in its economic aspects. The only positive advance it achieved in its educational component was the establishment in each of the nation's 21 provinces of a public university and a public teachers college. Under the new Suharto government in 1968 a series of five-year development programs was inaugurated, emphasizing improvement of the nation's major industry — agriculture — and exploitation of such natural resources as petroleum, mineral deposits, and extensive forests. To achieve their goals, economic planners sought foreign investors who would enter into joint-venture projects with the Indonesian government, bringing funds and expertise to Indonesia to hasten progress in a variety of fields. Since the late 1960s many millions of dollars have been invested in Indonesia by foreign firms, and millions more in loans for improving the nation's infrastructure (transportation, communication, administration) have come from international agencies. Over the past dozen years Indonesia's income from exports, particularly of petroleum products, has risen significantly. The country's increasingly favorable balance of trade in terms of exports and imports is illustrated in Fig. 2.1.

The success of the economic-development plans during the 1970s has influenced schooling in several ways. First, the first three five-year plans (1969–1973, 1974–1978, 1979–1984) laid out the guidelines for innovations which the Ministry of Education's new Research and Development Center would sponsor nationwide. Second, the infusion of funds into the government treasury from exports, loans, and grants permitted the country to finance educational expansion and quality-improvement at a level never before possible. The growing health of the economy in general enabled the supporters of private schools to improve private education as well.

The overall intention of the First Five-Year National-Development Plan (1969–1974) was to raise agricultural output, stimulate mining production (including petroleum), increase such industries as textile producers, and build up the infrastructure (communication, transportation) required for socioeconomic progress. (*Rentjana Pembangunan Lima Tahun 1969/70–1973/74*, 1968, Vol. I, pp. 15–30.) The educational component of the plan focused on attacking seven problems: (1) providing enough educational facilities to accommodate the entire school-age population, particularly at the elementary-school level, (2) altering secondary-school

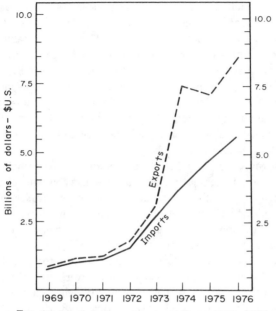

FIG. 2.1 Trends in import—export balance 1969—1976

enrollments from their present majority of students in general-academic curricula to a ratio that finds far more in vocational-training schools, particularly in agricultural institutions, (3) increasing the percentage of pupils who pass from primary into secondary education, particularly into vocational secondary schools, (4) reducing illiteracy in the adult population, (5) reducing the 50-percent dropout rate in the elementary school, (6) increasing the corps of qualified teachers, and (7) improving administrative efficiency. (*Rentjana Pembangunan Lima Tahun 1969/70–1973/74*, 1968, Vol. IIC, pp. 15–17.) In addition, the plan committed the nation to a family-planning-education program that might reduce the nation's birth rate substantially. This was an entirely new policy for Indonesia, since under the Sukarno government prior to 1966 the president had condemned birth-control efforts and, instead, encouraged population growth.

The 1969–1974 plan was pursued with encouraging success, despite a good many difficulties and shortfalls in achieving specific goals in both economic development and education. The subsequent 1974—1978 Second Five-Year National-Development Plan dramatically increased funds for educational development (beyond the budget for routine operations) by 666 percent over the First Plan, that is, from $192 (US$) to $1,283 million. The proportion scheduled for different segments of the school system was: primary education 38 percent, junior-high schools 15 percent, senior-high schools 14 percent, higher education 12 percent, and special vocational and youth-guidance programs 21 percent. (*Second Five-Year Development Plan,* 1974, p. 17.)

The following examples suggest the nature of the principal goals of the Second Plan. In terms of quantitative expansion, the Plan aimed to raise the proportion of children ages 7—12 attending school from 57 percent in 1973 to 85 percent by 1979. To accomplish this, the government planned the most extensive school building program in the nation's history and a large-scale teacher-education effort that would supply 38,000 new primary-school teachers each year. A total of 180 million new textbooks in basic subject-matter areas were to be published. To expand secondary education, 650 new junior-high buildings were to be erected and 1,500 more rehabilitated, while 518 senior-high buildings were scheduled for repair, and fully equipped chemistry laboratories were to be added. Over the five-year period, 30,000 new junior-high and 11,000 new senior-high teachers were to be trained. A total of 52 million textbooks would be printed.

A further goal in the Second Plan was to improve the relevance and quality of education. Not only were higher-quality textbooks to be published at all levels of the school system, but a number of curriculum-development projects were to be continued or initiated in both the formal and nonformal education sectors. Several inservice teacher-education programs of the First Plan were to be expanded. Finally, upgrading programs were planned for improving the supervisory skills of the nation's several thousand school inspectors. (Suriasumantri, Hasbullah, and Dachliani, 1976, pp. 1—24.)

The Third Five-Year Development Plan scheduled for mid-1979 to mid-1984 was designed to correct shortfalls in the Second Plan and extend the educational programs further in the general directions delineated for the Second Plan.

Governance of the Islands – the Historical Background

During several eras in the ancient past, the islands of the Indonesian archipelago and parts of its adjacent Asian land mass were collected into different patterns of empire. However, the present-day pattern that forms the Republic of Indonesia is not the result of conquests by ancient emperors. Instead, it is the consequence of Dutch colonialists' winning control over more and more island regions during the three centuries prior to the early 1900s. The Dutch first came to the Far East to vie with the Spanish and Portuguese for the spice trade which centered in the north-central islands of the archipelago – for clove and nutmeg that made food palatable in a Europe that lacked refrigeration. Although the Spanish managed to hold the Philippines until 1898, and the Portuguese kept the eastern half of the Indonesian island of Timor until the mid-1970s, the Dutch won the remainder of the territory that the British did not already control. They labeled the island colony the Netherlands East Indies and set up plantations for growing coffee, tea, rubber, and sugar cane, thus creating riches for the Netherlands.

The Dutch administered the islands through the medium of the traditional princes or sultans who controlled the separate princedoms when the Europeans arrived. Within each district or province, the local prince was the titular ruler, but a Dutch governor or district supervisor was on hand to serve as his "advisor". If the prince did not heed the advice, he would soon be out of office. During the 19th century the East Indies government established a "culture system" which set agricultural-production quotas for different parts of the country and required peasants to contribute free a designated portion of their time to the system.

During the early decades of the 20th century, indigenous islanders increasingly voiced nationalistic, anticolonial sentiments publicly and were jailed or banished to remote places for expressing such views. Although the amount of formal education of a Western type that was available to Indonesians was slight, enough young islanders did progress through the school system to produce a small corps of vocal and convincing nationalistic leaders. Among those leaders who were banished to isolated islands by the Dutch in the 1930s were Sukarno, Mohammad Hatta, and Sutan Sjahrir, who were freed by the Japanese armed forces in 1942 after the Japanese invasion. These three subsequently became the first president,

57

vice-president, and prime minister of the Republic of Indonesia in August 1945.

In 1950, the control of the government came securely into Indonesian hands, following the Revolution against the Dutch from late 1945 through 1949. However, a significant portion of the economy was still controlled by Europeans who owned plantations, oil fields, shipping facilities, banking establishments, and import—export firms. President Sukarno declared that under these conditions the Revolution was not over. The fighting had stopped, but the social-economic Revolution was still being fought. He proposed the establishment of an Indonesian variety of socialism. As a result, during the middle and latter 1950s the government took over more and more foreign firms. Among the strong supporters of Sukarno's efforts to eliminate Western capitalism and substitute a form of socialism was the Indonesian Communist Party. The Party, which grew from a relatively small organization in the early 1950s to an enormous mass movement by 1965, was at first closely associated with the Soviet Union. But by the mid-1960s it had become bound far more intimately to mainland China.

Over the decade 1955–1965 the Indonesian economy declined at an accelerating pace. The US-dollar to Indonesian-rupiah ratio was officially $1 to 11-rupiah in the mid-1950s, but by 1958 the ratio was $1 to 85-rupiah. During the early 1960s it climbed to $1 to 500-rupiah, then $1 to 1000-rupiah, and eventually $1 to 20,000-rupiah or more. The Eight-Year National-Development Plan, scheduled for 1961–1968, was ill conceived and badly executed, with the planners unreasonably expecting a range of economic improvements to arise from industrial development that would be founded on local initiative and investment without much input of foreign expertise, funds, or equipment. By the mid-1960s political tensions increased between (1) left-wing forces gathered around the Indonesian Communist Party and (2) their opponents among the military, religious parties, and college students and staff members. President Sukarno appeared to control affairs by playing one side against the other. However, by mid-1965 it was apparent that he was according greater favor to the left-wing faction.

The political tensions broke loose on the night of September 30, 1965 when an attempted coup by military units under the Communists brought retaliation from the army, Moslems, and students. From the turmoil of the following months arose a new government under an army general, Suharto, who continued as president in 1980. Sukarno was isolated to his home, the Communist Party was outlawed, and diplomatic relations with China were terminated. The new government placed Western-educated economists in charge of socioeconomic planning, and a system of encouraging foreign investments was vigorously promoted. Thus, the political and economic tack of the Sukarno years of 1955—1965 was reversed. The new five-year development programs operate under a policy of heavy foreign investments that are monitored, and the profits shared, by the Indonesian government. It is in this political-economic environment that the education system has operated throughout the 1970s.

The Evolution of Schooling in Indonesia

Three main streams have contributed to the nature of education in modern-day Indonesia.

First is the sort of informal training that children receive from the family and community. In the ancient past as in the present, the core of what young people know about the nature of their world, the customs and language of their ethnic group, roles people play in life, and one's occupation has been learned through direct participation in family and village life. Today, most Indonesians are farmers or fishermen or artisans, occupations still learned from parents and neighbors through on-the-job participation.

The second stream is that of Islamic religious instruction, offered through the institutions of the *langgar* (small prayer house) and *pesantren* (a non-graded school operated by a Moslem scholar).

The third stream was introduced by the European colonialists. It is the institution typically known as a "school" in Western societies. It consists of a special building in which pupils are enrolled in grades that parallel their age levels. The curriculum is composed chiefly of such secular subjects as reading and writing the vernacular, history, geography, mathematics, science, and — in the upper grades — foreign languages.

Although the Islamic and Western-secular schools still exist as two identifiable systems in Indonesia — with the former under the Ministry of Religion and the latter under the Ministry of Education and Culture —

recent decades have found them becoming more alike. To clarify the characteristics of these institutions and to picture recent trends in their development, we shall briefly trace their historical backgrounds.

ISLAMIC SCHOOLS – LANGGAR, PESANTREN, MADRASAH

For centuries the simplest level of Islamic educational center has been the *langgar,* a small prayer house in a city or at the edge of a village where children learn to chant verses of the Koran in Arabic under the tutelage of an adult respected for his knowledge of such matters. The course of this study usually lasts from a few months to a year, with pupils attending perhaps two hours in the morning and another two in the evening. To begin, children learn the Arabic alphabet, then advance to chanting passages of the Koran, being careful to intone the text in the sing-song pattern demonstrated by their teacher. As a social institution the langgar over the centuries has served to impress children with the realization that they are members of the great congregation of Moslems.

After completing the year at a langgar and reaching the early or middle teens in age, some youths attend a more advanced religious school known most often in Indonesia as a *pesantren,* or in certain areas as a *pondok.* Although Indonesia today is a predominantly Moslem land, the Islam of Indonesia is erected on a substructure of Hinduism that preceded the arrival of Moslems. And one modern-day evidence of the society's Hindu beginnings nearly two millenia in the past is the pesantren form of school. Originally it apparently consisted of a Hindu guru who collected youths at his home in a remote place to study holy writings. When Islam replaced Buddhist-Hinduism on the principal western Indonesian islands in the 13th through 17th centuries, the Hindu ascetic scholar's center was transformed into the Moslem pesantren directed by an Islamic scholar or *ulama,* customarily called *kiyai* or *ajengan.*

The traditional pesantren is a boarding school, usually located in a rural setting adjacent to a mosque. It is directed by one or more scholars who give lessons in their dwelling complex to students known as *santris* or "followers" who have come to the study center because of the scholar's reputation for expertise in a particular aspect of Islamic doctrine. Included in the school complex are simple dormitories, called *pondoks* or *asramas,* where students live a spartan existence, sleeping on mats and cooking their food over a small fire. The santris pay no fees but commonly contribute to the scholar's welfare with gifts of money or food, or they may work in the ulama's garden or rice fields part of the day.

A student may stay only a few months or may remain 10 years or longer, depending upon how profitable he finds his studies. Common subjects taught are the Arabic language, principles of Islamic faith (*Usuluddin*), laws interpreted from the Koran and the Hadits (traditions of the Prophet), and Arobiyah science of analyzing Islam in depth. A typical day for santris starts with morning prayer (*subuh*), followed by the first series of lessons. At midday santris may do volunteer work for the teacher or may study. After lunch and a rest period, they begin their lessons once more, with further study periods coming after the sunset prayer and evening prayer.

The precise number of pesantrens in Indonesia is unknown, for the institutions are private organizations with no formal responsibility to report to government bodies, though most of them apparently do so. In size they range from a dozen or so santris to a hundred or more, and in a few cases there are pesantrens enrolling over a thousand students. According to Ministry of Religion estimates, there were 4,752 pesantrens in the nation in 1977 with a total enrollment of 830,850 santris taught by 15,950 instructors.* However, figures for 1974 (Table 2.1) are far lower, so the true number is in considerable doubt.

In the early years of the 20th century, groups of Islamic leaders expressed dissatisfaction with the pesantren, noting that students attending this institution did indeed acquire religious knowledge but did not achieve command over the kinds of practical skills taught in the nation's Western-style secular schools. Hence, during the second decade of the century several Islamic organizations intent on modernizing their institutions introduced secular subjects to parallel religious studies in the curriculum. This new institution, representing an amalgam of Islam and worldly topics (reading and writing in the vernacular language, arithmetic, history, geography, natural science), was named the *madrasah*, a term imported from the Middle East.

*The source of statistics on schools, students, and teachers in Chapter 2 is the Office of Statistics, Research and Development Center, Ministry of Education and Culture of the Republic of Indonesia.

Madrasahs increased with some regularity during the 1920s and 1930s, but the marked upsurge in their numbers did not come until after World War II when the new Republic's Ministry of Religion directed its main efforts at expanding the madrasah in contrast to the traditional pesantren. Not only does the madrasah include typical secular subjects as at least half of the curriculum, but it resembles the Western secular school in other respects as well. It is graded, with elementary, junior-secondary, and senior-secondary levels preceding a college level. Diplomas are awarded upon completion of each of these levels. Furthermore, teachers are prepared in teacher-education institutions rather than being drawn from among the older students, as is true in the original pesantren.

In certain Indonesian provinces, madrasahs are public schools, receiving financial support under the Ministry of Religion or provincial government. Curricula and textbooks are authorized by the Ministry of Religion.

The numbers of madrasahs, students, and teachers reported by the Ministry of Religion in 1974 are shown in Table 2.1. As the figures indicate, there are nearly 11 times more madrasahs than pesantrens as reported earlier. There are also 18 times more students in madrasahs than pesantrens.

Although the foregoing descriptions distinguish precisely between the entirely-religious nature of the pesantren and the mixed religious—secular nature of the madrasah, in actual practice the distinction is not nearly so clear. In some pesantrens secular subjects are included along with Islamic studies. Furthermore, some pesantrens are day schools rather than boarding schools, and they are structured in grade levels. Thus, the names pesantren and madrasah may not always identify precisely the nature of a modern-day religious institution.

Knowing that a pupil attends a pesantren or madrasah or the simple langgar may tell us only part of the story of his schooling experience, for many children attend more than one institution at the same time. A typical pattern in many villages involves pupils attending a public secular school part of the day, then studying at a langgar, pesantren, or madrasah a few additional hours. This practice of double attendance causes obvious difficulties for educational planners, since they cannot arrive at an accurate count of the number of children in school nationally simply by totaling the enrollments of all secular and religious schools. Such totaling results in an overcount that influences plans for expanding the access to education. Sampling of enrollments in certain districts has

TABLE 2.1
Islamic Schools, Students, and Teachers 1974

School Type	Schools			Students			Teachers (Full-time)		
	Public	Private	Total	Public	Private	Total	Public	Private	Total
Madrasah series									
Primary 1–6 Madrasah Ibtidaiya	358	22,655	23,013	157,794	5,546,731	5,704,525	3,905	23,694	27,599
Junior Secondary 7–9 Madrasah Tsanawiyah	182	2,246	2,428	32,208	388,878	421,086	1,318	2,788	4,106
Senior Secondary 10–12 Madrasah Aliyah	42	323	365	7,249	56,433	63,682	252	277	529
Senior Secondary 8–12 Madrasah Diniyah		8,492	8,492		471,106	471,106		11,096	11,096
Teacher Training 7–10	146	730	876	41,887	61,326	103,213	1,502	1,977	3,479
Teacher Training 7–12	116	296	412	62,319	82,626	144,945	2,986	1,899	4,885
Traditional Pesantren Pondok/Pesantren		3,321	3,321		376,357	376,357		4,841	4,841
Total	844	38,063	38,907	301,457	6,983,457	7,284,914	9,963	46,572	56,535

(*Source:* Sumardi, 1977, p. 107.)

suggested that a substantial number of pupils in some provinces may regularly be attending two types of schools at the same time.

In summary, the Indonesian education system today includes a large quantity of Islamic schools at elementary and secondary levels, ones that trace their beginnings to centuries past. These schools, however, do not compare in number or, usually, in social status with the Western-style secular schools introduced by the European colonialists.

WESTERN-STYLE SECULAR SCHOOLS – GENERAL-ACADEMIC
AND VOCATIONAL

When the Portuguese and Spanish landed in the Spice Islands in the 16th century, they brought priests who established schools to spread the Catholic religion and teach some simple reading, writing, and arithmetic. One such school was a seminary for children of upper-class native families established on Ternate in the Northern Moluccas in 1536. Another was set up in Solor, where Latin was taught along with religion in the native tongue.

However, the spread of Catholicism was slowed and then reversed when the Dutch defeated the Portuguese and Spanish in their efforts to monopolize trade in the Indonesian archipelago. Under the Netherlands East Indies Trading Company the Dutch established schools in Ambon in the early 17th century, with a Dutch teacher giving instruction to children of prominent native families in reading, writing, praying, and Protestant Christian doctrine. The original intention was to offer instruction in the Dutch language, but problems students faced in mastering the tongue convinced the Dutch clergymen that Malay was a more practical medium.

Over the next two centuries, as the Dutch assumed control over more and more sections of the islands, the increase in schools was slow. In the main, the objective of those who sponsored schools was to provide educational opportunities to children of locally employed European and Eurasian families and children of native chiefs and princes. Not until the mid-19th century did the Dutch colonial government give serious attention to furnishing secular education for the general population of Indonesians, and the number of schools for the common people began to grow. In 1867, a colonial department of education was established so that the development of schools and the compilation of statistics became increasingly systematic. Pupils in indigenous primary schools increased from 16,000 in 1866 to 41,000 in 1882, then to 61,742 (of which 14 percent were girls) in 1900 in public schools and an additional 36,431 (18 percent girls) in private Christian and secular schools. Additional schools were conducted at the beginning of the 20th century for Europeans (public), for Chinese and Arabs (private), and for training native officials for government service.

A prominent feature of Dutch-colonial schools of the Western variety over the first four decades of the 20th century was their socially-stratified structure. Colonial society was itself carefully stratified, with Europeans at the top, the native aristocracy and prominent Eurasians (called *Indos*) next, the Chinese businessmen a step lower, and several layers of the native peoples serving as the broad base. (Thomas, 1970, pp. 278–291.) The European-style school system was stratified in a like pattern, not only reflecting the colonial government's view of society but serving to perpetuate the structure in coming generations. At the top of the system were the Dutch schools, identical in curricula and staffing to those in Holland and fully funded by the colonial government. At the bottom were village primary schools, furnishing a meager fare of subjects in the local dialect and funded by the native princes. In between these extremes were other institutions, including ones for Orientals in the Dutch language, that would enable apt pupils in the village primary schools to transfer (by continuation and linking schools) into the Dutch-language track of upper-elementary and junior-secondary schools. (Table 2.2.)

In colonial times, secondary schooling was virtually all in the Dutch language, thus eliminating the possibility that any youth who had not mastered Dutch would rise beyond the lowest primary grades in the secular school structure.

The number of Indonesians attending elementary schools in 1940 was over 20 times greater than the number attending in 1900. However, this did not mean that by the close of the Dutch period in early 1942 there was either universal primary schooling or universal literacy. Of children in the 6-to-14-year age group, only an estimated 20 percent were in non-Islamic schools. Of people over age 10, only an estimated 37 percent were literate. (Thomas, 1966, p. 280.)

When the Japanese captured the islands from the Dutch in 1942, they soon drastically altered the structure of the school system. They eliminated

TABLE 2.2

The Stratified Elementary School System 1940

Title of School	Instructional Language	Kinds and Numbers of Pupils		
		Europeans	Indonesians	Other Asians*
European	Dutch	40,851	5,150	1,281
Dutch-Chinese	Dutch	441	2,208	22,816
Dutch-Native	Dutch	498	70,364	1,114
Linking	Dutch	5	5,750	256
Continuation	Local Dialect	**	287,126	**
Village Primary	Local Dialect	**	1,896,374	**

*With the exception of a relatively small number of Arabs and Indians, "other Asians" were all Chinese.

**Although a few Chinese and Eurasians in remote areas might attend continuation and village-primary schools, government statistics did not distinguish the ethnic characteristics of the pupils of these institutions because pupils were almost invariably indigenous Indonesians.

(*Source*: S. L. Van Der Wal. *Het Onderwijsbeleid in Nederlands-Indie 1900–1940,* 1963, pp. 691–696.)

the stratified pattern of elementary schools and substituted instead a single-track, six-year elementary program. At the secondary level, they changed the Dutch-colonial pattern of general-academic and vocational schools into several types of vocational institutions, ones for teacher training, ship building, agriculture, and the like. The Japanese also eliminated the use of Dutch in the schools and substituted, instead, the Malay-Indonesian language which continues today as the medium of instruction.

Following the expulsion of the Japanese at the close of World War II and the end of the Revolution against the Dutch in late 1949, the independent Republic of Indonesia established its own education system, founded on the commitment in the 1945 constitution that: "Each citizen has the right to receive an education." In the Education Law of 1950/1954 this general intention was specified as:

> All children who have reached age six are permitted, and those who have reached age eight are obliged, to attend elementary school for a period of six years. (Soemardi Atmaprawira, 1962, p. 41.)

In addition to this formal pledge to furnish universal elementary schooling, there has existed since the early 1950s among Indonesians an informal, widespread feeling that almost everyone deserves further education as well, at least opportunities to finish some grades at the secondary level.

The structure of the school system sponsored by the Ministry of Education in the 1950s was patterned after the one-track, six-year elementary school of the Japanese-occupation era, 1942–1945, and at the secondary level after the mode of high-school education of Dutch-colonial times. Two characteristics of secondary education adopted from the Dutch pattern are of particular note. First, there was a general-academic stream leading to higher education, and a parallel set of vocational schools prepared students for the world of work rather than university study. Second, there were both public and private schools, with many of the private institutions receiving financial aid from the government. Although the ethnic bias (favoring Europeans) was eliminated from the secondary schools under the Republic, the status differential between academic and vocational education remained. Vocational schools continued to be, and remain today, less prestigious than general-academic schools. Furthermore, within the general-academic institutions of the 1950s there were three curricular tracks at the upper-secondary level – a mathematics–science track, a literature–languages track, and a social-sciences track. The first of these was the most ·prestigious, for it qualified students for the most desired higher-education specialties – in medicine, engineering, and the sciences as well as nearly any other specialization a student chose.

Over the 1960s and 1970s some simplification of the complex secondary-school system was effected. Compared with the past, today's students are not routed into a specialization track so early in their academic careers as the beginning of the junior-high school. Instead, most students now pursue a general-academic program at the junior-secondary level, waiting until senior high school to choose their area of emphasis. However, at the close of the 1970s there were still four types of junior-secondary schools and nine varieties of senior-high schools under the Ministry of Education. Furthermore, several other ministries also conduct a small number of specialized secondary schools designed either to train employees for service in their ministry or else to give vocational training in the realm of the ministry's expertise. For example, the nation's Bureau of Statistics today has one high school and the Ministry of Communications two more

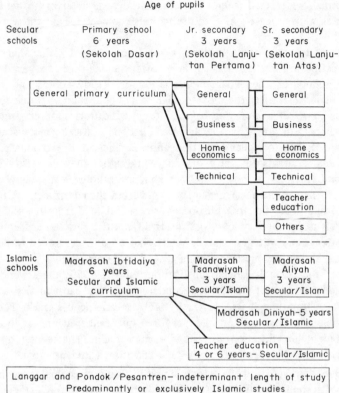

FIG. 2.2 Primary and secondary school system — 1970s

to train middle-level technicians for their staffs. The Ministry of Agriculture operates 62 junior-high and 103 senior-high agricultural schools, and the Ministry of Health has 62 junior-high and 358 senior-high institutions specializing in nursing and midwifery.

In summary, by 1980 the Indonesian elementary-school system was relatively simple in structure, while the secondary-school system was complex. (Fig. 2.2) The majority of elementary schools were secular, either public or private, providing a single six-year track of studies — reading and writing the Indonesian language and local dialect, mathematics, science, social studies, a small amount of religious instruction, and some simple vocational instruction in the final two years. Paralleling the secular schools were over 20,000 public and private Islamic madrasahs offering the same range of subjects as the secular schools but with a larger amount of each day devoted to religious subjects. In addition, some elementary-school-aged children attended pesantrens where they focused exclusively, or predominantly, on Islamic topics.

At the secondary-school level, most of the nation's youths were enrolled in the array of junior and senior high schools under the Ministry of Education and Culture. However, a substantial number attended pesantrens and madrasahs under the Ministry of Religion or the few special vocational schools conducted by six other ministries.

Formal Schooling in the 1970s — Problems and Solutions

In recent years the Indonesian government has sought to meet its commitment to universal education by means of both formal and informal institutions. To review these efforts, we shall first inspect the formal school system, then later turn to nonformal provisions.

As a vantage point from which to consider present-day schooling, we shall use the seven problems selected by educational planners as the focus of the First Five-Year National Development Program of 1969—1974. In the case of each problem, we first describe its nature, then identify ways the government has sought to solve it, and finally estimate what yet remains to be done in the 1980s.

MEETING THE SHORTAGE OF EDUCATIONAL FACILITIES

By the early 1970s, the nation found itself still far from the goals of universal literacy, universal primary schooling, and generous opportunities for secondary education. By 1973, only an estimated 60 percent of the general population over age 10 could read and write. Less than 55 percent of children age 7—12 were in secular elementary schools, with an estimated 20 percent in Islamic madrasahs. However, this total of 75 percent is deceiving, since it involves an unknown amount of double counting of children attending both types of school simultaneously. Thus, it might

69

be safer to speculate that perhaps 65 percent or so of the primary-aged population were in school. (*Pendidikan di Indonesia,* 1976, pp. 49. 63; Sumardi, 1977, p. 107.)

At the junior-secondary level in 1973–74 nearly 59 percent of primary-school graduates entered junior-secondary schools, while 75 percent of junior-secondary graduates entered senior-secondary school. (*Rangkuman Statistik Persekolahan 1978,* 1979, Tables 15–16.)

A major reason that enrollments fell short of the government's goal was a lack of sufficient school buildings. Hence, as an emergency measure to increase facilities rapidly, President Suharto in 1973 issued a special instruction (*Instruksi President* abbreviated as *Inpres*) providing extra funds from oil-export revenues to erect thousands of additional primary-school buildings each year. In the public-school sector by 1978 the number of such Inpres schools had reached 24,065, representing 30 percent of the nation's total of secular public schools. The 1979–1980 national budget provided for construction of 10,000 more, plus the addition of 15,000 new classrooms in existing schools and the repair of 15,000 existing buildings. (*Rangkuman Statistik Persekolahan 1978,* 1979, Table 2; *Indonesia Development News,* 1979, p. 8.)

At the secondary level, emphasis was placed on establishing or rehabilitating science laboratories, which were nonexistent in many sections of the country. In 1974–75 more than 1,000 laboratories and equipment were built at the junior-high level and 200 more at the senior-high level. Thirteen new technical high-schools were set up. Over 1,340 existing general high schools were rehabilitated along with 100 vocational schools of various types. These construction activities represented the most ambitious building program in the nation's educational history. (*Pendidikan di Indonesia,* 1976, p. 109.)

One of the major shortages suffered in nearly all schools throughout the 1960s had been that of textbooks and supplementary learning materials. To solve this problem, the government in the 1970s mounted a massive publication program, assisted in the effort by grants and loans from international agencies and by experts from abroad. In 1974–1975, over 13 million primary-school books were printed along with nearly half a million more for secondary schools and one-quarter million for people in nonformal educational programs. The revision and printing of texts continued at approximately this level throughout the latter 1970s.

While the government during the 1970s directed its most intense efforts at increasing primary-school facilities, private religious and secular groups were devoting more of their energies to increasing secondary-school opportunities. The total number of private schools under the Ministry of Education in 1974 (excluding Islamic schools under the Ministry of Religion) was 4,670 at the junior-high level and 1,759 at the senior-high level. By 1978 private junior highs had increased to 6,177 or by 32 percent and private senior highs to 2,402 or by 37 percent. These marked increases in so short a period of years reflect a strong social demand for schooling beyond the primary years and suggest the willingness and ability of private organizations to furnish such schooling if the government is unable to meet the demand. (*Pendidikan di Indonesia,* 1976, p. 73; *Rangkuman Statistik Persekolahan 1978,* 1979, Table 2.)

While at first glance the increase in government school facilities might appear unrelated to the growth of private schools, closer analysis shows that the two phenomena are actually linked. The term *school* in Indonesia refers to an administrative unit composed of a headmaster, teachers, and pupils under a sponsoring organization. Thus, one such *school* may be held in the morning in the same building that a different *school* uses in the afternoon or early evening. The morning group may be a public school using a building erected by the government, while the afternoon group may be a private school taking advantage of the same facilities. Hence, when the government invests in a new school building it may at the same time be assisting a private organization by providing the needed facilities. In addition, the Indonesian government since achieving independence in 1945–1949 has continued a policy of private-school subsidies inherited from the Dutch. In terms of economic support, then, there are three sorts of private schools: (1) those which receive full subsidy, (2) those which receive partial aid, and (3) those which are entirely on their own and receive no government funds. In 1978, of the total 6,177 junior highs, 86 percent were without government aid, while 7 percent were fully subsidized and another 7 percent assisted. Of the total 2,402 senior highs, 82 percent were unaided, 12 percent subsidized, and 6 percent assisted. In effect, the great majority of private secondary schools in the latter 1970s operated solely on their own funds, though many took advantage of public-school buildings when the public school was not in session. (*Rangkuman Statistik Persekolahan 1978,* 1979, Table 2.)

Schooling in the ASEAN Region

Despite the remarkable progress Indonesia achieved in the 1970s toward furnishing universal elementary-school and expanded secondary-school facilities, the nation faced the 1980s with much still to accomplish. While educational planners, public and private, were opening thousands of new schools and publishing millions of textbooks, the general population was increasing by over 3.5 million each year, forcing planners to pursue a constantly retreating target. By 1980 there were still perhaps only 75 percent of children ages 7–12 in secular and religious elementary schools and possibly 40 percent or so of youths ages 13–18 in secondary schools, secular and religious. The task of supplying enough school buildings, books, and other equipment to meet government goals and social demand was still unfinished in 1980.

ALTERING THE ACADEMIC–VOCATIONAL RATIO IN SECONDARY SCHOOLS

Like its ASEAN neighbors, Indonesia has continued to face an imbalance between enrollments in general-academic curricula and vocational programs. Economic-development plans call for large numbers of well trained technical, business, and agricultural workers at the intermediate level of skill produced by efficient high-school vocational programs. However, for a variety of reasons, enrollments in vocational schools have lagged far behind the needs for employees with such skills. At the same time, enrollments in the classical academic curricula have exceeded the demands of the economy. One cause for this imbalance has been the traditional higher status of academic studies. Vocational education continues to lack the prestige of academic studies, so that schools with an academic emphasis not only attract more candidates but also tend to attract students of greater ability. A second cause of low enrollments in vocational studies is the higher cost of equipping a technical, business, or home-economics institution as compared to an academic high school.

Thus in its series of five-year development plans the Indonesian government has sought to achieve a more acceptable ratio of academic to vocational secondary schools. The First Five-Year Plan called for rebuilding and equipping deteriorated technical schools, the erection of new vocational schools in each province, and construction of skills-development centers that would serve as central workshops for the students of surrounding high schools that lacked workshops or had inadequate facilities. In addition to building new vocational schools to accommodate larger numbers of candidates, the government planned vocational studies for students in academic curricula to follow as part of their high-school program. In other words, a small measure of vocational education would be introduced into academic tracks. In the early years of the Plan, agricultural-education facilities would be emphasized, while in the latter years more stress would be placed on increasing opportunities for technical and industrial education. (*Rentjana Pambangunan Lima Tahun 1969/70–1973/74,* Vol. II-C, pp. 21–22.)

The general pattern of progress toward achieving a higher proportion of vocational-education students compared to academic-track students over the period of the first two Five-Year Plans, 1969–1979, is indicated in Tables 2.3 and 2.4. The figures in the two tables show the numbers of schools of different types and enrollments in each type for the year before the first plan was formulated, 1967, and for the last full year of the second plan, 1978.

An initial fact to note is that the number of junior-secondary schools, both academic and vocational, increased by 54 percent over the 11-year period, while senior-secondary schools increased by 28 percent. But far more noteworthy was the growth in total number of students. Because the average enrollment per school rose significantly, the number of junior-high students increased 143 percent and of senior-high students 191 percent.

How, then, was this growth distributed between academic and vocational institutions? While at the junior-high level general-academic pupils increased by 155 percent, vocational pupils increased by only 91 percent. This disparity is likely due to two factors. First, the government was placing less emphasis on vocational specialization early in students' lives, so students were less likely to be pressed into a specialized vocational school at the junior-secondary level, that is, at ages 13 to 15. The idea of continuing in the general academic stream during these early teen-age years was more widespread than it had been in Dutch-colonial times or even during the first two decades of the Republic. Second, the greater prestige of college-preparatory, academic studies as compared to vocational studies continued to influence parents' choice of schools. Social demand still appeared to favor academic training. This inference is supported by

TABLE 2.3
Numbers of Public and Private Schools – 1967, 1978*

Type of School	Public Schools		Private Schools		All Schools	
	1967	1978	1967	1978	1967	1978
Primary (6 yr)	49,253	80,948	8,022	11,551	57,275	92,499
Junior High (3 yr) Total	2,414	3,328	3,748	6,177	6,162	9,505
General Academic	1,294	2,127	3,331	5,601	4,625	7,728
Vocational	1,120	1,201	417	576	1,537	1,777
– Business	316	455	141	257	457	712
– Home Economics	247	206	218	125	465	331
– Technical	557	540	58	194	615	734
Senior High (3 yr) Total	988	1,279	1,424	2,402	2,412	3,081
General Academic	397	548	878	1,031	1,275	1,579
Vocational	591	731	546	1,371	1,137	1,502
– Business	121	261	193	441	314	702
– Home Economics	27	62	46	98	73	160
– Technical	89	151	71	460	160	611
– Teacher Education	354	257	336	372	590	629

*Includes only schools under the Ministry of Education, not schools under the Ministry of Religion or other Ministries.

(*Sources*: 1967 data – *Statistik Indonesia 1968/1969*, 1971, pp. 78–79.
1978 data – *Rangkuman Statistik Persekolahan 1978*, 1979, Table 2.)

figures in Table 2.3 on the number of new private schools started during the 1967–1978 decade. The number of private schools rose by 68 percent (from 3,331 to 5,601), and students increased by 145 percent. Public academic junior-highs experienced similar growth, with schools increasing by 64 percent and students by 168 percent.

At the senior-secondary level the nation achieved a far more significant advance in altering the academic/vocational balance in the direction urged by the national-development plans. As shown in Table 2.4, in 1967 58 percent of the students were in academic curricula and 42 percent in

TABLE 2.4
Students in Public and Private Schools – 1967, 1978*
(in thousands)

Type of School	Public Schools		Private Schools		All Schools	
	1967	1978	1967	1978	1967	1978
Primary (6 yr)	10,420	16,775	2,052	2,300	12,472	19,075
Junior High (3 yr) Total	590	1,429	510	1,245	1,100	2,674
General Academic	408	1,092	481	1,179	889	2,271
Vocational	182	337	29	66	211	403
– Business	49	138	9	29	58	167
– Home Economics	25	34	12	10	37	44
– Technical	108	165	8	27	116	192
Senior High (3 yr) Total	265	665	178	635	443	1,290
General Academic	138	339	121	275	259	604
Vocational	127	326	57	360	189	686
– Business	31	110	12	101	43	211
– Home Economics	3	14	4	11	7	25
– Technical	31	84	13	154	44	238
– Teacher Education	62	118	28	94	90	212

*Includes only schools under the Ministry of Education, not schools under the Ministry of Religion or other Ministries.
(*Sources*: 1967 data – *Statistik Indonesia 1968/1969*, 1971, pp. 82–83.
1978 data – *Rangkuman Statistik Persekolahan 1978*, 1979, Table 3.)

vocational. By 1978 the ratio had reversed, with 53 percent vocational and 47 percent academic. While enrollments in all types of schools rose over the decade, the most striking increase came in the technical schools emphasized in the national economic plan – a gain of 441 percent (from 44,000 students to 238,000). The private sector contributed significantly to this growth, increasing the number of technical schools from 71 to 460 and the number of students almost twelve times.

In effect, over the period of the first two development plans, educational planners had made progress toward increased vocational education at the upper-secondary level, both in the numbers of students enrolled and in the ratio of academic to vocational enrollments. However, the popularity of academic curricula brought about marked growth of academic schools as well, with the percentage of students in public academic high schools growing by 146 percent and in private high schools by 127 percent over the 12-year period. However, the academic to vocational ratio was still short of the government's plan. An increase in agricultural and technical senior-high schools in the future was still the goal to be achieved.

INCREASING THE PROPORTION OF SECONDARY-SCHOOL STUDENTS

Two principal aims lay behind the government's ambition to increase the proportion of primary-school graduates who continued into secondary school. First was the desire to satisfy the expectations of the populace that the new generation would not only have an opportunity to complete a six-year primary education but would also have a chance for more advanced schooling. Second was the need for more workers trained at an intermediate level of vocational skill, a level that could be expected from secondary-school graduates.

The chief techniques employed to raise the number of secondary-school openings in the early and middle 1970s were to increase the number of junior-secondary schools and to enroll more students in each school and to increase the number of double and triple sessions in the same school building.

Over the seven-year period 1972–1978 steady progress was recorded in accommodating a larger number of primary-school graduates in junior-secondary schools, but the percentage of graduates entering the junior high rose as well from 55 percent in 1972 to 59 percent by 1974, to 65.5 percent in 1976, and finally to 70.5 in 1978. Thus, while 546,092 new students enrolled in junior highs in 1972, and 665,229 in 1974, the total rose to 815,003 in 1976, and to over a million (1,025,073) by 1978. In effect, junior-high schools by 1978 were accepting 88 percent more entering students than they had been seven years earlier. (*Rangkuman Statistik Persekolahan 1974*, 1976, pp. 45–46; and *1978*, 1979, Table 15.)

Despite this remarkable accomplishment, the rapid growth of the population which brought increasing numbers of pupils through the primary schools in the 1970s continued to frustrate educational planners' attempts to accommodate larger percentages in junior-secondary schools than the 70.5 percent of 1978. Therefore, in his independence-day speech on August 17, 1978, President Suharto announced an attempt to achieve further advances, particularly in rural areas, through the medium of a new nonformal educational institution to be known as the *open junior-high school*. In 1979, Ministry-of-Education curriculum experts laid initial plans for pilot trials of this venture, which would employ a variety of media for furnishing learning opportunities to primary-school graduates — media that would include self-instructional modules, radio broadcasts, and correspondence courses by mail. Whether the open junior-high in the future would be a permanent option paralleling the traditional junior-secondary school or would serve as a transition institution until enough traditional schools could be built was not yet clear at the beginning of the 1980s. If this nonformal institution worked well, it might serve as a model to other nations that had difficulty caring for rising numbers of primary-school graduates.

What did become clear during the decade of the 1970s was that marked progress was achieved in expanding opportunities for more students at the junior-secondary level, and there was good reason to expect further progress in the future.

REDUCING THE DROPOUT RATE IN THE ELEMENTARY SCHOOL

At the time the First Five-Year National Development Plan was being formulated in 1967–1968, two symptoms of inefficiency in the elementary-school system were the high dropout and repeater rates. Far less than half of the pupils who entered first grade reached grade six, and still fewer than that graduated. In addition, at all grade levels there was a significant number of pupils who were not passed to the next higher grade at the end of the school year but were held back to repeat the same grade again.

The high dropout rates seemed to be the result of a combination of factors. In some cases, children found school difficult and uninteresting, so they urged their parents to let them stay home. Parents who did not highly value schooling and who found their children of use in the family work force either encouraged or permitted children to drop out. And since a child with a primary-school diploma usually could not expect to get any better employment than a 12-year-old or 13-year-old who had finished only three or four grades, the occupational advantages of a six-year education over a three- or four-year education were doubtful. A further cause was the financial burden on the family. Although in the 1970s elementary schooling ostensibly was free, in reality there were costs to be met, usually for school fees as well as for books and clothing and sometimes transportation. A family with a meager income and six or eight children of school age found the expense often too burdensome to bear, so children stopped attending after two or three years.

The practice of charging fees in public primary schools was initiated by individual school staffs themselves without official permission from the Ministry of Education. The practice began in the 1960s, often through the medium of a parents' association, as an effort to maintain the school buildings and supplement staff salaries during the years of greatest economic deterioration in the country, that is, during the 1960–1966 era. But in 1973 the Minister of Education sought to systematize what had become a universal but uncontrolled fee-levying policy. He established rates of payment adjusted to parents' incomes. However, even modest charges often proved too much for economically distressed parents to pay, so schools were in danger of becoming increasingly the sort of elitist institutions which Indonesians had objected to in Dutch colonial times. Children whose parents had money could attend primary school. Those whose parents did not have money would need to drop out. To help remove this financial barrier to universal schooling, the government in 1976 revised the fee-payment plan so that children in the first three primary grades were exempted from all fees, and the government made up the loss to the schools through furnishing special funds from the national budget.

In addition to the foregoing funding maneuvers, the Ministry of Education sought to make school more attractive and useful to pupils by a large-scale textbook publishing program, the improvement of buildings and equipment, and more inservice teacher-training programs.

As a result of these efforts, the absolute numbers of pupils graduated from primary schools increased by 30 percent between 1971 and 1978. In addition, some progress was achieved in reducing the percentage rate of dropouts; however, the progress was comparatively slight. In 1971, an estimated 67 percent of pupils had dropped out before graduating from Grade 6, leaving 43 percent with elementary-school diplomas. By 1978, the retention rate had improved by only about 5 percent. Of all the children who had entered first grade in 1972, only 48 percent graduated from sixth grade in 1978. Once more, the pace of growth of the general population appeared to be an important element in frustrating educational planners' attempts to achieve universal elementary schooling for a full six years. However, it was not only population increase but also the other influences in the society — financial burden, the questionable value of full elementary schooling for the job market, inefficient and uninteresting instructional techniques — that continued to produce a high dropout rate. Yet, at the end of the 1970s there were signs that improvements could be expected in the future. Between 1973 and 1978, the retention rate for pupils in third grade had improved by 7 percent, and the rate in fifth grade had improved by 9 percent from 1975 to 1978. In the early 1980s, these improvements were expected to show up in reduced dropout rates by the end of sixth grade. However, the dropout problem in the 1980s would continue to pose one of the most serious challenges educators had to face.

Linked to the dropout problem is that of pupils repeating the same grade one or more times. Failure to progress regularly in school is an obvious motive for pupils to drop out. Furthermore, even when a pupil remains in school until he graduates, if he requires seven or eight years to complete the normal six-year course, he is doing so at undesirable cost to himself and society. A high rate of repeaters means that more school facilities are needed to care for all students or else some potential pupils cannot attend school because repeaters are occupying the desks that could accommodate them.

In 1971, the average repeater rate for elementary schools was 11 percent, with the highest incidence of repeating occurring in the lower-primary grades. Nearly 18 percent of first graders were held back to repeat, whereas only 11 percent of fourth-graders and 3 percent of sixth-graders were retained in the same grade. (*Rangkuman Statistik Persekolahan 1974*, 1976, p. 45.) By 1978, the average proportion of repeaters in primary grades was 12 percent, with the incidence ranging from 19 percent in Grade 1 to 11 percent in Grade 4 and 3 percent in Grade 6. (*Rangkuman Statistik Persekolahan 1978*, 1979, Tables 7 and 13.) In effect, no progress was made in reducing the repeater rate over the 1971–1978 period. The cause for this lack of progress was not clear. Did teachers throughout the decade hold students to the same standards for passing, yet teachers failed to improve their own instructional effectiveness, so repeater rates stayed the same? Or did teachers improve their instructional effectiveness and at the same time raise their standards for passing so that the incidence of repeaters remained constant? An investigation aimed at answering these questions could aid educational planners determine how best to reduce the numbers of repeaters in the future without sacrificing standards of achievement.

Although the goal of decreasing dropouts and repeaters in secondary schools was not a prime target of the first Five-Year Development Plan, this goal did become a serious concern of educators by the mid-1970s. A comparison of dropout and repeater figures in 1971 and 1978 indicated substantial improvement over the seven-year period. Whereas only 66 percent of the students who entered junior-secondary school in 1971 graduated in 1974, more than 80 percent of those entering in 1975 graduated in 1978, a reduction of dropouts by 14 percent. At the senior-high level the percentage completing the three-year sequence rose from 68 to 78 between 1975 and 1978, with the promise of even higher success rates in the near future. Repeater rates improved as well between 1971 and 1978, dropping from 13 to 2 percent at the junior-high level and from 12 to 3 percent in senior-high schools. Whether these dropout and repeater gains were due to a relaxation of achievement standards at the school level or to improved instruction, or perhaps to a combination of the two, is unknown. A special investigation of the causal factors in the early 1980s would appear desirable. (*Rangkuman Statistik Persekolahan 1974*, 1976, pp. 46–47; and *1978*, 1979, Tables 7, 13, 18, 19.)

Nonformal Education

A further national-development goal was to reduce illiteracy and to improve the quality of learning. Two major devices adopted during the 1970s to attack the problem of the quality of education were those of nonformal education programs and of improved curricula and teaching methods. We shall first consider nonformal innovations, then turn to curriculum development.

Nonformal education – in the sense of organized learning opportunities outside the regular school room – is nothing new for Indonesia. During the 1945–1949 Revolution against the Dutch, the beleaguered Republican government in Central Java encouraged all literate citizens to instruct any youths and adults not yet able to read and write. By 1947, these endeavors had assumed the formal status of a program under the community-education directorate of the Ministry of Education. Employees of the division were located in towns and villages throughout the archipelago, responsible for organizing literacy classes, teaching about health measures and child care, setting up village libraries so people would have reading matter on which to practice their newly gained literacy, and offering instruction in vocational skills of use in the community. Under the Five-Year Development Plans the directorate has continued its efforts in the face of a growing number of illiterates caused by the rapid population increase and by the pupils who drop out of elementary school and soon lose their embryonic reading skills through disuse. A variety of programs during the Second Plan of 1974–1979 were intended to reach 800,000 adults not yet literate or ones needing follow-up programs of basic knowledge and vocational skills.

The 1970s also brought an expanding array of nonformal efforts under both the community-education directorate and other agencies, both public and private. While the First Five-Year Plan gave priority to increasing adult literacy, the second expanded the assignment to furnishing lifelong education. The priority target for the Second Plan was identified as "the 10-to-24 age group who have never had the opportunity for formal schooling or . . . dropped out at the early stages." So as to achieve proper coordination of nonformal efforts without wasteful duplication, President Suharto in 1972/1974 allocated the responsibility for general and vocational education to the Ministry of Education, for training in specific vocational skills to the Ministry of Manpower, and for training of government employees to the Institute for State Administration. The range of informal programs conducted during the 1970s is illustrated by the following sampling of projects.

In the area of community health, each district within a province maintains a health center that people visit for aid in matters of illness, family planning, nutrition, and sanitation. Courses in midwifery and first-aid are also conducted.

To control population growth, family-planning workers contacting parents in home visits increased the number of parents accepting birth-control devices from 53,100 in 1970 to 2,246,100 in 1978. By 1978, there were 36,317 Family Planning Service Centers on the islands of Java and Bali and 980 more on other islands.

To help unemployed persons develop salable skills and open their own businesses, a "chain stimulus" program has offered training in such trades as brick laying and bamboo weaving. Then funds are loaned to trainees to launch self-operated businesses. When trainees become established and are earning their own way, they repay the funds which are then loaned to the next set of trainees in the chain.

To aid villagers and the urban poor improve their living conditions, mobile training units travel about the nation, staying for a three-month period in each location to furnish advice or education in whatever vocational skills appear useful in the area.

A series of rural radio broadcasts sponsored jointly by the Ministry of Agriculture and Ministry of Information is aimed at supporting the mass-education scheme for farm families so as to stimulate agricultural production. Agents of the Ministry of Agriculture located throughout the islands organize farmers into "listening groups" who gather to follow the broadcasts, then discuss how the suggestions in the radio lessons can be applied to their own work. The local agricultural agent may explain topics farmers do not completely understand and may demonstrate the use of new breeds of rice, methods of fertilizing, marketing crops, and the like. By 1977, there were 44 radio stations on the national network and 138 provincial stations broadcasting over 350 total hours per week to 19,818 listening groups across the nation.

The PAMONG program for primary-school dropouts (Chapter 1) and the open junior-high school for primary-school graduates are further examples of government-sponsored nonformal efforts.

In parallel with the foregoing programs conducted by public agencies, the private sector has contributed significantly to nonformal education. By the close of the 1970s, more than 5,400 private commercial organizations operated vocational courses covering a broad range of skills — foreign languages, home economics, dressmaking, vehicle and electrical-appliance repair, auto and truck driving, carpentry, typing, office management, and traditional and modern dancing. An estimated 900,000 participants were enrolled in such programs in 1979. In addition to commercial sponsors, religious and humanitarian organizations have contributed programs as well. In the main, the private programs are in urban areas, leaving most rural nonformal ventures in the hands of government agencies.

A clear implication in the second Five-Year Plan was that nonformal educational programs were not to be considered simply stop-gap measures conducted simply for facing present emergency needs, but they would become part of the nation's overall educational system to furnish a wide variety of life-long learning opportunities for Indonesians of all ages.

The Research and Development Center

Prior to the early 1970s, all curriculum development and the modest amount of educational evaluation carried out by the government were located in various divisions of the Ministry of Education. The primary-school division formulated its own nationwide curricula, the academic secondary-school division was responsible for academic high-school programs, and a vocational section was in charge of creating vocational curricula. However, in 1969–1970 an office was created in the Ministry to conduct a national assessment of education so planners might have a sound base of data on which to erect programs under the successive five-year development plans. (Beeby, 1979.) By the mid-1970s, the original small office had evolved into a full-fledged Research and Development Center, responsible for devising curricula and conducting evaluation of many varieties. By 1978, the Center occupied a five-story building on the Ministry grounds in Jakarta and was staffed by Indonesian educators trained both within the country and overseas. The Center made liberal use of educational consultants from abroad and enjoyed the financial support not only of the Indonesian government, but of foreign foundations and international agencies. Today, the main efforts in devising new curricula and assessing educational progress, both nationally and within special programs, are directed from the Center.

From the wide range of projects the Center has conducted in recent years, we shall briefly describe two as examples of the approaches used in the Center's work.

First is the *development-school* project, the most ambitious program in the Center from the viewpoint of pedagogical sophistication. This type of school since its inception in 1973–1974 has been an experimental institution operating on a tryout basis in eight sites, each associated with a regional Institute of Education. The chief focus is on matching primary- and secondary-school curricula closely to the needs of national development and pupils' personal characteristics. A key element of the school is its system of instructional modules. A module is a short learning unit, most often in the form of a pamphlet to be completed by the pupils over a period of several days. As far as possible, such modules are self-instructional, suited to individual learning rates, requiring active problem-solving by the student, and ensuring frequent self-evaluation for the learner so he can correct his errors and monitor his own progress. In addition to the self-instructional pamphlets, some modules include such multimedia activities as general class discussion, small-group discussion, demonstrations, audio recording (especially for foreign-language study), film presentations, radio-listening sessions, and excursions. *Basic modules* in each subject-matter area at each grade level are designed to be completed by about 85 percent of pupils in a normal class. *Enrichment modules* are provided for students who complete basic modules sooner than their classmates, and *remedial activities* are planned for the 15 percent or so of pupils who cannot keep up with their classmates in the basic modules. (Soedijarto, 1976.)

After a national assessment of the quality of education in 1972, the development-school project began in 1973 with a team of curriculum experts translating national-development goals into instructional objectives (stated in terms of desired student behaviors) for each subject-matter area at all elementary and secondary grade levels. Then other teams began in 1974 to write the learning modules. A computerized evaluation system has been developed to feed information to module authors about the strengths and weaknesses of the modules as they have been tried out in the eight experimental schools. Thus, shortly after a module has been tried, the author knows in what way it should be revised. As a result, module construction and revision is a continuing process. (Postlethwaite, 1978.)

An in-depth evaluation of the project is scheduled for 1981–1982 to compare the effectiveness of the modularized learning approach with traditional teaching methods and to estimate the feasibility of disseminating the methodology to typical schools nationwide. The project represents the first curriculum innovation in the nation's history that has been systematically developed and assessed in experimental settings for nearly a decade before a decision is reached about the desirability of disseminating it on a broad scale.

The second illustrative project from the Center is one designed to evaluate in a rather precise manner (1) how well students nationwide mastered learning goals in the final (sixth) year of the elementary school and (2) what factors seemed to influence their level of success. As noted earlier, the Center evolved out of a national-assessment project at the beginning of the 1970s, and since that time evaluation studies have continued to be an important part of its operation. The data in the sixth-grade study were gathered in 1975 by means of tests and questionnaires devised by local personnel who had been trained abroad, assisted by foreign experts imported for the term of the project. The following are several examples of results of the study which have since proven useful to policymakers in the Ministry who are responsible for upgrading the quality of schools. (Moegiadi, Mangindaan, and Elley, 1979, pp. 340–345.)

> Teachers who make use of group work, projects, field work, and experiments and who make some attempt to individualize their instruction produced significantly better results than more traditional teachers, who confine themselves to "chalk and talk". . . . Teachers who prescribe regular homework achieve better results than those who do not. . . . Schools where lighting was effective achieved better results on the whole. . . . Women teachers in Indonesia achieve better results than men at Grade 6 level. . . . Older teachers produce better results than their less experienced colleagues. . . . Children in urban areas generally achieve at higher levels than those in rural areas. . . . Children in large classes and large schools achieved at significantly higher levels than those in smaller units. . . . Strangely enough, pupils from homes where Bahasa Indonesia (the national language) is not spoken at all achieve just as well in most of their school work (which is offered in the national language) as those who speak it regularly (at home).

The sixth-grade survey of the quality of learning of 1975 has since been built into the education system as a periodic function, with the next intensive study of quality at that grade level scheduled for 1981. Similar intensive studies have also been instituted by the Center for grades nine and twelve, the final years of the junior- and senior-secondary schools.

In addition to the development-school and sixth-grade-evaluation projects, the Center has conducted a range of other programs, including the use of educational radio and television via the nation's communication satellite, the formation of the open junior-high school, a study of the financing of education nationwide, a revision of the country's entire teacher-education system, the evaluation of inservice teacher-training programs, and more.

In summary, the Research and Development Center has brought to the Ministry a level of professional expertise and coordination in devising new curricula, in compiling and reporting routine school statistics, and in evaluating many facets of schooling and societal forces that was missing prior to the 1970s.

Improving Administrative Efficiency

Efforts to achieve greater administrative efficiency in the educational system during the 1970s have assumed two general forms, alteration in the structure of the system and improvement of personnel.

An example of a structural change is found in President Suharto's Decision 34 of 1972 which assigned the Ministry of Education responsibility for coordinating all educational matters currently located in different ministries. The significance of this decision is perhaps best appreciated in terms of the division of power at the top levels of government. The structure of educational policy-making is shown in Fig. 2.3. At the highest level of authority as the foundation of all decisions is the Indonesian Constitution of 1945. At the next higher level is the People's Deliberative Council (Majelis Permusyawaratan Rakyat), composed of 920 elected and appointed representatives who meet once each five years to issue decisions for guiding the conduct of the government in the future. Below the Council are the President, appointed by the Council, and a permanent law-making Parliament of 460 members. In practice, the President is the more important of these two agents for the education system. Since members of Parliament in the past have found it difficult to reach unanimity on education laws, nearly all alterations of policy over the past 30 years have been implemented by means of presidential decisions rather than parliamentary laws. Beneath the President, are the executive divisions that actually carry out the business of government. Each is headed

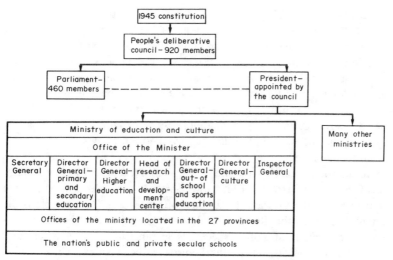

FIG. 2.3 Hierarchy of policy-making and administrative authority in Indonesian education.

by a minister who officially holds power equal to that of the other ministers and who is responsible to the President.

Since the early days of the Republic, the responsibility for the nation's schools has been divided among several ministries. Although the Ministry of Education and Culture has had jurisdiction over all secular secondary and higher education and over the curricula of primary schools, Islamic religious institutions have been under the Ministry of Religion, and the finance and upkeep of all secular primary schools have been relegated to the Ministry of the Interior. Furthermore, such ministries as those of Agriculture and of Social Welfare have conducted schools emphasizing their own specialties. This dispersion of authority has resulted in considerable administrative inefficiency caused by lack of coordination, duplication, experts in one ministry not being available to solve problems in another, and jealousy and competition between agencies. Consequently, in his Decision 34 in 1972 the President shifted the Ministry of Education into a superordinate position over the other ministries in matters of education. The Ministry of Education would henceforth be the coordinating authority for all matters educational, no matter which ministry currently operated the educational institutions.

However, since 1972 it has become apparent that implementing such a policy is far more difficult than first establishing it. Although some marked progress in coordination has been achieved, there is still far to go. As is true in perhaps all governments, agencies that conduct schools are usually reluctant to give up their power and control to another agency, such as the Ministry of Education, which ostensibly is on the same level of authority. Hence, officials in the Indonesian Ministry of Education have had to move cautiously in gaining more control over educational matters in other ministries, a caution dictated by the need to avoid unproductive conflicts among ministries.

In addition to such structural changes in the upper levels of government, a series of structural alterations have been carried out within the Ministry of Education and in regional offices as well. An example is the establishment of the Research and Development Center that permitted the concentration of skilled specialists in curriculum development and evaluation in one division of the Ministry rather than expecting all divisions to mount high-quality research and development activities on their own.

The improvement of educational personnel so as to enhance administrative efficiency has taken the two forms found in most organizations. Existing personnel have been upgraded through on-the-job training, short-term courses, workshops, and study abroad. People who could not be brought to the desired level of efficiency through such training have been removed from their jobs, either by retiring older workers or by assigning inadequate personnel to jobs for which their talents seem better suited. To ensure that staff members in the Ministry and in regional offices command the latest skills and knowledge of the international educational community, the government has made widespread use of fellowships for personnel to study abroad and of foreign consultants sent to Indonesia under the auspices of such organizations as UNESCO, the Ford Foundation, the U.S. State Department's Agency for International Development, the British Council, and others.

Thus, over the past decade changes to increase the efficient administration of education have been made. However, as population growth requires expansion of the school system and the nation seeks to furnish a greater variety of formal and nonformal learning opportunities for both children and adults, the enterprise that must be administered becomes larger and more complex. At the beginning of the 1980s, there was still much that needed improving.

Improving the Supply of Teachers

During Dutch colonial times most teachers for secondary schools were imported from Holland, while teachers for the three-year village schools and for more cómplete elementary schools were prepared in teacher-training programs in the islands. After 1950, when the Republic was free from colonial ties, a series of teacher-education programs was established to fill the need for instructors in the rapidly expanding primary and secondary school system. Many teachers participated in evening or correspondence courses while teaching primary or secondary classes during the daytime. Others attended three-year or four-year preservice schools that were just one academic step above the level in which they would soon teach. A junior-secondary school (*sekolah guru B*) prepared elementary-school teachers. A senior-secondary school (*sekolah guru A*) prepared teachers also for elementary grades, but because the shortage was so great in secondary schools, graduates of this institution in the 1950s and early 1960s often taught in secondary grades.

During Dutch and Japanese times, there had been no higher-education institutions, such as teachers colleges, for teacher education. However, in 1954 the Indonesian Ministry of Education began establishing a system of higher-education teacher-preparation institutions which evolved into the present-day colleges of education, with one or more in each province. The largest of these are independent Institutes of Teacher Training and the Science of Education (Institut Keguruan dan Ilmu Pendidikan), while smaller ones are faculties attached to universities. All offer bachelor-degree and master-degree programs, while a few offer doctorates in education.

In the closing years of the 1970s, teachers of secular subjects in the elementary school were prepared in the nation's 585 secondary-school teacher-training programs (*sekolah pendidikan guru*), while Islamic religious-education teachers graduated from nearly 1,300 four-year or six-year secondary schools (*pendidikan guru agama*). In 1978, enrollment in the secular-subject teacher-training schools exceeded 200,000. In 1974, enrollment in the Islamic teacher-training programs was 248,000. Forty-four special secondary schools for training athletic coaches enrolled over 10,000 students in 1978. (*Rangkuman Statistik Persekolahan 1978,* 1979, Tables 2–3; Soemardi, 1977, p. 107.)

The principal source of secondary-school teachers since the late 1950s has been the 17 public and 22 private institutes of education along with the 12 faculties of education attached to universities. Officially graduates of the three-year bachelor-degree program are authorized to teach in three-year junior-secondary schools, while candidates who complete a two-year master-degree program following their bachelor diploma are authorized to teach in three-year senior-secondary schools. However, the supply of teachers from these higher-education institutions has been insufficient to fill the demand, so an earlier discontinued emergency program for preparing junior-high teachers was revived in the 1970s to meet the need. The course is two years following candidates' graduation from a general-academic senior-high school.

Throughout the history of the Republic, upgrading programs designed for teachers currently in service have always been an important part of the teacher-education system. However, at no time was inservice training given greater attention than in the 1970s. In terms of numbers of teachers reached, the most notable of these efforts has been that designed to furnish three-week workshops in the use of new textbooks for nearly all the nation's 600,000 teachers in secular primary schools. The training staff consists of 1,200 specialists that form 120 provincial mobile teams equipped with four-wheel-drive vans and motor launches containing audiovisual aids. By 1976, some 90,000 teachers had been upgraded, with like numbers reached in subsequent years.

A further major endeavor has been a system of radio broadcasts beamed to 100,000 teachers in Central Java and nine remote outer-island provinces four times a week, 20 minutes a day.

Inservice training for secondary-school teachers has been conducted in two different settings, at existing teacher-education colleges and at a series of new inservice training centers. By 1979, two such centers were in operation, five more were under construction, and eight others were in the planning stage. Each center has been designed to accommodate 150 trainees in a course lasting six weeks, usually organized around a particular subject-matter field such as mathematics, science, language arts, and the like. When the network of training centers has been completed it will have the capacity to upgrade 18,000 teachers a year. Each center has been located near a teachers college on which the center depends for staffing.

Frequently in recent years, officials in the Ministry of Education have expressed strong dissatisfaction with the teacher-education system. Critics have charged that there is little or no coordination between the secondary schools that prepare primary-grade teachers and the institutes of education that prepare secondary-school instructors. They have charged further that the institutes do not have teacher-preparation as their serious goal, so that the educational programs are not properly designed to graduate skilled instructors and many graduates fail to enter the teaching profession. The quality of preparation at all levels of the system has also been criticized, with analysts claiming that the most effective modern methods of teacher training are not used in teacher-preparation institutions. Inservice education presentations have often been irrelevant to teachers' needs.

To correct such shortcomings, the Ministry during the last half of the 1970s initiated two major steps. First, committees under the Research and Development Center identified competencies modern Indonesian teachers needed, then used these as the source of specific learning objectives and instructional methods for devising new programs in the schools preparing primary-grade teachers. One aspect of the new programs is a far more extensive practice-teaching experience for candidates during their final year of training.

The second major step was the inauguration of a massive project, funded by a multi-million-dollar World Bank loan, aimed at a renovation of the entire teacher-education system. In 1978, a team of 40 teacher educators spent six months visiting teacher-training centers overseas in preparation for designing the intended revision of Indonesian teacher education in the 1980s.

How successful these efforts will be is unknown until assessments are carried out in the latter 1980s.

In conclusion, the decade of the seventies ended with the nation striving to prepare increasing numbers of teachers to keep up with the growing school population and, at the same time, to improve the quality of teacher training. Inservice programs to upgrade teachers currently staffing the schools were reaching more teachers than ever before. However, many problems remained to be solved. Although the government in 1973 had raised teachers' wages by 400 percent — to a higher comparative level than had been true for decades — teacher-training programs still did not attract the country's most talented youths. Outside activities prevented instructors in teachers colleges from dedicating sufficient time to their students and to improving instruction. And graduates of teachers colleges often entered occupations other than teaching. Solving these problems was the challenge of the years ahead.

Future Problems and Prospects

As in the past, the most serious problems for educational planners in the future will continue to be the rising number of candidates for schooling. Unless the population growth rate can be decreased substantially, there appears little hope that even the present levels of enrollment can be maintained. The goal of universal primary schooling for six years is still only a hope. More schools will need to be built and more teachers trained just to keep the present level of school attendance. Beyond the primary school, the expectations of both the public and the government for expanding educational opportunities for youths and adults significantly increases the magnitude of the educational-planners' task. Even greater efforts will be required, if public demand is to be met. And the aim of achieving a system of "lifelong learning" rather than only universal primary schooling has opened a panorama of new assignments for educators. Such nonformal projects as PAMONG and the open junior-high school may help, but care will be needed to ensure that these projects work well in their experimental stages and that later they are disseminated efficiently throughout the nation.

The best hope for reducing the gap between the rising number of candidates for schooling and the nation's educational facilities is found in the family-planning program that is designed to decrease the birth rate. The program achieved a secure foundation in the 1970s, and by the close of the decade there were signs of some small reduction in the pace of population growth. However, more vigorous efforts to inform parents of the advantages of planning and, in particular, more effective sanctions to encourage their cooperation in reducing family size will be required in the coming decade, if the growth rate is to be reduced to a point at which the economy will permit implementation of universal primary schooling and of secondary education for more than half an age group.

Further hope for providing enough educational facilities for all potential students lies in the nation's growing economic strength and in the willingness of both the government and private bodies — including parents — to contribute substantial amounts of their income to education. If there is further improvement in the economy in coming years, there will likely be more liberal financing of education, resulting in more school buildings, more books and laboratory equipment, and more attractive salaries for teachers.

In addition to the problem of furnishing ever-greater quantities of education, Indonesia faces the task of solving the deficiencies in the quality of schooling that were identified during the 1970s. A good foundation for improving quality was laid during the decade of the first two Five-Year Plans, 1969—1978. A significant step early in the decade was the establishment in the Ministry of Education of the Research and Development Center which, by 1980, sponsored a series of well-designed efforts at quality improvement. Furthermore, great strides were made in building the Center's capability for carrying out assessment studies, so that a staff with sophisticated techniques and equipment is ready in the 1980s to evaluate the efficiency of several quality-improvement programs that will soon reach the end of their tryout periods. Plans have been laid for comparing the effectiveness of the modularized learning system of the development-school with traditional teaching methods, for comparing the success of mobile-team upgrading of primary teachers with radio-broadcast courses for such teachers, and for appraising the outcomes of the PAMONG project described in Chapter 1. Although the quality of work of the Research and Development Center has been impressive, the Center has been producing primarily prototype programs, while the bulk of traditional textbook development and teacher training has been conducted by other agencies within the Ministry of Education. However, the other agencies have much progress to make before they emulate the quality of work of the Research and Development Center. Thus, better coordination of the efforts of these agencies with the Center appears desirable. Within the Center, it can be expected that further efforts will be made in the 1980s to increase the number of qualified personnel to tackle the tasks faced in the years ahead.

Earlier, we noted that at the close of the 1970s both primary and secondary schools displayed symptoms of inefficiency in their continuing high rates of dropouts and repeaters. Although more careful investigation is required to determine the reasons that different students drop out and repeat, it is clear from studies in the 1970s that problems of finance, low-quality instruction, lessons that appear irrelevant to students' needs, and unsuitable standards held by staff members were among the causes. The matter of families lacking sufficient funds to keep children in school may be solved, at least partially, by the sort of supplementary funding the government furnished for the primary grades in the late 1970s. If similar extra funding can be provided for the lower and upper secondary grades, more families near the poverty level may feel encouraged to keep their children in school. Hope for more relevant and interesting instruction lies in the curriculum experiments in progress, particularly the development-school project. These same experiments should help teachers establish more reasonable standards for pupil achievement so the repeater and dropout rates decline.

The dropout and repeater problems are linked to the system of examinations on which decisions about pupils' passing and failing are based. Prior to 1968, the Ministry of Education each year produced examinations to test pupils' performance at the close of the primary, junior-high, and senior-high years. However, because of the difficulties of shipping examinations to all schools in the archipelago and the high costs involved, responsibility for preparing and administering tests was shifted gradually to the schools, so by 1972 the responsibility for examinations was borne fully by school staffs. With this development, new problems occurred. Even though the Ministry provided booklets to guide teachers in preparing tests, the examinations varied greatly in quality from one school to another, since those who constructed the tests lacked the skill and care of the experts in the Ministry. Thus, one major task ahead is the improvement of tests, probably through the Ministry's furnishing an item bank from which to draw well-devised test questions and through inservice training of test constructors. (Nasoetion *et al.,* 1976.)

Additional problems to be solved in the future were identified in the nationwide assessment of sixth-graders' achievement in the mid-1970s. Two of the most serious were the wide discrepancy in the quality of learning by pupils in one province compared to those in another and the

94

discrepancy between urban and rural pupils' achievement. As possible steps toward solving these differences in coming years, the evaluation team recommended:

> ... national subsidies could be tied to enrolment ratios; incentives might be given to competent teachers to move to the poorer areas; inservice training might be stepped up in deprived regions; teacher exchange schemes might be encouraged, local research and development centers established. ... (Moegiadi, Mandinaan, and Elley, 1979, p. 341.)

The evaluation results of many of the innovations in both formal and nonformal schooling will only be known early in the 1980s. Further innovations will be tried out. Assuming that the innovations prove to be successful, a broadscale effort at disseminating reform measures throughout the nation's school system can be expected in the coming decade.

These, then, are some of the major problems and some of the possibilities for their solution which Indonesia's educational planners carry into the final years of the 20th century. The ideal of establishing a unified nation of people using a common national language, as voiced in the Indonesian Youth Pledge, was securely achieved by the end of the 1970s. But the job of ensuring lifelong education for the entire populace, suited to their individual needs as well as national-development goals, was still to be completed.

References

ATMAPRAWIRA, SOEMARDI (1962) *Mengisi Pantjawardhana* (Filling in the Five Developments). Pusataka Dewata, Jakarta.

BEEBY, C. E. (1979) *Assessment of Indonesian Education: A Guide in Planning.* New Zealand Council for Educational Research and Oxford Press, Wellington.

"FY 79/80 Draft Budget: Growth with Equity" (1979) *Indonesia Development News,* 2, No. 5, January.

MOEGIADI; MANGINDAAN, C.; and ELLEY, W. B. (1979) Evaluation of Achievement in the Indonesian Education System, *Evaluation in Education: International Progress* (B. H. CHOPPIN and T. N. POSTLETHWAITE, eds.), Vol. 2, No. 4.

NASOETION, N.; DJALIL, A.; MUSA, I.; SOELISTYON, S.; CHOPPIN, B. H.; and POSTLETHWAITE, T. N. (1976) *The Development of Educational Evaluation Models in Indonesia,* International Institute for Educational Planning (UNESCO), Paris.

Pendidikan di Indonesia (Education in Indonesia) (1976) Departemen Pendidikan dan Kebudayaan, Jakarta.

POSTLETHWAITE, T. NEVILLE (1978) "Evaluation Feedback to Curriculum Developers: An Example from a Curriculum Development and Evaluation Project in Indonesia", *Studies in Educational Evaluation,* Vol. 4, No. 3.

Rangkuman Statistik Persekolahan 1974 (Summary of 1974 School Statistics) (1976) Departemen Pendidikan dan Kebudayaan, Jakarta.

Rangkuman Statistik Persekolahan 1978 (Summary of 1978 School Statistics) (1979) Departemen Pendidikan dan Kebudayaan, Jakarta.

Rentjana Pembangunan Lima Tahun 1969/70–1973/74 (Five-Year Development Plan 1969/70–1973/74) (1968) Departemen Penerangan, Republik Indonesia, Jakarta.

Second Five-Year Development Plan (1974) Embassy of the Republic of Indonesia, Washington, D.C.

SOEDIJARTO (1976) *The Modular Instructional System as the Teaching-Learning Strategy in the Indonesian Development School.* BPPPK and UNESCO, Jakarta.

Statistik Indonesia 1968–1969 (1971) Biro Pusat Statistik, Jakarta.

SUMARDI, MULJANTO (1977) *Sejarah Singkat Pendidikan Islam di Indonesia 1945–1975* (A Brief History of Islamic Education in Indonesia 1945–1975) Departemen Agama, Jakarta.

SURIASUMANTRI, JUJUN S.; HASBULLAH, CHALIDIN; and DACHLIANI, YENNY (1976) *Program dan Sasaran Replita II: Pendidikan* (Program and Target of the Second National Development Plan: Education) Departemen Pendidikan dan Kebudayaan, Jakarta.

THOMAS, R. MURRAY (1966) Literacy by Decree in Indonesia, *School and Society,* Summer, pp. 279–283.

THOMAS, R. MURRAY (1970) Who Shall Be Educated? – The Indonesian Case, *The Social Sciences and the Comparative Study of Educational Systems* FISCHER, J., ed. International Textbook Co. Scranton, Penn.

VAN DER WAL, S. L. (1963) *Het Onderwijsbeleid in Nederlands-Indie 1900–1940* (Education Policy in the Netherlands-Indies 1900–1940) J. B. Wolters, Groningen.

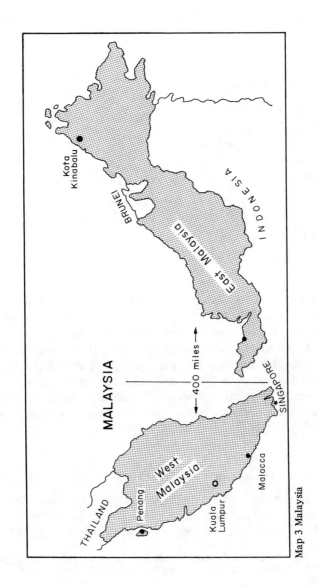

Map 3 Malaysia

Pendidikan ibarat benih yang baik
jatuh ke laut menjadi pulau.

Education is like a good seedling,
should it fall into the sea it would
grow to become an island.
                        Malay Saying

3

Malaysia

Arfah A. Aziz and Chew Tow Yow*

SINCE gaining independence from Britain and forming their own constitutional monarchy in 1963, Malaysians have striven to form a unified and
stable, peaceful and prosperous nation out of a multiracial and physically
divided populace. To illustrate the role performed by the education system
in pursuing this nation-building goal, we begin by inspecting demographic,
political, and economic conditions that have influenced the way educators
have carried out their assignment. Subsequently we describe the backgrounds of the education system itself and the state of the system at the
close of the 1970s.

The Country's Geography and Ethnic Groups

Malaysia occupies two distinct geographical areas: Peninsular Malaysia,
comprising the Malay Peninsula to the south of the Isthmus of Kra, and
East Malaysia (the States of Sabah and Sarawak) consisting of the north

*The authors would like to thank Dr. Isahak bin Harun, Deputy Dean, Faculty of
Education, University of Malaya, Kuala Lumpur, for his comments on the draft of
this chapter.

and western regions of the island of Borneo. Both parts are separated by about 400 miles of the South China Sea. The total land area of Malaysia is about 130,000 square miles, of which Peninsular Malaysia occupies 52,000 square miles and East Malaysia 78,000 square miles.

Peninsular Malaysia consists of the eastern and western coastal plains divided by the central mountain ranges. The greater part of the country is covered by jungle and swamp, but in cleared areas — mainly in the west and north-east and along the principal river valleys — there are towns, rubber plantations, tin mines, rice fields, palm-oil estates, and coconut holdings. Peninsular Malaysia is divided into eleven states.

East Malaysia consists of an alluvial and often swampy coastal plain with rolling country farther inland, rising to mountain ranges in the interior. Both states are largely jungle-covered, but on the coastal plains there are settlements with rice fields, rubber plantations, pepper gardens, and other crops.

Whereas communications are good in Peninsular Malaysia, there are no integrated road networks in Sabah and Sarawak, and the main means of communication are by river and air. River transport is by launch or boat, and certain inland areas are completely isolated from modern influences. The capital of Sabah, Kota Kinabalu, is one thousand miles from Kuala Lumpur, the capital of Malaysia, and Kuching, the capital of Sarawak, is 900 miles from Kuala Lumpur. These distances and modes of communication have been barriers in the past to the efficient running of education in Malaysia as a whole.

The earliest Malay Kingdom was the Buddhist Langkasuka, astride the Kra Isthmus, which probably came into existence in the second century. From then on, the history of Malaysia was for many centuries interwoven with the rise and fall of Buddhist, and later Hindu, empires of the region. The capture of Malacca by the Portuguese in 1511, a sultanate which had adopted Islam in the previous century and had grown into an important military and commercial power and a center of Islamic culture, marked the beginning of European influence in the region. In 1641, Malacca fell to the Dutch.

Britain's connection with Peninsular Malaysia, then known as Malaya, began with the establishment of trading settlements at Penang in 1786. In 1826, Singapore, Malacca, and Penang were incorporated into the colony of the Straits Settlements. From 1874—1884 a series of treaties were concluded with Britain by which four state rulers accepted British protection. These four states were Perak, Selangor, Negri Sembilan, and Pahang. In 1895, these four states were constituted by treaty into the Federated Malay States, with a British Resident-General and a system of centralized government. Between 1910 and 1930, treaties of protection were concluded with Britain by which the states of Kedah, Perlis, Kelantan, and Trengganu, accepted British Protection. These four states and Johore came to be known as the Unfederated Malay States. Singapore and the northern regions of the island of Borneo were also British colonies. After various acts of federation, self government, and independence, Malaysia, as described at the beginning of the chapter, came into existence in 1963; and Singapore became a separate independent state in 1965.

The *population* of Malaysia in 1975 was estimated at 12,249,000. (Government of Malaysia, 1976, p. 138.) About 85 percent or 10,385,000 live in Peninsular Malaysia, 751,000 in Sabah, and 1,113,000 in Sarawak. The annual growth rates for the intercensal years 1921–31, 1931–47, 1947–57, and 1957–70 were about 2.4, 3.0, 1.8, and 2.8 percent respectively. About 45 percent of the population is below the age of 15, and 26 percent is in the age group 15–29.

Malaysia is characterized by an uneven pattern of population distribution which reflects geographical, historical, and economic factors that have accounted for more rapid rates of economic development in areas of higher population concentration. Taking urban centers as gazetted areas of population of 10,000 and above, the percentage of urban population in Peninsular Malaysia in 1970 was only 28.7 percent, representing an increase of 2.1 percent over 1957. With very few exceptions, natural increase rather than rural–urban migration was the main source of urban growth. (Government of Malaysia, 1976, p. 149.)

This high growth rate creates a major problem for providing a place for every child of school-going age. Although more schools have been built since 1957, overcrowdedness in the classroom is still widespread. Many primary school classes have fifty children in them. A further problem is the disparity in allocation of resources between rural and urban areas; schools in urban areas are better established, and thus tend to be better equipped in terms of facilities and teacher supply. This disparity is reflected in the level of achievement where urban schools have higher achievement than rural schools. The rate of dropout from the school system is higher in rural schools than in urban schools. (Murad, 1973.)

One notable feature of Malaysia is its multiracial composition, with distinct cultural diversity. Of the total population in Malaysia, 55 percent are Malays and other indigenous people (Bumiputras), 34 percent Chinese, 9 percent Indians, and 2 percent others.

The state religion is Islam, but freedom of worship is guaranteed in the Constitution. Practically all Malays are Moslems. The Chinese are predominantly Buddhist, the Indians predominantly Hindu, but there is a sizeable Christian minority among both the Chinese and Indian groups.

Bahasa Malaysia is the national language and the sole official language in Malaysia. English is widely used and is a compulsory subject in schools. For the most part, each community has kept its mother tongue and dialects. In East Malaysia, English remained the official language until 1973, but the Sabah Government began using Bahasa Malaysia in March, 1972.

The different ethnic and language groups had developed their own school systems using various languages as the medium of instruction. Thus, at the primary level, there were Chinese, Indian, and English medium schools, besides schools in Bahasa Malaysia; and at the secondary level the medium of instruction was English or Chinese. Each school followed its own curriculum. Steps were taken by the government to bring all schools into a national system of education with a common content syllabus and using Bahasa Malaysia as the medium of instruction. Both steps were part of the drive towards developing a common Malaysian outlook and attitude. From 1958 onwards secondary schools using Bahasa Malaysia as the medium of instruction were established, and since 1970 English and Chinese as media of instruction at the secondary level have been phased out. (Hussein bin Onn, 1971.) Primary education is now offered in three language media, either Bahasa Malaysia, Chinese, or Tamil, and parents can select the medium of instruction for their child.

It must be noted, however, that in East Malaysia all groups (and there are about sixteen groups) have at least one distinctive language. Malay is widely understood for every day purposes, but the cohesion of the people through language is no minor undertaking.

The high rate of *illiteracy* continues to be a matter for concern. According to the 1970 census, of the population above 10 years of age, 61 percent were literate, 5 percent were considered as semi-literate, and 34 percent were illiterate. Over two thirds of the males and less than half of the females were literate. Sixty percent of the urban population was literate as compared with 54 percent of the rural population.

This higher proportion of illiteracy among the older age group in rural areas has, to some extent, affected the implementation of development programs for the rural population. Immediately before and after the country's independence, literacy classes were organized for that age group under an extensive Adult Education Program in the First Malaysian Economic Plan. The Ministry of Agriculture, through its Community Development Division, is currently implementing a comprehensive plan for rural areas of which an important component is the Functional Literacy Program.

However, the problem of illiteracy is, to a certain extent, compensated for by the availability of mass-media, especially transistor radios. This has been an important element in the dissemination of information to the rural population on current events and development programs, including modern techniques of agricultural production, nutrition, health habits, and sanitation.

SOCIO-ECONOMIC BACKGROUND

Malaysia is a producer of primary commodities and its economy is largely dependent on exports. Its predominant position as a producer and exporter of rubber and tin has enabled it to achieve one of the highest standards of living in Asia, with a per capita income of M$ 1000 (about US$ 400.00)

Despite the increase in recent years of the per capita income in Malaysia, inequality in income distribution among Malaysian households is still great. About 27 percent of the households in Peninsular Malaysia have incomes below M$ 100 per month. (Midterm Review of the Second Malaysia Plan 1971–75.) Overall in 1970, the top 20 percent of households accounted for 56 percent of the total household income, and the bottom 60 percent received only 25 percent of the total income. The incomes of rural households are distributed more equally than urban households. The mean income of rural households is less than half that of urban households (M\$ 435). About 90 percent of households with monthly incomes of less than M\$ 100 are to be found in rural areas.

Natural rubber continues to be the most important contributor to the Malaysian economy. In 1974, it accounted for about 30 percent gross export receipts and a little over 17 percent of the GNP. Malaysia remains the world's leading exporter of tin. Recent emphasis on the cultivation of oil palm has made the country one of the leading palm-oil producers; the same is true for hardwood timber. Peninsular Malaysia now produces about 80–85 percent of its yearly rice needs, but East Malaysia relies greatly on rice imports for its requirements. Petroleum production has recently increased and Malaysia hopes to develop its oil exports to a significant level.

Industrialization is now rapid. Manufacturing contribution to the GNP rose from 13.4 percent in 1970 to nearly 23 percent in 1973. Industrial production increased 11.3 percent in 1974 over the previous years. However, East Malaysia remains primarily agrarian.

The government has an aggressive strategy of industrial development which encourages foreign investment and participation. Several government organizations have been established to assist domestic and foreign investors as well as to furnish equity and participation in ownership of selected industry. The rapid industrialization, including diversification of primary products and manufacturing, has resulted in a corresponding diversification of educational programs provided in the school system at upper and postsecondary levels. More technical and vocational schools are being built, offering training in a variety of subjects. This is supplemented by training programs which are organized by other agencies, including the Ministry of Labour and Manpower, the Ministry of Youth and Culture, and the Ministry of Agriculture. These agencies provide industrial and technical training for skilled and semi-skilled labor. Training for highly skilled and professional labor is provided by several institutions at tertiary levels, including the Institute of Technology MARA, Politeknik Ungku Omar, Kolej Tunku Abdul Rahman, and the University of Technology Malaysia. These institutions offer a variety of technical and applied science courses such as engineering, architecture, and accountancy.

The unemployment rates from 1965–1975 and estimates for 1980 and 1990 are presented in Table 3.1.

TABLE 3.1

Labor Force, Employment and Unemployment, Malaysia (Estimates from Second and Third Malaysia Plans)

	1965	1970	1975	1980	1990
Labor Force	3,246,000	3,606,800	4,255,800	4,972,800	6,587,100
Employment	3,048,000	3,339,500	3,927,800	4,670,500	6,347,700
Unemployment	198,000	267,800	297,200	302,300	239,400
Unemployment % of Labor Force	6.1	7.4	7.0	6.1	3.6

Several labor-force surveys revealed that unemployment was most serious among young school leavers between the ages of 15–19. These are young people from urban areas seeking a job for the first time. In rural areas, while the unemployment rates are lower, underemployment continues to be a problem.

In 1975, nearly half (49.3 percent) of the entire Malaysian labor force was engaged in agriculture, forestry, and fishing. In second place, far behind the agriculture–fishing sector, was the public-service sector (public administration, education, defense) with 13 percent of the total work force. A close third was wholesale and retail trade with 12.6 percent, followed by manufacturing at 10.1 percent. (Government of Malaysia, 1976, p. 140.)

Thus, despite progress in industrialization, unemployment remains a serious problem, and a new economic policy has been adopted which aims at an accelerated program of industrial development and the creation of greater employment opportunities. (Government of Malaysia, 1976, p. 138.)

The economic policy of the government could be gleaned from the stated objectives of the New Economic Plans. The overriding objective is national unity. The objectives of the NEP are two pronged:

> Seeks to eradicate poverty among all Malaysians and to restructure Malaysian society so that the identification of race with economic function and geographical location is reduced and eventually eliminated, both objectives being realized through expansion of the economy over time. Based on an intensive review of the nation's policies and priorities and involving close consultation with and deliberation among all segments of Malaysian society, the NEP has come to constitute a positive commitment by the Government to the task of creating a united, secure, socially just and progressive nation. (Government of Malaysia, 1976, p. 7.)

Malaysia is now an elective constitutional monarchy. The Supreme Head of State, the Yang Di Pertuan Agong, and the Deputy Supreme Head of State, the Timbalan Yang Di Pertuan Agong, are elected by the nine hereditary Malay rulers from among their own number, for a period of five years. There is a Conference of Rulers, consisting of the nine hereditary rulers, the Governors of Malacca, Penang and Sarawak, and the Yang Di Pertuan Negara of Sabah, which has power relating to Muslim religious matters and certain appointments, and which may deliberate on questions of national policy.

However, the executive power in Malaysia is invested in the cabinet, led by the Prime Minister, the leader of the political party that wins the most seats in a Parliamentary election. The cabinet is chosen from the members of Parliament and is responsible to that body. Parliament consists of a Senate and a House of Representatives. All members of the Senate sit for 6-year terms. The members of the House of Representatives are elected for maximum terms of 5 years. Legislative power is divided between Federal and State Legislatures.

The Federal Government has authority over external affairs, defence, internal security, justice (except Islamic and native law), Federal citizenship, finance, commerce, industry, communications, education and other matters.

The Education System

GENERAL BACKGROUND OF THE SCHOOL SYSTEM

The school system in Peninsular Malaysia, Sabah and Sarawak is essentially inherited from the British system. The pre-Second World War educational policy had been to provide free primary education through the vernacular to Malay children, to provide subsidized primary and secondary school education in English for children of all races, to control loosely the schools which the Chinese had provided mostly at their own expense and to subsidize primary schools provided by estate owners for the children of their Indian employees as part of the welfare policy in the Labour Code. (Ministry of Education, EPRD, 1975, p. 1.)

Education for the Malays was seen by the British administrators within the general policy of the "protection of the Malays", but with a certain apprehension about the dangers of "over-education" of the natives. The majority of the Malays, especially the rural Malays, were provided with vernacular Malay education up to the primary level only. The effect of the limited rural-biased Malay primary education was the isolation of the majority of Malays in their rural peasant agriculture, with few opportunities for further advancement in education or participation in the modern non-agricultural sector.

The Chinese community organized their own primary and secondary education. The development of Chinese Schools in Peninsular Malaysia came about partly as a result of political interest and change in mainland China during the first two decades of this century. Chinese leaders came to Malaya to help overseas Chinese establish schools in 1900–1910. (Loh, 1975.) After 1911, when the Kuomintang was established, the Chinese Schools in Malaya were taught by teachers from China using textbooks and curricula from mainland China. Some amount of Chinese nationalism and anti-British attitudes seeped into the classroom. Thus, in 1920 the government passed the Registration of Schools Ordinance whereby these schools were brought under close government supervision.

Indian education was closely associated with the rubber plantations. Owners of large plantations were required by law to provide a vernacular (usually Tamil) school whenever ten or more of their workers' children were within the school age range, i.e. between seven and fourteen. A small per capita grant, based on examination results and attendance, was given annually by the government. But generally these schools were poorly run and staffed. The curriculum was arbitrary, depending on whatever textbooks could be acquired from India or at the initiative of the teachers. Education in Tamil was limited to the primary level.

Over and above these vernacular schools was the English school system run by Christian missionaries (Catholic, Church of England and Methodist), and Government, using English as its medium of instruction. The Christian mission schools were begun in Peninsular Malaysia in 1816 in Penang and in East Malaysia in 1848. They constituted a source of manpower for the junior administrative service and the British-owned commercial houses. Unhappily for the future development of the country they served almost exclusively the urban, immigrant population. Only a small proportion of Malays attended these schools, mainly because most Malays lived in rural areas and also because most Malays were Moslem.

From the point of view of national development it might be said that the education system before World War II was unplanned. There was no clear policy on the part of the government with regard to the role of education in the development of Malaysian society. The educational institutions were essentially a divisive force in this society, tending to sustain its ethnically plural character.

The search for a "national system" of education which could lay the foundation for integrating the various ethnic groups, as well as being an instrument for socio-economic development, became one of the main preoccupations of the Malaysian elites after World War II and continued after Independence in 1957. After Independence, the government developed a "new" educational policy based on the Razak Report (1956) and Rahman Talib Report (1960). What is basically new in the reorganized national system of education is the program of "common-content" curriculum with a Malaysian orientation for all schools, the use of Bahasa Malaysia as the medium of instruction, supported by a reorganization of public service examinations, teacher training programs and the teaching service structure.

THE EVOLUTION OF POLICY

In the years immediately before Independence, the representative government which came into power in 1955 gave priority to education as the primary force for cementing the diverse ethnic communities into a nation. The Education Committee, formed in September 1955 under the then Minister of Education, was given the task of formulating a national system of education which would be "acceptable to the people of the Federation as a whole (and) which will satisfy their needs and promote their cultural, social, economic and political development as a nation, having regard to the intention to make Malay the national language of the country whilst preserving and sustaining the growth of the language and culture of other communities living in the country." (Government of Malaysia, 1958, p. 1.)

The Report of the Education Committee in 1956 (popularly known as the Razak Report) became the fundamental educational policy document of the country. On the question of the goal of education, the Report stated: "the ultimate objective of educational policy in this country must be to bring together the children of all races under a national educational system in which the national language is the main medium of instruction, though we recognise that progress towards this goal cannot be rushed and must be gradual." (Government of Malaysia, 1958, p. 3.)

On the question of education content, the Committee recommended a radical departure from the then practice of allowing each community to develop its own form of schooling. The Report stated that: "One of the fundamental requirements of educational policy in the Federation of Malaya is to orientate all schools, primary and secondary, to a Malayan outlook." (Government of Malaysia, 1958, p. 17.) The Report elaborated this 'fundamental requirement' as follows:

> We cannot over-emphasize our conviction that the introduction of syllabuses common to all schools in the Federation is the crucial requirement of educational policy in Malay. It is an essential element in the development of a united Malayan nation. It is the key which will unlock the gates hitherto standing locked and barred against the establishment of an educational system 'acceptable to the people of Malaya as a whole'. Once all schools are working to a common content syllabus, irrespective of the language medium of instruction, we consider the country will have taken the most important step towards establishing a national system of education which will satisfy the needs of the people and promote their cultural, social, economic, and political development as a nation.
> We do not consider that the order in which the material is treated is of major importance but priority should be given to the Malayan aspects of each subject and non-Malayan elements in the syllabus should only be admitted either if they are of international value, or if they provide the necessary background. (Government of Malaysia, 1958, p. 18.)

The recommendations of the Education Committee were incorporated into the Education Ordinance, 1957, the year the country became an independent state. Under the Ordinance, a six-year primary-school education was provided for all children between the ages of 6 and 11. At the end of the primary-school stage, pupils were selected on the basis of their performance by the secondary-schools selection examination for another three years of lower secondary-school education which led to the Lower Certificate of Education. The Lower Certificate of Education examination was a terminal certification examination as well as a selection examination for pupils proceeding to the upper secondary-school stage, a two-year course leading to the Cambridge School Certificate and the Federation of Malaya Certificate. A small number of pupils who were highly successful in these examinations were selected for a two-year pre-university sixth-form course.

Under the Education Act of 1961, which incorporated the findings of the 1960 Education Review Committee, a policy was implemented of raising the school leaving age to 15 years through the provision of two types of three-year nonacademic schools, the Secondary Continuation School and the Rural Extension School, for pupils who were not successful in gaining admission to the academic type of lower secondary school. There was general dissatisfaction with these nonacademic schools, and in 1965 a comprehensive type of lower secondary education was introduced for all pupils. The secondary-schools selection examination was abolished, thus providing nine years of uninterrupted primary and lower secondary education for all pupils leading to the Lower Certificate of Education.

The overall educational policy which has evolved now aims at providing the educational foundation for the inculcation of national identity and unity, the growth of the national culture and social mobility, as well as meeting the manpower needs of the country through a nine-years basic education program for all pupils and a further two years of differentiated upper secondary education in the arts, science, technical, and vocational streams.

Increased social mobility is based on the premise that with increased opportunities for formal education, and thus a higher level of educational certification, school leavers will have greater and better access to employment opportunities beyond menial jobs. However, the extent to which this can be realized is dependent on the anticipated increase in employment opportunities envisaged in the Third Malaysia Plan (1976–1980).

How education can contribute toward the manpower requirement of the country is a perennial problem. Except for the technical and vocational schools, which have courses of studies more directly related to specific fields of manpower requirement, general education, at best, provides a broad base preparation for meeting the manpower needs of the country.

CURRENT AIMS

The statements contained in the Third Malaysia Plan (1976–80) exemplify the current aims:

(1) Strengthen the educational system for promoting national integration and unity through:

(a) the continued implementation, in stages, of Bahasa Malaysia as the main medium of instruction at all levels;

(b) the development of personality, character and good citizenship and the promotion of moral discipline through curriculum and extracurriculum activities;

(c) narrowing the gaps in educational opportunities between the rich and the poor, and among the various regions and races in the country, through a more equitable distribution of resources and facilities; and

(d) the eventual integration of the educational system in Sabah and Sarawak into the national system.

(2) The orientation and expansion of the education and training system toward meeting national manpower needs especially in science and technology.

(3) The improvement of the quality of education in order to reduce wastage and increase its effectiveness for nation building.

(4) The expansion of the research, planning and implementation capacity to meet the above objectives. (Government of Malaysia, 1976, p. 391.)

To achieve these objectives, the Third Malaysia Plan, *inter alia,* has provided for:

(a) the improvement of school buildings and increased facilities to replace the existing substandard school buildings and facilities especially in the rural areas;

(b) seven additional (to the present eleven) residential science schools for rural children to pursue their education in science, mathematics, and related subjects;

(c) nine more vocational schools providing industrial trades, home science, agricultural science, and commercial courses;

(d) the strengthening of the teaching of science and mathematics through the increased provision of teaching materials and expansion in the number of science and mathematics teachers;

(e) increasing the enrollment of students in science, technical, and vocational courses at the upper secondary level to account for 81.6 percent of total enrollment at this level in 1980 as compared to 39.4 percent in 1975;

(f) pre-school child development and other compensatory education facilities to reduce dropout rate at the primary and secondary levels; and

(g) the improvement of educational research, planning, and coordination within the agencies of the Ministry of Education.

Present School Structure and Enrollment

FORMAL SCHOOLS

Malaysia has a 6–3–2–2 system of primary, secondary, and upper/ postsecondary levels with pupils entering the system at 6+ years. The organization chart showing the formal system of education is presented as Fig. 3.1.

At the primary level, there are six standards (grades) with automatic promotion between standards. This is followed by three years of lower secondary education, again with automatic promotion. After the lower secondary level, pupils are selected by examination and move to the upper secondary level for a further two years. At this level, there are separate types of schools for the Academic, Technical and Vocational

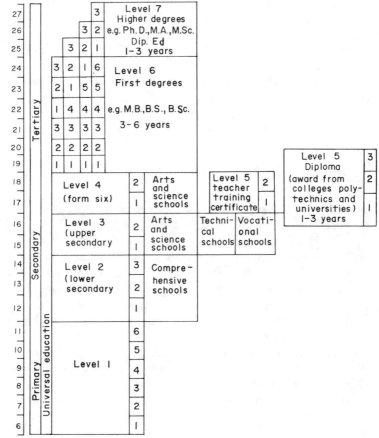

FIG. 3.1. *Organization chart of formal system of education*

groups. This is followed by two years (Grades 12 and 13) at the Form-Six level, which is essentially in preparation for the university. The upper levels of education, also known as the tertiary level, are composed of universities and colleges.

Most schools are either government or government-aided schools. These schools receive financial aid as well as their supply of teachers from the Ministry of Education. There is a small number of private schools which provide education at all levels, from kindergarten to Form 6, and training in vocational, commercial, and technical subjects for employment.

Primary education, lasting six years, is free but not compulsory. All primary schools, in any of the language media, use a common content syllabus. This is to ensure that all pupils will follow the same course content reflecting a Malaysian outlook. Each school conducts its own evaluation of pupils. Tests are administered regularly, whether weekly, monthly, or termly, according to the decisions of the headmaster/ headmistress. In addition, centralized assessments are conducted yearly for all pupils in Standards III and V. The tests in Standard III are diagnostic in nature aimed at identifying areas of pupil weaknesses and assisting teachers to provide remedial activities for the pupils. The tests are school based, and most of the grading is done by the teachers in the school. The Standard V Assessment is used to determine the level of pupil achievement and to determine the remedial activities required before the pupils enter secondary schools.

At the *lower secondary school level (3 years)*, pupils receive a comprehensive type of education. In addition to the academic subjects, subjects of a prevocational nature such as industrial arts, home science, agricultural science, and commercial studies are also included in the curriculum. Each pupil is required to take at least one of the prevocational subjects, the main aim being to expose them to some practical subjects. At the end of Form Three, pupils sit for the Lower Certificate of Education Examination. Based on the results in this examination, pupils are selected to proceed to the upper secondary level and are channelled into various streams such as science, arts, technical, and vocational.

At the *upper secondary school level (2 years)*, education consists of academic (arts or science), technical, and vocational streams. Pupils in the academic and technical streams sit for the Malaysian Certificate of Education Examination at the end of the second year. This examination provides entry qualifications for posts in the public and private sectors. It is also utilized as a basis for selection into postsecondary level (Form 6) or for entry to the various courses at the tertiary level. Pupils in the vocational streams are given courses in such areas as engineering trades, commerce, home science, or agriculture as a preparation for employment in the commercial and industrial world.

At the *post secondary school level (2 years)*, education is streamed into science or arts. Pupils are selected for this level of education based on their performance in the Malaysian Certificate of Education Examination. At the end of the two years, pupils sit for the Higher School Certificate Examination. This examination serves as a basis for selection and entrance to the universities. It is also a qualification for appointment to the government service and private sectors.

Tertiary education, comprising college and university education, is normally attended by youths who leave school at about 18 or 19 years of age. It takes the form of general or specialized studies. Some courses combine higher education with practical training for professions such as teaching and medicine. Off-campus courses are also offered for people in employment. College diploma courses normally last from two to four years. University degree courses generally extend over three to four years, though medicine and dentistry require between five and six years. There are three institutions at the college level: Politeknik Ungku Omar, Institute of Technology MARA, and Kolej Tunku Abdul Rahman. There are five institutions of university status in the country: University of Malaya, University of Science Malaysia, the National University (Universiti Kebangsaan), University of Agriculture (Universiti Pertanian), and University of Technology Malaysia (Universiti Teknologi Malaysia).

SCHOOL ENROLLMENT

Enrollment of pupils in primary, secondary, and post-secondary schools in Peninsular Malaysia, Sabah, and Sarawak has increased over the years. The total enrollment for years 1970, 1975, and target enrollment for 1980 are presented in Table 3.2.

Total enrollment in primary education increased by 12.8 percent from 1970 to 1975. The more significant increases were in Sabah and Sarawak.

TABLE 3.2
Developments in the Educational System 1970–80

	Enrollment			Increase (%)	
	1970	1975	1980	1971–75	1976–80
Primary					
Peninsular Malaysia	1,421,469	1,586,909	1,815,600	11.6	14.4
Sabah	110,607	133,179	166,140	20.4	24.7
Sarawak	150,111	177,100	227,300	18.0	28.3
Total	1,682,187	1,897,188	2,209,040	12.8	16.4
Lower Secondary					
Peninsular Malaysia	378,535	561,471	676,100	48.3	20.4
Sabah	25,068	41,835	68,492	66.9	63.7
Sarawak	17,041	46,400	67,530	172.3	45.5
Total	420,644	649,706	812,122	54.5	25.0
Upper Secondary					
Arts and Science					
Peninsular Malaysia	84,925	153,415	241,900	80.6	57.7
Sabah	3,619	6,518	16,743	80.1	156.9
Sarawak	4,384	7,120	19,130	62.4	168.7
Vocational &					
Technical	4,899	14,338	25,920	192.7	80.8
Total	97,827	181,191	303,693	85.4	67.4
Post Secondary					
Peninsular Malaysia	10,619	16,335	35,970	53.8	120.2
Sabah	272	293	618	7.7	110.9
Sarawak	641	1,360	2,320	112.2	70.6
Total	11,532	17,988	38,908	56.0	116.3

(*Source:* Government of Malaysia 1976, p. 405.)

In the same period, enrollment at the secondary level grew by 60 percent. At the lower secondary level, enrollments increased significantly as a result of improvements in survival rates from primary to lower secondary classes. This improvement in survival rates could be due, in part, to the realization of the importance of education and the negative effects of early dropouts from the school system as indicated by the report on the dropout problems published in 1973. (Murad, 1973.) In Sarawak, the major increase in enrollment at the lower secondary level resulted from the abolition of the Common Entrance Selection Examination for entry to lower secondary classes and the improvement in survival rates as a result of the takeover by the Government of primary schools previously managed by local authorities. An important feature of upper secondary education was the establishment of eleven fully residential schools, with a total enrollment of 9,240, to provide expanded educational opportunities for pupils from rural areas. (Government of Malaysia 1976, p. 386.)

Based on the total relevant age-group population, *enrollment ratios* at the various levels of education are as follows:

	1974	1975	1976
Primary level	90.5%	96.0%	96.3%
Lower secondary level	65.1%	69.5%	71.9%
Upper secondary level	28.5%	32.7%	34.5%
Post secondary level	2.8%	3.5%	3.9%

Comparatively, the enrollment ratio of pupils at the primary level and secondary levels is quite high. This is surprising when it is realized that primary school is not compulsory. The high rate of attendance could be due to the increasing importance placed on education as a vehicle for social mobility, and the fact that education is now available in remote areas and villages so that a child does not need to travel far to reach a primary school.

The *transition rate* in 1976 of pupils continuing from primary to lower secondary school was 85 percent, from lower to upper secondary was 62 percent and from upper to postsecondary was nearly 16 percent. In the upper secondary school the vast majority of pupils were in the academic stream (85.8 percent), with only 9.6 percent in the vocational stream and 4.6 percent in the technical stream. In the post-secondary school, the pupils were enrolled in approximately equal numbers in the arts and science streams. The overall picture of enrollment by type and level of education for the period 1974—76 is presented in Table 3.3.

NON-FORMAL EDUCATION

The agencies, apart from the Ministry of Education, responsible for out-of-school training programs include the Board of National Unity of the Prime Minister's Department, the Agriculture and Community Development Division, the Veterinary and Fisheries Department of the Ministry

TABLE 3.3

Quantitative Development in the Education System 1974–76

Level and Type of Education	Enrollment			% Increase for period to 1976	% Enrollment by level of education		
	1974	1975	1976		1974	1975	1976
Primary level	1,547,331	1,586,909	1,602,635	3.6	68.6	67.1	65.8
Lower secondary level	518,001	561,471	597,720	15.4	23.0	23.7	24.5
Upper secondary level	142,461	164,727	175,992	23.5	6.3	7.0	7.2
Academic (Arts & Sciences)	132,319	153,415	162,808	23.01	–	–	–
Technical	3,382	3,683	4,295	26.8	–	–	–
Vocational	6,757	7,629	8,889	31.6	–	–	–
Post secondary level	13,889	16,335	19,369	29.5	0.6	0.7	0.8
Arts	6,512	7,880	10,265	57.6	–	–	–
Science	7,377	8,455	9,104	23.4	–	–	–
Teacher training	5,657	6,182	8,616	52.3	0.3	0.3	0.4
College level	13,654	15,612	16,600	21.6	0.6	0.7	0.7
University level	12,984	14,063	15,805	21.7	0.6	0.5	0.6
Grand total	2,253,979	2,365,308	2,436,737	88.1	100	100	100

of Agriculture and Rural Development, the Manpower Department of the Ministry of Culture, Youth and Sports, the Ministry of Welfare Services, the Department of Prisons of the Ministry of Home Affairs, and the Department of Broadcasting and Information of the Ministry of Information. The programs they provide are mainly concerned with development of technical skills either for on-the-job training or in preparation for employment.

Training for manpower needs in specific technical skills is coordinated by the National Industrial Training and Trade Certification Board (NITTCB) which was established to provide common trade standards and to improve syllabuses and course structures for vocational training institutions. The Division of Manpower in the Ministry of Labour runs Industrial Training Institutes (ITI's) for the workers already in different industries as well as job-oriented vocational training programs for children of school-going age who are found to profit more from such courses than from academic courses. The Malayan Railway Administration trains apprentices in various skills related to railway maintenance. The Telecommunications Department provides several courses, including courses in radio and microwave. The Postal Department provides training courses for clerical staff, uniformed staff, and senior postal officers. The Public Services Department at its Staff Training Centre offers courses on land administration management, supervision and local government. The Town and Country Planning Commission provides training for tracers, craftsmen, town planning assistants, and technical cadets. The Customs Department provides specialized courses for members of the Customs and Excise. Other departments such as Drainage and Irrigation, Radio Malaysia, Veterinary, Agriculture, Fisheries, Social Welfare, and Health provide specialized training in their respective fields. Short-term management training courses are also conducted by the National Productivity Centre (NPC), Institute of Technology MARA, the National Institute of Public Administration (INTAN), and the Malaysian Institute of Management.

In an effort to provide maximum opportunities for the rural population, MARA (Malay and Rural Development Agency) and the Community Development Division of the Ministry of Agriculture have developed training programs geared mainly towards youths from the rural areas. MARA has established several centers in various regions of the country and offers training in such skills as electronic repairs, woodwork, and dressmaking. Other agencies, such as the Federal Land Development Authority (FELDA) and the Farmers Association (Persatuan Peladang), organizes training in modern agricultural techniques so that the level of agricultural production can be improved.

The Community Development Division of the Ministry of Agriculture has a comprehensive program which includes the following components:

(1) Family Development Programs: to increase women's contributions in the development of the nation.

(2) Pre-school Program.

(3) Adult Education Program: Basic Literacy Classes, Functional Literacy Classes, Work Oriented Classes.

(4) Establishment of Rural Libraries.

(5) Organizing economically viable community projects, e.g. classes in agriculture, fish-farming, etc.

An important program specifically for the rural population is the *Functional Literacy Programme* (Rancangan Pedoman Tugasan). It is essentially a program to eradicate illiteracy, and at the same time to develop skills, knowledge, and information in order to raise the daily standard of living of the rural population within their social and economic contexts. This program, now in an experimental stage, develops the participants' skills in reading, writing, arithmetic, and other related skills so that their level of productivity will rise.

All out-of-school training programs are run independently of the formal school system in the Ministry of Education. However, the curricula of all these programs complement the vocational and technical subjects which are offered in the schools. Links are maintained with the Ministry of Education through the participation of officers and teachers, who are brought in from time to time to assist in the preparation of the curriculum and to conduct specific portions of the training program.

Administrative Structure

After the Razak Report in 1956 a second committee, the Rahman Talib Education Review Committee, was set up in 1960 to review the Razak policy and its implementation. Its recommendations were duly incorporated in the Education Act of 1961. The present system of education is largely the result of the implementation of the Education Act, 1961.

GENERAL ADMINISTRATION

The education system operates at two levels: Federal and State. At the *Federal* level, the Ministry of Education is responsible for the implementation of the education policy and administration of the entire educational system. The Minister of Education is responsible for making decisions on all policy matters either singly or in consultation with his Cabinet colleagues.

The Minister is assisted by two Deputy Ministers and a Political Secretary. The chief executive officer in the Ministry is the Secretary-General; he is directly responsible to the Minister and has overall control of the administrative functions of the Ministry.

The head of the professional side, the Director-General of Education, advises the Minister and the Secretary-General in all professional matters. He is assisted by two Deputy Director-Generals of Education. There are two major operating divisions in the Ministry of Education:

The *Administrative Division* comprises divisions of Finance and Accounts, Development and Supply, Scholarships and Training, Establishment and Service, Administration, Higher Education, and External Affairs.

The *Professional Division* comprises divisions of Educational Planning and Research, Schools, Education Media Service, Teacher Training, Federal Inspectorate of Schools, Examination Syndicate, Technical and Vocational Education, Curriculum Development Centre, Registration (Schools and Teachers), and Islamic Religious Schools.

At the *State* level, the State Director of Education is the executive Head through whom the Ministry of Education operates. He implements the Government's educational policy in his State and performs administrative functions relating to registration, examinations, finance, scholarship, staffing, etc. He is also responsible for the proper management of all schools. The staff in a State Education Office consists of education officers, organizers, assistant organizers on the professional side and a number of other executive, clerical, and lower staff personnel.

The Ministry of Education does not run any schools itself, but it sets minimum standards in various matters. It controls the training and supply of teachers and lays down principles for the recognition of teachers as qualified. It provides financial grants to schools and other educational institutions including colleges and universities.

Educational planning is done at two levels. At the national level, it forms part of the overall economic planning conducted by the National Development Planning Committee which operates through the Economic Planning Unit attached to the Prime Minister's Department. Educational planning at this level is undertaken within the context of general considerations such as the economic policies of the country and the manpower requirements of the country.

At the Ministry level, the planning of education is coordinated by the Educational Planning and Research Division. Plans are submitted to the Educational Planning Committee for consideration and policy decision. This committee is a high-powered decision-making body chaired by the Minister himself, and its functions are mainly to consider and, if necessary, to approve educational development plans and annual operational plans and budgets for implementation. The Educational Planning and Research Division maintains close contact and liaison with other divisions of the Ministry of Education, the State Education Departments, and other agencies whose work and programs may have relevance to educational needs.

FINANCE

Education is free at the primary level. Students pay a tuition fee in those secondary schools which were previously English-medium schools. Schools are allowed to collect fees for miscellaneous expenditure such as library and sports activities. In addition, the government gives assistance, in the form of money for recurrent expenditure to purchase necessary equipment and materials for such subjects as science, arts, and home science. The amount is based on the number of pupils enrolled in the school.

The cost of education, both capital and recurrent, is financed mainly from public revenue. The Finance and Accounts Division in the Ministry of Education is responsible for making yearly estimates of expenditure and for the payment of grants to states for recurrent as well as capital expenditure on education. Different divisions of the Ministry of Education send their estimates to the Estimates Committee in the Treasury. The budget is tabled in Parliament some time towards the end of each year. A ceiling is generally fixed for the total budget of each Ministry by the Cabinet. After the budget has been passed by Parliament, expenditure can be incurred by the Ministry directly. Tables 3.4—3.5 present information on Public Development for Education and Training programs, and expenditure on education.

The *development expenditure* in education during the Second Malaysia Plan period (1971—1975) was $573.8 million. For the Third Malaysia Plan period (1976—1980), $1,430 million is allocated for development expenditure, giving a 149.2 percent increase over the Second Malaysia Plan period. The percentage distribution of development expenditure according to level and type of education is as follows for the period 1976—80 (Fact sheets, Ministry of Education, Kuala Lumpur):

Level/type of education	% allocation of development expenditure
Primary	24.8
Secondary	26.1
Technical & vocational	4.5
Hostels	1.7
Teacher training	6.1
College level	5.1
University level	27.9
Other programs	3.8

The per pupil expenditures for the different levels of education are (Fact sheets, Ministry of Education, Kuala Lumpur):

Level/type of education	cost per pupil ($)
Primary school	240
Secondary school	345
Technical/vocational school	950
Residential school	2,200

As more and more places are provided for lower and upper secondary

TABLE 3.4

Public Development Expenditure for Education and Training Programs
1971–80 (M$ million)

Program	Estimated Expenditure 1971–75	Allocation 1976–80
Peninsular Malaysia	438.2	1,068.1
Primary Education	80.2	210.0
Secondary Education	138.0	200.7
Vocational & Technical Education	25.7	20.7
Higher Technical Educ.	6.6	22.7
Teacher Training	3.6	77.2
Sabah	44.9	195.0
Primary Education	14.3	76.1
Secondary Education	22.9	95.3
Vocational Education	3.9	16.5
Sarawak	55.2	186.9
Primary Education	10.4	68.0
Secondary Education	41.2	82.7
Vocational Education	2.01	4.3
Other agencies:	92.6	221.3

(*Source:* Adapted from Government of Malaysia, 1976, p. 405.)

education, the cost of education will increase gradually. This rise in cost is caused by the increased facilities required, especially for science, technical, and vocational subjects. The cost will continue to rise until the number of students entering both primary and secondary schools stabilizes.

INSPECTORATE SYSTEM

School inspection is carried out by the Federal Inspectorate of Schools through a regular program of school visits. School visits are of three types: the ordinary school visit, the full inspection, and the block inspection.

The ordinary school visit is usually undertaken by one or two members of the inspectorate and is limited to one day per school. After each inspection of a school followed by a discussion with the Headmaster and teachers, a written record of the inspection is sent to the headmaster of the school

TABLE 3.5
Expenditure on Education, 1974–1976

Year	Recurrent Expenditure Amount (M$ million)	Increase	Capital Expenditure Amount (M$ million)	Increase	Total Expenditure Amount (M$ million)	Increase	% of Educational Expenditure as compared to the National Expenditure
1974	1051	30.6	187	31.7	1238	30.7	22.8
1975	1158	10.2	212	13.4	1370	10.7	19.6
1976*	1474	27.3	261	23.1	1735	26.6	18.8

* Estimate
(*Source*: Fact sheets, Ministry of Education, Kuala Lumpur)

with copies to the Director-General of Education, Director of Education of the State and to the divisional heads of the Ministry of Education.

The full inspection of a school takes a whole week. The aim is to inspect thoroughly every aspect and activity of the school. The teaching and learning of every subject is observed and evaluated. The number of inspectors taking part in a full inspection is determined by the size of the school and the number of subjects taught in the school. At the end of the full inspection, a comprehensive report is prepared and submitted to the Ministry of Education.

In a block inspection, many schools, both primary and secondary, in a district or area, are inspected by a team of inspectors to assess the standard of teaching and learning. A report of the inspection together with the recommendations of the inspecting team are sent to the Director of Education of the State concerned, with copies to the Director-General of Education and the heads of division. A record of the visit is also sent to the headmaster of each school that has been visited.

In addition to the normal school visits, the Federal Inspectorate also organizes courses and seminars for teachers on specific strategies for classroom teaching. As the need arises, it also conducts surveys to assess the appropriateness of teaching-learning situations in the school. The findings from such a study are conveyed to relevant divisions in the Ministry for further action. In 1979, for example, the Inspectorate conducted a survey to assess the level of reading of primary school children in one of the states in Peninsular Malaysia.

The full establishment of the Inspectorate Division comprises one Chief Inspector of Schools, a Deputy Chief Inspector, several senior inspectors, and a full complement of inspectors. Six divisional offices have been established for the Federal Inspectorate in various regions in Peninsular Malaysia. Normally all members of the Inspectorate are selected from the pool of experienced teachers in the field. They are then given on-the-job training and also some professional training in institutions of higher learning through a yearly allotment of fellowships and scholarships within the overall program for staff development in the Ministry of Education. At present, the number of inspectors is not adequate for satisfactory inspection of all schools, with the result that many schools are only infrequently visited. There is a concerted effort to increase the number of inspectors, and to place them in regional centers so that their role as supervisors and inspectors of the school system can be made more effective.

Curriculum

THE FORMAL CURRICULUM

The formal Malaysian school curriculum for the various levels of the school system is contained in the following sets of official documents:

(1) *The Schools (Courses of Studies) Regulations, 1956*: the latest notification came into force in January 1968 with subsequent amendments circulated as Professional Circulars. The gazetted notification sets out the schedule of approved subjects to be taught and the minimum time allocation for each subject in each year of schooling;

(2) The Subject Syllabuses issued by the Ministry of Education from time to time;

(3) The approved lists of textbooks circulated to all schools by the Textbook Bureau of the Ministry of Education; and

(4) Centralized Examination Requirements issued by the Examinations Syndicate, Ministry of Education, principally the Syllabus *Guide and Regulations for the Lower Certificate of Education Examination* and the *Joint Examination for the Malaysia Certificate and the G.C.E.*

From these sets of official documents the teachers construct their instructional curriculum. Tables 3.6 to 3.8 present the Course of Studies for the primary, lower secondary and upper secondary levels of school education.

CURRICULUM DEVELOPMENT

The principal focus of curriculum development is in the development of subject syllabuses and their implementation in schools. Prior to January 1973, curriculum development was coordinated by the Curriculum Section of the Educational Planning and Research Division of the Ministry. Curriculum development was and is subject based. In other words, it consists mainly of the preparation of subject syllabuses, the development of teachers' guides and teacher retraining, and the supervision of textbooks

TABLE 3.6
*Courses of Studies for Primary Schools – Prescribed subjects and
minimum time in minutes per week by year of schooling
(Bahasa Malaysia Medium)*

Subject Year/Standard	Minimum number of minutes per week					
	I	II	III	IV	V	VI
Islamic Religious Knowledge* ⎫						
or ⎬						
Pupils' Own Language** ⎭	120	120	120	120	120	120
Bahasa Malaysia	300	300	300	300	300	300
English	300	300	300	300	300	300
Mathematics	210	210	210	210	210	210
Science	90	90	90	120	120	120
Art and Craft	120	120	90	80	80	80
Physical Education	80	80	90	60	80	80
Health Education	50	50	60	30	40	40
Local Studies	30	30	30	–	–	–
Geography	–	–	–	80	80	80
History	–	–	–	80	80	80
Civics	–	–	–	40	40	40
At the discretion of						
the head Teacher	80	80	90	70	200	200
Group Activities	–	–	60	60	120	120
Total minimum number of						
minutes per week	1380	1380	1440	1500	1720	1720

(*Source*: Ministry of Education)
* Compulsory for all Muslim pupils
** Chinese or Tamil, optional for Chinese/Tamil pupils when parents of 15 or more
   pupils request such instruction.

produced by either the Dewan Bahasa dan Pustaka (the Language and Literacy Agency), a statutory body of the Ministry, or by authors in the private sector.

In 1973, the Curriculum Development Centre was set up within the Ministry of Education to play a major role in the following curriculum development activities:
(1) to identify national needs and aspirations and to translate them into curricular specifications;
(2) to conduct curriculum research and experimentation;
(3) to plan and develop curricular programs for continuous, systematic, and qualitative development in education;

TABLE 3.7
Courses of Study for Lower Secondary School –
Prescribed subjects and minimum time in minutes
for Form I to Form III

Subject	Minimum number of minutes per week
Bahasa Malaysia	240
English	240
Islamic Religious knowledge OR Pupils' own language	120
Mathematics	200
Science	200
Art & Craft/Music	80
Physical Education	80
Health Education	40
Civics	40
Geography and History	120
Industrial Arts/Home Science/ Commercial Studies/Agricultural Science	160
Optional subjects (approved by the Registrar of Schools)	80
Group Activities	180
Total minimum number of minutes per week	1780

(*Source*: Ministry of Education)

(4) to develop and produce curriculum materials such as syllabuses of instruction, teacher's guidelines, pupil learning materials, evaluation instruments, audiovisual aids and prototype science and other equipment;

(5) to disseminate information on curricular innovations and practices to teachers in schools and others in the community;

(6) to organize pilot inservice teacher-education courses to communicate innovation, changes, and revisions; and

(7) to conduct surveys and analysis of significant worldwide trends and development in curriculum specifications and teaching practices.

With the institutionalization of curriculum development at the Curri-

TABLE 3.8

*Course of Studies for Upper Secondary Schools – Prescribed
subjects and minimum time in minutes per week for Form IV
and V by streams*

Subject	Minimum number of minutes per week					
	Arts Subjects	Science Subjects	Technical	Agricultural	Commerce	Home Science
Bahasa Malaysia	200	200	200	200	200	200
English	160	160	160	160	160	160
Islamic Religious knowledge OR Pupils' Own Language	120	120	120	120	120	120
Literature	120	–	–	–	–	–
Mathematics	200	160	160	160	160	160
Additional Mathematics	–	160	–	–	–	–
General Science	200	–	–	–	–	200
Additional General Science	160	–	–	–	–	–
Physics	–	200	200	160	–	–
Chemistry	–	200	160	260	–	–
Biology	–	200	–	200	–	–
Art & Craft and/or Music	80	–	–	–	80	80
Physical Education	80	80	80	80	80	80
Civics	40	40	40	40	40	40
Social Studies/History/ Geography	–	120	120	120	–	–
Geography	120	–	–	–	120	120
History	120	–	–	–	120	120
Geometrical & Building Drawing/Geometrical & Mechanical Drawing	–	–	120	–	–	–
Surveying/Additional Mathematics	–	–	120	–	–	–
Engineering Workshop Practice/Building Construction	–	–	160	–	–	–
Agricultural Science	–	–	–	200	–	–
Commerce	–	–	–	–	160	–
Principles of Accounts	–	–	–	–	–	160
Two of the following: Cookery, Needlework & Dressmaking, General Housecraft	–	–	–	–	–	320
At the discretion of the Head Teacher	–	–	–	–	–	–
Group Activities	180	140	140	180	180	180
Total number of minutes per week	1780	1780	1780	1780	1780	1780

(*Source*: Ministry of Education)

culum Development Centre, a base has been provided for making curriculum reforms for the on-going improvement of the school curriculum. Besides the periodic review of the subject syllabuses, increasing resources are being directed towards curriculum research and evaluation and experimentation of alternative approaches and procedures for the improvement of the curriculum-in-use. However, it must be pointed out that the Curriculum Development Centre is not the sole institution responsible for curriculum development in the Ministry of Education. The Technical and Vocational Education Division is responsible for the specification and development of the technical and vocational subjects of the curriculum.

While the Curriculum Development Centre and the Technical and Vocational Education Division of the Ministry are responsible for the planning, development, and evaluation of the school curriculum, the final authority for all aspects of curriculum planning and implementation is the *Central Curriculum Committee*, chaired by the Director-General of Education, who is the chief professional executive of the Ministry. The permanent members of the Central Curriculum Committee are the Directors of the professional divisions of the Ministry, the Secretaries of the Finance and Accounts Division and the Staff and Establishment Division, and a representative from a local university.

The major task of implementing curriculum changes in the schools is undertaken by the various State Departments of Education through the Schools Division of the Ministry. The Inspectorate of Schools, with its headquarters and field inspectors, is responsible for the quality control of educational standards and the implementation of change in schools. Summative evaluation in general and the certification of educational achievement is undertaken by the Examinations Syndicate by means of the prescribed centralized examinations conducted yearly.

The goals and objectives of the curriculum are derived from the educational policy defined by Parliament. The Minister of Education is responsible for the execution of the government policy, and he is empowered to make rules and regulations concerning the operation of the educational system. The actual task of the interpretation of the educational policy into curriculum objectives is in general delegated to the Director-General of Education assisted by the Central Curriculum Committee. The *Curriculum Development Centre*, acting as the secretariat for the Central Curriculum Committee, has the responsibility of actually identifying and formulating the curriculum objectives.

The Central Curriculum Committee is free to receive and consider recommendations concerning the curriculum from members of the public, divisions of the Ministry, State Curriculum Committees chaired by the respective State Directors of Education, and members of the teaching profession. However, any anticipated curriculum change which would involve changes in any aspect of the school system requires the approval of the Educational Planning Committee, chaired by the Minister himself.

With the formation of the Curriculum Development Centre, the process of systematic cyclic curriculum improvement is increasingly being undertaken by the Centre which develops its own professional staff and administrative resources as well as calling upon professional expertise and assistance from outside the Centre.

As an illustration of current practice, the revision of a subject syllabus is a good example. Following a decision to review a subject syllabus by the Central Curriculum Committee, a subject committee or a project consisting of curriculum officers from the Centre, administrators, school inspectors, teachers, and where necessary, subject-matter and general-education experts, is formed to develop the desired syllabus following a review of the current syllabus and its implementation. The draft syllabus developed by the committee is then subject to a series of revisions following evaluation by teachers and others who are considered to be useful to the task. After appropriate revisions, the proposed syllabus and follow-up activities are submitted to the Central Curriculum Committee for approval. Following the approval of a new or revised syllabus and its plans for implementation, the Centre is given the task of organizing the development of the required curriculum materials, which may be in the form of teachers' guides, resource materials, teaching aids, and pupils' textbooks. The Centre works closely with the Textbook Bureau.

In the case of primary-school textbooks, the Centre, the Textbook Bureau, and the Language and Literacy Agency work together with a team of writers to produce the textbooks. Secondary-school textbooks, on the other hand, are written by writers working independently with editors of the commercial publishing houses, using guidelines laid down by the Centre and the Textbook Bureau. All drafts of such books are submitted for evaluation to the Textbook Bureau, if they are to be approved for subsequent listing in the approved textbook lists.

Changes in syllabuses of instruction, following approval by the Central

Curriculum Committee, are tried out in selected schools. Such try-outs are normally undertaken by the Centre with the cooperation of the State Departments of Education and the Heads of the schools concerned. The usual practice is for the syllabus and teachers' and pupils' materials to be tried out in prepublication form.

Once a new or revised set of curriculum materials has been approved for implementation, the program of implementation depends on the extent and nature of the change. The Schools Division of the Ministry is the primary agency for overseeing the process of implementation of curriculum programs and materials. When teacher retraining is involved, the Centre is responsible for the organization of the training of key personnel, the change agents operating in the field. Administratively, the Teacher Training Division of the Ministry is responsible for the budgetary provisions for teacher inservice programs as well as modifications to the preservice training programs in the light of the new syllabus or curriculum change requirement. The Schools Division, and the State Department of Education in particular, are the chief executors of the retraining programs and other aspects of implementation. The monitoring of the implementation of new or revised curriculum programs and materials is undertaken by the Centre as a means for considering further improvement of the resources for improving implementation. The Inspectorate is concerned with the actual monitoring and on-the-spot improvement of curriculum implementation and other aspects of school administration and organization.

Curriculum development is increasingly being viewed as more than the development of subject syllabuses, teachers' guides, and pupils' textbooks. The need to improve the quality of teaching practices and effectiveness in pupil learning has recently been receiving greater attention from the Centre in particular and by the Ministry as a whole. The need to provide a more diversified range of curriculum programs and materials within a common-content curriculum has yet to be resolved. The need to provide an alternative to the lock-step progress by school year rather than by the idiosyncratic characteristics of pupils is another problem that will require bold but well-considered departure from current practices. The whole problem of evolving and sustaining change as an integral part of curriculum implementation will require systematic investigations with insightful, yet economic, approaches. The issues and problems associated with the theoretical and conceptual approaches to curriculum planning and development will need further work in the years to come. Two further important areas requiring much more research are those of teaching—learning strategies and the problem of teacher training to ensure that teachers are trained to implement the new curriculum efficiently in the classroom.

Examinations

The Federation of Malaysia Examinations Syndicate is the corporate body responsible for the conduct of all examinations in the school system. It was established by the Education Ordinance of 1957. The Syndicate is administered by the Director of Examinations who is responsible to the Director-General of Education. In accordance with the Education Act of 1961, the Syndicate is responsible not only for the conduct of public examinations organized by the Syndicate itself, but also for those organized by examining bodies overseas.

The Examinations Syndicate is a relatively large organization. It comprises several units, each with its own responsibility for such matters as the determination of policies regarding examination regulations, the administration of examinations, which entails the selection of examiners and invigilators, the marking of examination scripts, the development, printing and distribution of question papers, and the processing and issue of certificates. The Biological Unit of the Syndicate is responsible for the supply of materials for science practical examinations. Most examinations up to the Lower Certificate of Education use the multiple-choice format, and the Electronic Computer unit of the Syndicate is responsible for the processing of examination entries, the marking of answer sheets, the collating of results, the processing for selection for promotion, and the issuing of certificates. In the actual conduct of school examinations at the school level, the Syndicate is assisted by the State Department of Education which has an examination unit headed by an officer of the Syndicate.

In the primary school the Syndicate is responsible for two assessment examinations. The main objective of the *Standard III Assessment Examination,* introduced in 1973, is to assist educational planners in general and teachers in particular in ascertaining the progress of the pupils in acquiring the basic skills in mathematics and the languages prescribed for the first three years of primary education. Except for a selected number of schools which have been sampled to provide measures for the determination of the national norms of pupil performance, the answer scripts of this examination (about 80 percent of the national total) are now marked and the results processed by the teachers themselves. This action has been undertaken to strengthen the immediate feedback of information concerning pupil performance, the diagnosis of pupil learning difficulties and the planning and implementation of remedial action by the teachers.

The purpose of the *Standard V Assessment Examination* introduced in 1967, is to assess pupils' achievement in the key subjects: the language of instruction and the second language, mathematics, science, geography, and history at the end of the fifth year of primary education, so that appropriate measures can be taken to remedy weaknesses that have been identified. Over the years, it has also been found that pupils' achievement in this examination is a useful device for the selection of pupils into fully residential schools.

At the secondary school level, the Syndicate is responsible for two examinations. The *Lower Certificate of Education (LCE)* examination is conducted once a year in the month of October for pupils who have completed three years of lower secondary education. It may also be taken by private candidates who can show evidence that they have completed the equivalent of the three-year lower secondary education provided in government schools. Since 1978, the examination has been conducted entirely in Bahasa Malaysia. The examination has two main objectives. Firstly, it is a national examination for the selection of pupils into upper secondary schools as well as a basis for channelling them into the various streams: arts, science, technical, and vocational. Secondly, it serves to evaluate the development and progress of lower-secondary education for planning and research purposes.

The Examination Syndicate currently offers a total of twenty-two subjects for this examination. To obtain the full certificate and be eligible for promotion to the upper-secondary schools, candidates have to fulfill the following requirements:

(1) obtain a pass in Bahasa Malaysia, English, Mathematics, and History or Geography;

(2) obtain a pass in one of the following subjects: Science, Industrial Arts, Agricultural Science, or Home Science;

(3) obtain at least a total of 34 units (performance grades) from five subjects altogether. Three subjects must be from (1) above, one subject from (2) above, and one other subject from either (1) or (2).

The performance of candidates in each subject is graded on a nine-point scale, with grades 1 and 2 being distinction pass, 3 to 6 being credit pass, 7 and 8 being a pass only, and 9 being failure in the subject.

The Lower Certificate of Education is awarded with one of three grades: *Grade A* entitles the candidate to promotion to Form IV, and is awarded to a candidate who has fulfilled the three conditions mentioned above; *Grade B* is awarded to a candidate who has fulfilled conditions (1) and (2) but not (3); and *Grade C* is awarded to a candidate who fulfills only condition (1) and obtains a pass in at least five subjects. All other candidates are issued statements for subjects passed.

Until such time as the Ministry of Education decides to assume full responsibility, the *Joint Examination for the Malaysia Certificate of Education (MCE) and the General Certificate of Education (GCE)* is conducted by the Malaysian Examinations Syndicate in collaboration with the University of Cambridge Local Examinations Syndicate in the United Kingdom. The examination is conducted in two languages, Bahasa Malaysia and English. Both bodies are responsible for the examination in English while only the Ministry of Education is responsible for the examination in the medium of Bahasa Malaysia. This examination, which is held at the end of the upper-secondary stage, provides the statement of educational achievement required for entry into most employment in the public and private sectors. Pupils' performance in this examination is also used as a basis for selection into the sixth form in fully assisted schools.

Like the LCE examination, pupils' performance in each subject is graded on a scale from 1 to 9, 1 being the highest and 9 the lowest. To be awarded a full certificate, a candidate must satisfy at one and the same examination the following conditions:

(1) reach a satisfactory general standard as judged by his performance in his best six subjects (the maximum number to be offered is nine); and either

(2) pass in at least five subjects (including Bahasa Malaysia) with credit in at least one of them, or

(3) pass in at least four subjects (including Bahasa Malaysia) with credits in at least two of them.

Another examination, also conducted by the Malaysian Examination Syndicate and taken by pupils in the vocational and technical schools (end of upper secondary stage), is the *Malaysian Vocational Certificate of Education Examination.* Success in this examination results in a certification of educational achievement. This certificate is gaining in status and is attaining recognition as equivalent in status to the Malaysia Certificate of Education.

Teacher Education

PRE-SERVICE EDUCATION

Prior to 1956, full-time teacher training for Malay Primary Schools was available at Sultan Idris Training College in Tanjung Malim and Malay Women's Training College in Malacca. In addition, teachers for various media primary and secondary schools were trained by a system of weekend training at normal Training Classes or Teachers Preparatory Classes. Some teachers were trained at two teacher-training colleges in the United Kingdom. A small number of teachers for upper-secondary classes in the English-medium schools were trained at Raffles College, Singapore.

The system of training during the period 1956—70 showed a gradual transition towards the national educational policy as contained in the Razak Report. The various teacher-training programs were coordinated so that teachers who graduated from these colleges would have comparable qualifications and would therefore be able to serve in all government assisted schools, irrespective of the medium of instruction. In institutions for primary teacher training, students were trained to teach as general purpose teachers in any one of the four language media: Bahasa Malaysia, English, Chinese, and Tamil. Since 1970, all students in the institutions for primary teacher training have been instructed in Bahasa Malaysia, with English as a compulsory second language.

Institutions for teaching the lower secondary level were at first organized as general purpose colleges where all subjects for secondary schools could be studied. Since 1964, institutions for secondary training have been organized on the basis of specific fields of study, i.e. mathematics and science, language and arts subjects, technical and vocational subjects, agricultural science, and home economics.

Essentially, teacher education in Malaysia is organized at two levels:
(a) graduate level, at which graduate teachers are trained at all five local universities, and
(b) nongraduate level, at which nongraduate teachers are trained by the Ministry of Education through its Teacher Training Division in twenty-five teachers colleges — nineteen in Peninsular Malaysia, three in Sabah, and three in Sarawak.

Trained teachers are classified according to the level of school in which they will teach:
(a) Primary School Teachers for Standards I to VI;
(b) Lower Secondary School Teachers for Forms 1 to 3; and
(c) Upper Secondary Schools Teachers for Forms 4 to 6.

Those in category (c) should be graduate teachers. Those in category (a) and (b) are nongraduate teachers. The nongraduate teachers are of the same status from the standpoint of salary scale and terms of service. Their entry qualification to the respective colleges for preservice training is also the same, namely the Malaysian Certificate of Education or the School Certificate (equivalent to G.C.E. "O" level), but a small number of them will have the Higher School Certificate of Education (equivalent to G.C.E. "A" level). Table 3.9 presents the enrollment in teacher training colleges in 1970 and 1975 and the targets for 1980.

At the nongraduate level all the twenty-five colleges conduct a two-year teacher-preparation course, with the exception of three which also conduct either a three- or one-year course, as follows:
(1) The Technical Teachers Training College in Kuala Lumpur conducts a three-year course in Trade subjects, and a one-year course in Commercial Studies.
(2) The Specialist Teachers Training Institute in Kuala Lumpur conducts a one-year supplementary course for qualified teachers in various subjects not normally offered at the university level, e.g. librarianship.
(3) The Kent Teacher Training College in Sabah conducts a three-year course for candidates with only the Lower Certificate of Education qualification.

The two-year program was launched in 1973, and is based on an integrated approach. The program is divided into two parts, each lasting one year. In the first year, students follow a core curriculum to prepare them to teach Standard IV to Form One. In the second year, students are channelled into one of two groups, A or B. Group A specializes in the teaching of lower-primary classes, Standards I to III, with an additional component to prepare them to handle preschool classes. Group B specializes in handling lower secondary classes, Forms One to Three. Group A students are trained to teach all subjects in the primary-school curriculum, whereas Group B students are given the choice of specializing in *one* or *two* special subjects.

In addition, each teacher trainee is also trained in the utilization of school libraries and the conduct of cocurricular activities, including a field game, such as netball or hockey, and a volunteer group such as Girl Guides or Boy Scouts, St John Ambulance Brigade, or the Red Cross. The components for proficiency in both English and Bahasa Malaysia and in Civic Education have been strengthened. These new elements have been included in the new system in order to prepare teachers to be more versatile and enable them to play a more important and dynamic role not only in the school but also in the community in which they serve.

The teaching staff of the training colleges comprises both nonuniversity graduates and university graduates with a Diploma in Education.

The selection of lecturers to work in teacher-training colleges is based on their years of experience, and subjects of specialization. The nonuniversity graduates are selected from teachers who have had considerable teaching experience in primary and secondary schools in the country. Besides their teaching experience they should also have attended some courses at certificate or diploma level in certain relevant subjects such as Physical Education, Home Sciences, or Audiovisual Education. University graduates should have at least three years' teaching experience in school.

Members of staff typically follow a training program to update their knowledge and skills. Training programs include:

(a) seminars and workshops to discuss problems and possible solutions in certain subject areas;

(b) short courses ranging from one to two weeks in certain fields of specialization — such courses are normally conducted by specialists from either local or overseas universities;

(c) three-month or sandwich courses at the University of Science of Malaysia in Penang, offered to lecturers who wish to pursue in depth their subject of specialization — this is more or less on the same pattern as the sabbatical leave granted to university lecturers;

TABLE 3.9
Enrollment in Teacher Training Colleges 1970–1980

	Enrollment			Increase %	
	1970	1975	1980 (target)	1971–75	1976–80
Peninsular Malaysia					
Primary	1,435	2,735	7,680	90.6	180.8
Secondary	1,123	3,544	4,260	215.6	20.2
Sabah*	630	782	924	24.1	18.2
Sarawak*	699	879	2,200	25.8	150.3
Total	3,877	7,940	15,064	104.3	89.7

(*Source*: Government of Malaysia, 1976: p. 385)
*Separate figures for primary and secondary schools not available.

(d) an Advanced Training Program which provides an opportunity for lecturers to work for higher degrees. The non-graduate lecturers can pursue a program leading to a degree at any one of the local universities or overseas, while those with a first degree may go for courses leading to a higher degree.

The Teacher Training Division of the Ministry of Education is constantly evaluating its program with a view to raising the quality of teachers in keeping with the demands of a fast-developing country. Officers from the division and lecturers from colleges, from time to time, go overseas to study the "latest methods" in teacher preparation. They come back with new ideas, some of which are being adapted to local conditions. Other lecturers are exposed to new ideas through seminars and courses. Some of the ideas which are currently being tried out in Malaysia are: micro-teaching, utilization of resource centers, strategies for remediation, and the teacher's role in cocurricular activities.

In the middle of the 1960s, the biggest problem facing the Teacher Training Division was the problem of teacher supply. When the Comprehensive School system was introduced and all children were given a place in the school for nine years, there was a shortage of teachers. A crash program to produce trained teachers was conducted at regional centers. Contract teachers were also employed, mainly from Indonesia. The number of trained teachers, for the primary as well as secondary levels, began to stabilize at the end of the seventies except for teachers of mathematics and science of whom there is still a shortage. There is also concern for the level of proficiency in the English language, and at present there are some English teachers on contract from Great Britain. They are working with their local counterparts in projects in order to improve the teaching of English particularly in the rural areas.

With the demand for and supply of teachers now thought to be reaching equilibrium, efforts are being made to improve the quality of teaching. The two-year program is considered to be inadequate for exposure and internalization of the basic principles of teaching and education. The length of preservice teacher training is now being increased to three years, so that teacher trainees will be able to have more classroom contact hours. It is hoped that the longer time for training may improve the quality of teachers trained in the training colleges.

INSERVICE EDUCATION

Inservice education is the responsibility of the government or government-sponsored agencies. (Lokman bin Musa, 1974, p. 38.) The Teacher Training Division of the Ministry of Education is responsible for the planning, administration, and financial control of inservice education for teachers. This division works through the Inservice Education Planning Committee consisting of the Director of Teacher Training as its Chairman and heads of other divisions as members. Proposals for inservice courses outlining their objectives, curricular content, modes of implementation, and financial implications are submitted to the committee by members of the other divisions and teacher-training colleges. Approved courses are implemented by various course organizers who are assisted by instructors drawn from teachers in the schools, lecturers from training colleges and universities, and other professional people.

While preservice teacher education is designed to introduce the would-be teacher to basic attitudes, knowledge, and skills that will be useful to him in his personal and professional development, inservice training has the overall aim of assisting him to keep abreast of developments in knowledge, methods, and techniques in his field through formal or informal programs.

139

One exception is the training of temporary, untrained teachers in the basic methodology of teaching. These teachers have been recruited to supplement the trained teachers in the school system. A large number of them are teaching in the primary schools, in all three media of instruction. They have been teaching for many years without any formal teacher training. This system of teacher training through the inservice approach allows these teachers to be in school during term time, thus alleviating to some extent the problem of teacher shortage. The number of untrained teachers is on the decrease. In 1977, the number of untrained, temporary teachers was 10,535, and in 1978 it was 9,058.

Specifically, inservice programs aim to:
— provide a basic academic and professional education for temporary, untrained teachers;
— upgrade the academic and professional knowledge and experience of trained teachers in various subject disciplines;
— orient trained teachers towards new developments in teaching methods and techniques;
— assist teachers to gain proficiency in the use of Bahasa Malaysia as a medium of instruction;
— upgrade the competency of teachers of English as a second language;
— provide an introduction to school administration and management for head teachers and organizers of schools;
— provide exposure to new curriculum programs for use in classrooms.

The budget for inservice education is gradually increasing, and in 1979 it was M$8,000,000. Evaluation of inservice teacher training courses is being built in to most courses to help improve them.

Problems and Priorities

The overriding objective of education in Malaysia is national unity. It is firmly believed that through a unified national educational system with common curriculum content the foundation of a united and harmonious nation will be laid. Education is also regarded as an important means to achieve the twin objectives of the New Economic Policy, namely,
(a) the eradication of poverty by raising income level and increasing employment opportunities of all Malaysians irrespective of race; and

(b) the acceleration of the process of restructuring Malaysian society to correct economic imbalances so as to reduce and eventually eliminate the identification of race with economic functions.

In this respect the school system is expected to play a complementary role in manpower planning programs. The various streams in the upper secondary schools, that is to say the arts, science, technical and vocational streams, are immediately related to the planning of the manpower requirements of the country. These are supplemented by training programs provided by other agencies to train semiskilled and skilled labor and professionals.

One major educational policy objective is to integrate the educational systems of the states of Sabah and Sarawak, which at the moment are under the control of their state governments. One problem associated with the process of integration is the supply of an adequate number of teachers competent to teach in Bahasa Malaysia. The Teacher Training Division is conducting courses in language proficiency and competency so that teachers will be able to use Bahasa Malaysia as the medium of instruction in both Sabah and Sarawak.

The need for rapid expansion of educational facilities to meet the increasing school population has gradually eased in the last few years. Increasing attention is now being paid to the consolidation of the educational system and curriculum improvement with priority being paid to the improvement of the quality of education, the reduction of wastage and increasing the effectiveness of education for nation building. This effort is reflected in the establishment of the Curriculum Development Centre (1973) and the Ministry of Education Staff Training Institute (1979). The problem of the qualitative improvement of education is multifaceted. It is related to the continuing need to make the curriculum relevant to the emerging and changing needs of the nation as it moves towards rapid urbanization and rural modernization. It is also related to the process of initiating and sustaining improvement in individual classrooms in diverse locations, staffed by teachers with different motivations and differing competences, and filled by pupils whose individual differences have still to be catered for.

The enrollment ratio (expressed as a percentage of the actual enrollment over the estimated population of school-going age) has improved over the years. At the primary school level, it stood at 94 percent for the year 1978. The enrollment ratio in the same year for the lower secondary school level was 79 percent and for the upper secondary level it was 39 percent. The Ministry's Drop-Out Study Report, 1973, has highlighted the factors that appeared to contribute to the dropout problem. Since the publication of the report a number of steps have been taken to resolve the problem. For example, the textbook loan scheme has been launched to provide free textbooks to all primary-school children and to secondary-school pupils whose parents' income level is low.

At the primary-school level, projects have been undertaken to study ways of remedying pupil learning difficulties in the early years of schooling so that their progress would not be impeded. A school guidance service for secondary school pupils has been started and is gradually being extended to the primary schools.

The problem of large class size, particularly in the urban areas, and the converse problem of multiple-class teaching in small rural schools will require further study. A project has been started by the Ministry to identify ways of assisting teachers to manage multiple-class teaching more effectively.

Four educational resource centers will be established in the next two years as a pilot project to coordinate efforts at the ground level to improve the quality of education. To augment the efforts of the teachers in the classrooms, the Educational Media Service, incorporating the Education Television Service (ETV), the audiovisual aids program, and the school radio service, will be further expanded during the Third Malaysia Plan (1976–1980) to provide wider coverage of the nation's schools. To increase the resources for pupil learning, school library facilities are being increased, particularly in rural primary schools. At the Ministry level, research, planning, and implementation capabilities are being improved within the context of improving the quality of education.

With the gradual implementation of Bahasa Malaysia as the main medium of instruction, eventually encompassing tertiary education, the task of developing a national lingua franca to unite the diverse races of the Malaysian nation will be achieved. It is hoped that, with a common Malaysian outlook actively pursued in curriculum development and implementation, a body politic committed to national well-being and individual progress and able to adapt to rapid social, cultural, and economic changes will be successfully created.

References

Government of Malaysia (1958) *Report of the Education Committee 1956,* Government Printer, Kuala Lumpur.

Government of Malaysia (1976) *Third Malaysia Plan 1976–1980,* Government Printer, Kuala Lumpur.

HUSSEIN BIN ONN (1971) *Education in Malaysia,* Department of Information, Kuala Lumpur.

ISAHAK BIN HARUN (1977) Social Class and Educational Achievement in Plural Society: Peninsular Malaysia, unpublished Ph.D. thesis, University of Chicago, Chicago.

LOH FOOK SENG (1975) *Seeds of Separatism: Educational Policy in Malaya 1874–1940,* Oxford University Press, Kuala Lumpur.

LOKMAN BIN MUSA (1974) Continuity and Changes in Inservice Teacher Education in Malaysia, *Jurnal Kementerian Pelajaran* (Ministry of Education Journal), 49, No. 19.

Ministry of Education, EPRD (1975) *Education in Malaysia,* Dewan Bahasa dan Pustaka, Kuala Lumpur.

MURAD BIN MODH. NOOR (1973) *Study of Opinion about Education and Society,* Dewan Bahasa dan Pustaka, Kuala Lumpur.

World Population Data Sheet 1975 (1975) Population References Bureau, Washington, D.C.

Map 4 The Philippines

Ang sa taong karunungan
kayamanan di manakaw.

Learning is wealth that
cannot be stolen.
TAGALOG PROVERB

4

The Philippines

Josefina R. Cortes

EDUCATION in the Philippines today is the product of four eras of
cultural influence.

The first era extended from prehistoric times until European voyagers
appeared in the Far East to trade and establish colonies. During this pre-
colonial period education consisted mainly of the young learning indigenous Filipino tribal customs and vocations through informal instruction and observation in the family and village. However, there were also
apparently schools of a sort in which children were taught reading and
writing in a seventeen-letter native script. (Alzona, 1932, p. 1–10.)

The second era began in 1521 with the arrival of Ferdinand Magellan,
the Portuguese explorer in the service of the Spanish crown. This event
led to the gradual colonization of the islands and ultimate full political
control of the area that now makes up the Philippine Republic. Side
by side with the Spanish soldiers came the Spanish priests, dedicated
to the mission of teaching Catholicism among the peoples of the islands.
Thus, for nearly three-and-one-half centuries, 1565–1898, the dominant
type of formal education in the Philippines was of a Roman Catholic
nature.

The third era began when the United States in 1898 took the
Philippines from Spain by force of arms. This inaugurated the period of

145

American influence on the Filipino school system, an influence that directly guided the form and content of education till World War II.

Following the war, in 1946, the Philippine Republic was established, opening the fourth era, which has found Filipinos themselves seeking to mold a nation and its education system in a form that accommodates for both traditional ways of life in the islands and the demands of the modern world.

In this chapter we picture the present-day Philippine educational enterprise against a backdrop of these four eras and within the current geographical and cultural environment. We begin with a description of geographic, social-class, economic, and political features of the nation that significantly affect educational practices. Then we turn to the education system itself — its goals, structure, administration, curricula, teacher-supply system, and plans and problems for the future.

The Islands and the People

The Philippines is a nation of 7,100 islands and small coralline islets extending north and south over 1,000 miles and east and west for nearly 660 miles. Only 45 islands have areas of more than 100 square kilometers, and they account for 98 percent of the nation's total land area of 299,404 square kilometers (115,660 square miles). The three largest islands are Luzon with a total land area of 104,688 square kilometers, Mindanao with 94,630, and the Visayan Islands with a total of 52,801. The country has almost all varieties of topographical features from low swamps to high mountain masses. (Philippine Almanac Printers, 1977.)

The estimated population of the Philippines in 1980 was 47.5 million, making it the sixth largest in Asia and fifteenth largest in the world. And it is increasing rapidly, growing at 2.6 percent annually in the late 1970s compared to a world average of 1.9 percent.

Since the nation is composed of islands, communication and transportation have been gigantic problems, compounded by the country's developing state. Some adverse consequences of this situation are uneven development and unequal distribution of population, government resources, and opportunities for social and economic advancement. This has meant that the process of effecting national unity has been slow. All these consequences have had corresponding negative impacts on education. Teachers have tended to crowd into more populated, more affluent schools. In contrast, the physically isolated and depressed communities have been faced with a shortage of teachers and resources, resulting in vast inequalities of educational opportunity between affluent and depressed areas. Schools in depressed regions are usually mission institutions run by Catholics, by Protestants, and, in Muslim communities of the southern islands, by Islamic leaders who conduct madrasah schools where the main subjects taught are Islam and the Arabic language.

The rate of urbanization in the Philippines is rapid. The number of people living in cities doubled between 1948 and 1970 (from 5.1 million to 11.7 million). If this trend continues, the country will have an urban population of 28 million or 34 percent of the total population by year 2000. (Metro Manila Philippines, 1976.)

The population is also getting younger. The median age changed from 20.2 years in 1903 to 16.3 in 1972 so that over 56 percent of the people were below age 20 in the early 1970s. (NEDA-POPCOM-NCSO, 1978.) This means that the school system has faced an increasingly heavy burden of educating the young.

Ethnic and religious diversity have posed additional challenges for educational planners.

Most people in the islands trace their origins to Malay ancestors. However, today Filipinos are actually a cultural and ethnic mixture of East and West because of the long period of commercial and cultural contact with China, Japan, and other Asian neighbors (contact which can be traced to as far back as the third century AD) and with Westerners through nearly three-and-one-half centuries of Spanish colonization followed by over four decades of American rule. The presence of Chinese and Spanish blood is specifically apparent among Christian Filipinos. (Shahani, 1970.)

The Philippines is predominantly Christian, with the population in 1970 85 percent Roman Catholic, 8.3 percent Protestant (including Aglipays and Iglesia Ni Kristo, both local sects), 4.3 percent Moslem, and the remainder a few other non-Christian tribes. The Moslems and non-Christian tribes are found mostly in the hinterlands of Mindanao, Palawan, Calamian Islands, Mindoro, the Visayas, and the Northern Philippines.

Otley Beyer, the leading authority on Philippine ethnology, lists at least 43 distinct ethnic groups speaking 87 dialects. However, in terms

147

TABLE 4.1

Filipino Population by Language Groups – 1970

Major Languages	People	% of Population
Tagalog	8,979,719	24.5
Cebuano	8,844,966	24.1
Iloko	4,150,596	11.3
Panay-Hiligaynon	3,745,333	10.2
Bikol	2,507,156	6.8
Samar-Leyte	1,767,829	4.8
Pampango	1,212,024	3.3
Pangasinan	838,104	2.3
Others	4,638,729	12.9
	36,684,486	100.0

(Source: NEDA–NCSO, 1977, p. 86)

of major tongues spoken, Filipinos can be grouped into the categories shown in Table 4.1.

In terms of literacy (able to read and write a simple message), the population in 1970 was 76.39 percent literate among those age six and above. Literacy was higher in urban areas (86.6 percent) than rural areas (71.47 percent). Males were slightly higher (76.9 percent) than females (75.9 percent). The lowest literacy was in Western Mindanao (68.4) and Eastern Visayas (69.95). (NCSO.)

Since the beginning of the century, measured illiteracy has fallen. For those over age ten, it was 79.8 percent in the 1903 census, 51.24 in 1939, 40.1 just after World War II in 1948, and only 27.9 in 1960. (NEDA–NCSO, 1972, p. 9.)

The Economy and Education

In the Philippines, as in all countries, there is a reciprocal relationship between the education system and the economic system. The economy serves the education sector by providing funds and defining skills that students, as future workers and consumers, should command. The education system serves the economic sector by furnishing trained workers and, it is hoped, enlightened consumers and citizens.

The sector of the economic establishment that has always contributed the most to the country's net domestic product (NDP) has been the agriculture, fishery, and forestry cluster, with 52.3 percent (8,069 million workers) of the work force in this sector in 1976. Commerce ranked second in 1976 with 12.2 percent of the workers. Manufacturing was third with 10.9 percent. Of the total, 41.2 percent were wage and salary workers, 35.8 percent self-employed, and 22.6 percent unpaid family workers. The bulk of the self-employed and unpaid workers were in agriculture. (NCSO, 1976.)

The country's leading exports in 1975 included centrifugal sugar, coconut oil (crude), copper concentrates, copra, logs, gold, bananas, pineapple in syrup, molasses, and processed copra. These items accounted for 69 percent of total exports in 1975. (NEDA-NCSO, 1977, p. 883.) The Philippines imports much machinery and transport equipment, so in 1975 mineral fuels and lubricants topped the country's imports.

In the typical pattern for modern developing nations, the Philippines has organized its growth programs around a series of five- and ten-year plans, with education assigned an important role in the programs.

The 1972—1977 period witnessed the implementation of the First Five-Year Plan under the New Society, after the declaration of Martial Law. At present the country is pursuing simultaneously the 1978—1982 Five-Year Plan and the overarching 1978—1987 Ten-Year Plan. The First Five-Year Plan placed great emphasis on increased production in agriculture and industry to attain the goals of self-sufficiency in food by means of the eradication of tenancy through land reform, massive government support to boost agricultural production, financial support for small and medium scale industries, infrastructure projects, and social-development programs. Under this plan, education's main role was to train people for the social and economic programs.

The Second Five-Year Plan of 1978—1982 and the Ten-Year Plan of 1978—1987 aim to correct shortfalls of the immediate past and correct bottlenecks foreseen as the economy develops. The prime objective is a better quality of life for the great masses of Filipinos through "industrialization hand in hand with agricultural modernization and the development of human resources." (Sicat, 1978, p. 158.) The main thrust of government efforts is countryside development where nearly three-fourths of the population live. Education is to focus mainly on human resources development, especially in the rural and depressed areas through formal and nonformal programs, educating and enskilling people of all ages. The educational objective is a balanced development of the individual as a social, economic, and political being, including the reduction of illiteracy in depressed areas through such programs as adult literacy classes.

The need for more balanced socioeconomic development is seen in figures on income distribution. In the Philippine population:

> The richest 20% enjoy an income nearly triple the average. The middle 20% enjoy only two-thirds of the average mean income; the second poorest, only two-fifths of it; and the very poorest, less than one-fifth of it... (Development Academy of the Philippines, 1975, p. 13.)

There has been no narrowing of this gap since 1950. So the present government's policy is to widen and equalize access to economic and social opportunity by means of land reform and emphasis on rural development.

In effect, the nation's educational planners are charged with formulating programs that will contribute to greater general prosperity and equal access to the good things of life for all Filipinos, not simply a select elite.

Governance of the Philippines, Past and Present

The Philippines was a colony of Spain for almost 350 years, 1565–1898, and of the United States of America from 1898 to 1946. From 1916 onward the United States established the Philippine Legislature, intended to prepare Filipinos for self-government. However, the American period was interrupted in 1941 by the outbreak of World War II in the Pacific, so that Japanese forces occupied the country until August 1945.

The Philippine Republic established in 1946 was organized according to the Philippine Constitution of 1935. This charter, as amended in 1940, provided for a democratic presidential government with the principle of separation of powers – executive, legislative, and judicial. However, in 1973 a new constitution was adopted, providing for a parliamentary government with legislative power vested in the National Assembly. The prime minister with his cabinet was to exercise executive power, while judicial power was vested in the courts. Under this new form of governance the country has been divided into 13 regions. Then each region is divided further into traditional political units: (1) chartered cities and their subunits called *barangays* and (2) provinces that parallel the cities and that oversee towns and their subunit barangays. In the 1970s, there were 72 provinces, 60 chartered cities, 1,471 towns, and 42,000 barangays.

With this picture of the main demographic, economic, and political features of the country as a background, we turn now to the school system and its historical origins.

The Historical Roots of Today's Schools

Although the present system of education is essentially American in origin, it owes its foundation to values in Philippine society that can be traced to the pre-Western incursions and to Spanish times.

THE SPANISH REGIME – 1565–1898

Prior to the arrival of the Spanish, Filipinos already had an alphabet of 17 letters, and children were taught "reading, writing, reckoning, religion, and self-defense." (Alzona, 1932, pp. 1–10; UNESCO-Philippine American Educational Foundation, 1953, p. 67.)

Under the Spaniards the early schools were mainly in the hands of Catholic missionaries who taught Christian doctrine, religious songs, and prayers. Because of the difficulty of communicating in Spanish, the missionaries learned the local dialects and translated Christian writings into these tongues. Classes were usually held in a convent in "a roofed and closed structure without any interior provision for the various objects needed in a classroom". (Alzona, 1932; D. Abella, 1965, p. 23.)

Although the colonial government urged friars to educate the natives, no legislative provisions were made until the Educational Decree of 1863 was issued by the Spanish crown, ordering the establishment of a public elementary-school system and the creation of a normal school for men. The decree prescribed one school for boys and one for girls for every 5,000 inhabitants. Attendance was to be compulsory and the language of instruction Spanish. In creating the normal school, colonial authorities envisioned eventual transfer of the task of education from the Spanish clergy to laymen.

151

By another royal decree in 1865, a secondary-school system was to be set up, but because the clergy continued to control education and few laymen could teach in Spanish, neither the 1863 or 1865 decree was fully implemented. The Moret Decree of 1873 represented a further attempt to wrest the control of education from the hands of the friars, but because of the Catholic authorities' strong protest, this plan was shelved. (Alzona, 1932.) As a result of religious and political pressures, the use of Spanish in Filipino elementary and secondary schools was not widespread, thus essentially closing the doors of higher education to Filipinos, since all higher education was in Spanish.

For the large masses of Filipinos in Spanish times the curriculum of the schools was chiefly composed of doctrines of Christianity, prayers, and religious songs. However, a few technical and vocational schools were also set up, most of them in the later 1800s — an agricultural institution in Manila, a nautical school, a school of commerce, a trade school, and one focusing on fine arts. But they all languished from lack of government patronage and from small enrollments. The nautical school established in 1820 continued to operate and remains today as Spain's legacy to vocational education. (Alzona, 1932.)

THE AMERICAN PERIOD – 1898–1946

Schools established under the Spaniards had practically ceased to function during the Filipinos' revolution against Spain toward the close of the 19th century, so by the time of the Filipino-American War in 1898 the educational system had to a great extent collapsed. Scarcely three weeks after the surrender of Manila to the Americans (August 13, 1898), the U.S. military government reopened seven schools with soldiers of the U.S. Army as teachers.

In 1901, the Second U.S. Commission in the Philippines issued Act 74, creating a Department of Public Instruction to "insure a system of free primary instruction for the Filipino people". (UP Law Center, 1977, Vol. 1.) This marked the beginning in the Philippines of a public school system patterned after the United States in organization, curriculum, and methods of instruction. With the system came American textbooks, equipment, and English as the teaching medium.

The first public-school teachers were American soldiers joined by American civilian teachers who arrived on the ship *Thomas* in August 1901, earning them the name Thomasites in the history of Philippine education. Act 74 specified that the Americans would be detailed as instructors until they could be replaced by Filipinos who would be trained in a newly created Philippine Normal School, known today as the Philippine Normal College. Early in 1904, around 100 young Filipinos were sent to the United States as government *pensionados* or grantees, several of whom later became the first Filipino educational leaders.

From 1901 to 1935 when the Philippines assumed commonwealth status in preparation for the independence that would come in 1946, the Department of Public Instruction was headed by an American as secretary of instruction. During the same period the number of American teachers gradually decreased, so that in 1935 only 160 remained. The first Filipino secretary of instruction was Sergio Osmena, under whose office as vice-president of the Commonwealth government the Department was placed in 1935.

In 1925, a decade before the Commonwealth, a joint educational committee was organized by the Philippine Legislature. It was headed by Dr Paul Monroe to survey the condition of Philippine schools. The Monroe Survey reported the following problems:

(1) Most teachers in primary and intermediate schools were professionally untrained, were inexperienced, and were dissatisfied.

(2) About 82 percent of pupils did not continue beyond grade four.

(3) At all grade levels many pupils failed and were kept back to repeat the grade.

(4) All the curricula were ill adapted to Philippine society.

(5) Education was bookish and artificial, since the textbooks had been prepared for schools in the United States.

(6) The skills of facing new situations and solving problems met in real life were neglected.

(7) Filipinos had great difficulty learning English. While pupils studied the new language 25 hours a week, whatever gains they made were canceled out by the pervasive influence of the local dialect. This situation was aggravated by the fact that Filipino dialects are almost totally unlike English. Whereas English is a highly staccato and accented language, the Tagalog, Ilocano, Visayan, and other dialects are dominated by a singing, unstressed monotone.

153

(8) Schools were inadequately financed. (The Board of Educational Survey, 1925.)

These problems remained unsolved during the Commonwealth period, and in many respects they were increased during the Japanese occupation of the Philippines during World War II (1941–1945). The Japanese at first converted the schools into quarters for their soldiers. Later, when a state of some normalcy was restored, the Japanese ordered the schools to reopen. But the few that did open suffered irregularity of attendance and a lack of teachers and supplies. More often than not these schools would again close because of fear by the Filipinos that there would be Japanese–Filipino guerilla encounters.

The liberation of the Philippines from the Japanese in 1945 was followed a year later with the establishment of the Philippine Republic. The problems of education that faced the new republic included not only those identified by the Monroe Survey of 1925 but also those arising from the adverse effects of the war.

THE PHILIPPINE REPUBLIC – 1946–1980

Educational development after 1946 reflected both a great social demand for schooling on the part of the populace and a strong effort of the government to fulfill an earlier commitment to universal education.

The hunger for education unleashed after the liberation of the country from the Japanese by American forces in 1945 was evidenced by the mushrooming of "old and new schools . . . out of the shambles and ruins" of the war. (UNESCO–PAEF, 1953, p. 108.) The government built on the foundation laid down in the 1935 Philippine Constitution, which continued to serve as the fundamental law of the Republic, a constitution that stipulated that:

> All educational institutions shall be under the supervision and subject to the regulation of the State. The Government shall establish and maintain a complete and adequate system of public education, and shall provide at least free public primary institutions and citizenship training to adult citizens. (Art. III, Sec. 5.)

The 1946–1955 decade saw the Republic direct great effort to rebuild the school system and expand it sufficiently to meet the needs of the large numbers of youths of school age whose schooling had been disrupted and delayed by the war. In an effort to cope with the problem, the government ordered the implementation of Commonwealth Act 581 which prescribed the following measures:

(1) Reduction of elementary education from seven to six years.
(2) Adoption of double sessions in elementary schools.
(3) One-teacher-to-one-class plan in the intermediate grades. (Vol. 1, UP Law Center, 1977.)

In addition, during this period 31,460 extension classes were opened. (Swanson, 1960, p. 35.) However, before long complaints poured in from parents and concerned citizens about the adverse effects on the quality of learning that resulted from the retrenchment measures. Public opinion became so strong that in 1953 the Philippine Congress passed Republic Act 896 providing for the restoration of the seventh grade, discontinuance of the double sessions, and adoption of a three-teachers-to-teach-two-classes ratio in intermediate grades. (Vol. III, UP Law Center, 1977.) In short, attempts to ensure that large quantities of young people had access to school caused problems in maintaining the former quality of schooling.

The rapid growth of elementary and secondary schooling during the first quarter century of the Republic is shown in Table 4.2. Between 1948 and 1970 elementary schools increased by 238 percent and secondary schools by 242 percent. In the early half of this period, great social demand by the populace for schooling is reflected in the number of private schools set up at both levels. When the government could not keep up with the rising demand, private groups took the initiative to do so. Prior to 1970, the majority of secondary schools were private, indicating a trend that carried over from the American colonial period of the 1920s and 1930s. At that time the colonial government's main effort was at the elementary level, so the people's appetite for secondary schooling was filled to a great degree by private organizations. By 1970, the government's secondary-education building program had enabled the public sector to pass the private sector in the number of schools by a narrow margin, 52 percent as against 48 percent.

The problem of regulating the rapidly increasing number of private schools prompted the Philippine Legislature to adopt Republic Act 74 in 1946, providing additional funds for supervising private institutions.

TABLE 4.2
Elementary and Secondary Schools 1918–1970

Year	Elementary Schools					Secondary Schools				
	Public	Private	Total	% Increase	% Public of Total	Public	Private	Total	% Increase	% Public of Total
1918	5,867	203	6,070		96.6	50	34	84		59.5
1948	16,472	189	16,661	174.4	98.9	288	613	901	972.6	31.9
1960	29,052	1,073	30,125	80.0	96.4	376	1,328	1,704	89.1	22.1
1970	37,755	1,820	39,575	31.3	95.4	2,144	1,975	4,119	141.7	52.1

(Sources: Data for 1918 are from the US–Philippines Commission Report, 1918, and for 1948, 1960, and 1970 from the NEDA *Statistical Yearbook*, 1976, pp. 486–487, except for the 1948 private elementary data which are from records in the Office of Planning Service, Ministry of Education and Culture.)

TABLE 4.3
Public and Private School Enrollments 1903–1970
(In Thousands)

Year	Elementary Students					Secondary Students				
	Public	Private	Total	% Increase	% Public of Total	Public	Private	Total	% Increase	% Public of Total
1903	279.4	80.3	359.7		77.6		9.3	9.3		
1918	665.2	99.0	746.1	112.4	87.0	16.9	6.5	23.4	152.8	72.1
1939	850.2	63.4	1,915.6	150.7	96.6	90.6	63.6	154.2	558.2	58.7
1948	3,693.2	114.3	3,807.4	98.8	96.6	193.3	220.4	413.8	168.4	46.7
1960	4,003.3	196.4	4,199.7	10.3	95.3	192.1	417.6	609.7	47.3	31.5
1970	6,715.2	341.2	7,056.479	68.0	95.2	673.8	956.4	1,630.2	167.5	41.3

(Sources: Public-school enrollment for 1903, 1918, 1939, and 1948 are from UNESCO's *Philippine American Education*, 1953, p. 93, and from NEDA *Statistical Yearbook*, 1974, pp. 356–357. Private-school enrollment for 1903, 1918, 1939, and 1948 are from Carson, 1961, p. 112, and from NEDA *Statistical Yearbook*, 1974, pp. 356–357.)

The following year, the Bureau of Private Schools was delegated the authority to maintain a suitable standard of education in private schools.

A growing awareness of the mismatch between the products of the educational system and the needs of Philippine society for certain types of manpower reached its peak in the mid-1960s. There were growing numbers of "educated unemployed", and heightened student activism toward the end of the 1960s resulted in student demands for greater relevance of schooling for the socioeconomic and political realities of the country. Consequently, President Marcos constituted the Presidential Commission to Survey Philippine Education (PCSPE) in 1969, a body assigned: (1) to analyze the performance of the education system with reference to national development goals, (2) to recommend specific ways of improving the system, and (3) to identify critical areas for more detailed research. In 1970, the Commission submitted its Survey Report with the following general observations:

> (1) The members were impressed by the basic strength of the education system. The strength flowed from the virtually unanimous high regard in which schooling was held by the people, resulting in some of the highest enrollment ratios in the world and supported by consistently high levels of public and private expenditure on education.
>
> (2) At the same time the Commission could not overlook forces that reduced the system's capacity to meet peremptory development needs and which mitigated the optimization of social benefits that could be expected from education.
>
> (3) Philippine education was plagued by serious imbalances between: popular expectations and educational standards; facilities and enrollment; the supply of graduates and demand for specific manpower skills; location of educational facilities and actual regional development needs; and national investments in economic enterprises. (Presidential Commission to Survey Philippine Education, 1970a.)

As an offshoot of the PCSPE recommendations, President Marcos issued the Educational Development Act of 1972 (Decree 6-A), stipulating that "It is the policy of the government to ensure, within the context of a free democratic system, maximum contribution of the educational system to the attainment of national development goals." The Act generated reforms envisioned to evolve a truly Philippine-based and needs-oriented educational system. The inertia of tradition and the historical ties with the American schooling system may require some time to alter so as to achieve a system of education responsive to Philippine conditions, but the current efforts being taken in this direction are gaining momentum, powered by the Filipinos' increasing determination to optimize the contributions of the educational system to their general well-being.

The Formal School System Today

Filipinos' faith in education as "wealth that cannot be stolen" is as strong today as it has always been. Notwithstanding the growing disillusionment associated with the inability of schools to produce high national-achievement test scores and with the unsettling presence of "educated unemployed", the Filipino would still go through all kinds of personal sacrifices so a son or daughter could attend school and eventually obtain a college diploma. It is not surprising, therefore, that by 1975 the formal school system was a huge enterprise of 46,879 schools, 358,124 teachers, and 11.3 million students. (NEDA–NCSO, 1977, p. 234.)

Structurally the formal system today consists of six years of elementary education (by law seven years, but as yet unimplemented for lack of funds except in some private schools), of four years of secondary education, and of at least four years to obtain a college diploma.

Public schools are managed and funded by the government, while private schools are under corporations (stock or non-stock) and foundations, some of them sectarian and some secular. The private system antedates the public. Both secondary and higher education actually began with private schools, the oldest founded as early as the 16th century.

From the standpoint of national development, one traditional problem has been the imbalance between academic and vocational secondary schools. In the 1960s and before, 90 percent of the secondary enrollment was in academic curricula. However, by 1972, the government's efforts to increase enrollments in vocational courses brought the proportion of students in agriculture (41,884), in commercial (764), in fishery (13,055), in trade (58,565), and in special vocational programs (4,895) to over 16 percent. Nearly all of these vocational students are in public schools. (National Board of Education, 1974, p. 5.)

The Philippine school system has been very successful in pursuing its goal of universal primary schooling. Among children in the age group of seven to twelve year-olds, only 80 percent were in school in 1957 compared to 100 percent in 1964. At the secondary level for the thirteen to sixteen year-olds there were 26 percent in school in 1951 compared to 58 percent in 1971. (Development Academy of the Philippines, 1975, p. 8.)

Part of the reason for the higher enrollment percentages in recent years has been the reduction of dropouts from the school program. In 1925, the Monroe Survey found that of every 100 pupils entering grade one, 45 reached grade four and only 18 reached grade six. In 1960, the Swanson survey showed that of every 100 pupils in grade one in 1953, 64 reached grade four and 35 grade six. By 1970 nearly 56 percent of those who had entered grade one had reached grade six, over 25 percent had reached the last year of high school, and 11.5 percent had finished college. (Presidential Commission to Survey Philippine Education, 1970a.) Therefore, even though the holding power of elementary schools improved over the years, in 1970 42 percent had dropped out by grade six. Hence, the task of reducing dropout rates was still far from over.

As noted earlier, inequities between regions and between rural and urban areas in opportunities to learn continue to be a problem for educational planners. Elementary schools are found in nearly every town and barrio or barangay. The average national pupil—classroom ratio at the elementary level is 42 pupils to one classroom. However, this average is made up of varied ratios ranging from 207-to-1 in one district to 28-to-1 in others. Likewise, the national average of 29 pupils per teacher is composed of ratios varying from 90-to-1 in Region VI (Western Visayas) to a low of 17-to-1 in Region XI (Southern Mindanao). (Task Force on Human Settlements, 1975, p. 44.)

At the secondary level, the number of schools rose from 84 in 1918 to 4,119 by 1970. However, they are distributed unevenly throughout the nation, with as few as three in the northernmost province of Camiguin to 37 each in Pampanga and Pangasinan. (Task Force on Human Settlements, 1975.)

The total number of teachers at all levels of the school system, elementary through tertiary, reached 358,124 in 1975, with an average of five public-school teachers for each private-school teacher. However, this preponderance of public over private teachers is caused by the dominance of the public sector at the elementary level. At the secondary-school and college levels the relationship is reversed, with three private-school teachers for every one in public schools. (NEDA—NCSO, 1977.)

159

Such are the general characteristics of the schools today. And paralleling the formal educational system is a growing nonformal sector.

Roles for Nonformal Education

The term *nonformal education* has been defined by the Ministry of Education as "any organized and systematic educational activity carried on outside the framework of the formal school system to provide selected types of learning to particular sub-groups in the population, adults as well as children." (J. Manuel, 1978.) This definition, however, is still vague considering that nonformal education is taking place even within the formal school system. The proposed Education Code of the Philippines (1979) prepared by a Committee convened by the Law Center, University of the Philippines, defines nonformal education as "any organized learning program or activity undertaken by the Ministry of Education and Culture and other agencies aimed at attaining specific learning objectives for particular clienteles, distinct and separate from the hierarchically structured and chronologically graded formal education. It can be an alternative and not just a supplement to formal schooling." (UP Law Center, 1979, p. 12.)

The vital role of nonformal education in the total educational effort of the country has long been recognized. However, the extent and nature of nonformal activities was not assessed before the late 1970s. A first step in this direction was made with the creation in 1977 of the position of Undersecretary of Nonformal Education in the Department of Education and Culture (in 1978 made into a Ministry) with responsibility to "establish linkages with institutions with similar programs, both government and non-government, and to ensure effective and integrated implementation of these programs." (Office of Non-Formal Education, DEC, 1977, p. 6.)

The Five-year Philippine Development Plan of 1978–1982 recognized nonformal education as a "complement and supplement" to formal education. The nonformal objectives are: (1) to provide opportunities for the acquisition of skills necessary to enhance employability, efficiency, productivity, and competitiveness in the labor market, (2) to ensure functional literacy, numeracy, and general education, and (3) to improve the quality of family and community life. Clienteles for nonformal education include: (a) people in the work force either unproductively employed or unable to find a job, (b) employed or unemployed school leavers who are interested in rejoining the mainstream of formal education, (c) adults age 15 and over who need compensatory education, and (d) technical workers and professionals who need constant upgrading to improve their performance. (NEDA, 1977.)

The Ministry of Education and Culture has a number of nonformal programs, including ones in agricultural extension and farmers' training, adult literacy, and occupational skills. These programs employ mass media and such forms of delivery as mobile schools and correspondence courses (distance study). In addition, current policies of the Ministry stress greater student involvement in such nonformal activities as the Youth Civic Action Program, community outreach programs, extension services, and development-oriented teacher-education programs such as the Masters in Teaching Elementary Agriculture. (Manuel, 1977.)

Practically all agencies of the government conduct some kind of nonformal activities. An agency outside the Ministry of Education and Culture created specifically for occupational-skills training is the National Manpower Youth Council. It works closely with the Ministry's vocational schools in nation-wide skills-training programs, utilizing the facilities and teachers of vocational schools for instruction in industrial, agricultural, and service skills. The teaching methodology in NMYC programs features "training modules", especially for instruction in industrial skills.

Nonformal education by most government agencies can be grouped into three types in terms of target clienteles: (1) upgrading of the agency's work force, (2) education and information for the agency's publics, and (3) skills training for members of the community in the agency's specialization. For instance, education and information programs are carried out by the Ministry of Public Information, and skills training is offered by the National Institute of Science and Technology and the Bureau of Plant Industry in such areas as food processing and preservation, mushroom culture, biogas generation and utilization, and the like.

Government policy encourages the private sector to undertake nonformal education in the form of apprenticeship, on-the-job-training, and entrepreneurship programs. With education fast becoming a lifelong process, nonformal education in the Philippines will surely become a learning system equal in importance to the country's formal education system.

The Administrative Structure of Schooling

Prior to the government reorganization in 1972, the formal education system was highly centralized and bureaucratic, a condition attributed to two major factors: (1) the Filipino people had acquired an authoritarian orientation after centuries under authoritarian rule and (2) when the public school system began, local governments were incapable of conducting the schools efficiently. In other words, the highly centralized school-administration structure had its roots in the nation's colonial history.

THE HISTORICAL BACKGROUND

The Americans' organic law (Act 74) in 1901 provided for a Department of Public Instruction which was given control over all existing schools and those to be established. Heading this office was a General Superintendent of Public Instruction appointed by the U.S. Commission in the Philippines. For the purpose of school administration, the country was divided into ten school divisions, each headed by a superintendent. Every division consisted of school districts, with each town or pueblo designated as a district. A principal headed each school within a district. Thus, at the division level a superintendent was the highest official, in charge of division supervisors, supervising teachers, and school principals. These offices, from the top down to the principals, were all filled by Americans until 1934. The Secretary of Public Instruction was appointed by the U.S. President, and the General Superintendent by the Civil Governor of the Philippines. Other officials were appointed at the recommendation of the next higher ranking official above them. Private schools after 1910 were placed under the Office of the Superintendent of Private Schools. (Alzona, 1932; Act. 447 in Vol. 1, UP Law Center, 1977.)

In 1934, under the new Commonwealth Government, the Department of Public Instruction came under the Vice-President of the Commonwealth, who concurrently held the position of Secretary of Public Instruction. For the first time a Filipino, Vice-President Sergio Osmeña, became the head of public instruction. However, the administrative structure remained the same.

PRESENT-DAY ADMINISTRATIVE ORGANIZATION

In 1972 President Marcos issued Decree 1, directing the reorganization of the national government according to a plan of the Commission on Reorganization. The striking administrative differences between the Department of Education's structure under this plan and under the previous ones were: (1) the abolition of the Bureau of Public Schools and Bureau of Private Schools and their replacement by three staff bureaus, one each for elementary, secondary, and higher education, and (2) the establishment of regional offices, each headed by a director responsible for supervision, evaluation, and coordination of Department activities in the region, with the director accountable directly to the Secretary of the Department. Under the regional director are staff divisions of elementary, of secondary, and of higher education as well as an administrative and a finance-and-budget division. The creation of regional offices as the implementing arms of the Department was intended to stimulate decentralization in the operation of education. (Presidential Commission on Reorganization, 1973.)

As noted above, the dichotomy in regulating public and private schools was removed. Likewise, the same office supervises schools at all levels. A province and a chartered city under the new plan are considered school divisions, and the superintendent of schools remains as head of a school division, assisted by an assistant superintendent in the larger divisions.

As in the pre-1972 organization, the National Board of Education is responsible for formulating long-range educational plans. However, its membership has changed to include more secular members and exclude religious bodies. The chairman of the National Science Development Board, the Deputy Minister of Education and Culture, and three prominent citizens (one representing nongovernmental educational institutions) serve on the Board along with the three directors of the elementary, secondary, and tertiary bureaus of education (who are nonvoting members). Catholic, Protestant, and Muslim associations are no longer represented on the Board.

In June 1978, the former Department of Education was renamed Ministry of Education and Culture, with the Secretary assuming the title of Minister. However, the body's structure was not altered with the change in name.

Schooling in the ASEAN Region

The goal of administrative reorganization in the 1970s, then, was to effect greater efficiency in the school system and better service the needs of different regions through encouraging decentralization, yet at the same time maintaining general guidance and support for the schools at the Ministry of Education and Culture in the nation's capital.

Trends in Curriculum Development

Since the establishment of the Philippine Republic in 1946, curricula for the schools have been based on policies from the Philippine Constitution and pronouncements and education laws adopted by the government. Article XV of the 1973 Constitution requires that "all educational institutions shall aim to inculcate love of country, teach the duties of citizenship, and develop moral character, personal discipline, and scientific, technological, and vocational efficiency." (Sec. 4.) In further clarifying this mandate, Presidential Decree 6-A (the Educational Development Act of 1972) provides objectives specific to the three levels of the formal educational system. Under the decree elementary and secondary schools are directed to:

> ... provide for a broad general education that will assist each individual, in the peculiar ecology of his own society, to (1) attain his potential as a human being, (2) enhance the range and quality of individual and group participation in the basic functions of society, and (3) acquire the essential educational foundation for his development into a productive and versatile citizen. (Sec. 3, a.)

Furthermore, secondary schools and post-secondary institutions below four-year degree-granting colleges are "to train the nation's manpower in the middle level skills required for national development." (Presidential Decree 6-A, Sec. 3, b.)

The Ministry of Education and Culture is responsible for implementing such policies and also those plans formulated by the executive and legislative branches of government and by the National Board of Education. The Board is the agency that approves curricula plans prepared by the Ministry's bureaus of elementary and of secondary education. Each bureau has a curriculum division whose task, among others, is to formulate objectives, instructional methods and materials, and instruments to evaluate the result of instruction. The actual production of curriculum materials and textbooks, however, is carried out in several special centers. Science and mathematics materials are prepared in the Science Education Center of the University of the Philippines, communication-arts materials in the Language Development Center of the Philippine Normal College, and social-studies materials in the Social Studies Center of the Ministry itself. Work-education materials are developed in the Philippine College of Arts and Trades (recently raised to the status of a Technological University), while industrial and agricultural resources are the responsibility of the Central Luzon State University.

Items produced in these centers are tried out nationwide through Regional Science Development and Staff Centers which were originally set up for trying out mathematics and science textbooks, but the centers now serve all subject-matter fields. Not only do the regional centers direct curriculum-material tryouts, but they conduct summer institutes for elementary and secondary teachers and act as distribution posts for the nation's Textbook Production Project that was initiated in 1975.

The Textbook Project is a massive effort involving both the centers' staffs and local writers, who generally are teachers in the field organized for this task, with their work supervised by the Educational Development Projects Implementing Task Force under the Ministry of Education and Culture. The goal of the project is to achieve a pupil-textbook ratio of two-pupils-per-book by 1980. A survey conducted before 1975 revealed that at the primary level there were 9.8-pupils-per-book and at the intermediate level 11.5-pupils-per-book. The survey further showed that 79 percent of the textbooks used were from five to ten years old. (Perfecto, 1977, p. 303.) The Textbook Production Project is intended not only to improve access to quality basic education but also, if possible, to end dependence on foreign-authored texts purchased at prohibitive costs — foreign texts whose contents are irrelevant to Philippine needs and realities.

Present-day academic subjects in elementary and secondary schools are essentially the same types as those of the first schools organized during American rule in the Philippines — reading, writing, arithmetic, science, history, civics, and government. But there is a major difference between past and present in the orientation, organization, and content of the subjects. Until the 1960s much of the content was Western-oriented and interpreted in terms of values and experience of Western living. In contrast, today there is a systematic effort to relate the content to Philippine realities and values, with the view to developing in students a commitment to improve the quality of life in their country. Moreover, the subjects today are taught in a more integrated rather than separated manner as in the past.

Elementary education today is a combination of academic and work-education courses. The basic academic subjects, cast in their integrated form, include:

(1) Communication arts taught in English, using science and health-education concepts as the main content.

(2) Communication arts taught in Pilipino language, using social-studies concepts (history, government, Filipino life) as major content.

(3) Mathematics, taught as a separate subject and stressing practical applications to problems in real life. Mathematics is taught in English, since Pilipino in its present form does not have sufficient technical terms for efficient instruction in mathematics. Furthermore, use of English gives students an additional opportunity to learn the language under the Philippine government's bilingual policy — Pilipino and English.

(4) Work education taught as a separate subject from Grade 1 to Grade 6 for both boys and girls.

(5) Character education which is integrated into all the other subject areas.

At the secondary level there are two broad categories of schools on the basis of curricular types: (1) general and (2) vocational/technical schools. The latter group can be subdivided into agricultural, fishery, technical, and commercial schools. Secondary institutions are also differentiated in terms of their genesis and funding as provincial, city, municipal, barrio, and barangay high schools. Nearly all of these follow a curriculum combining academic and vocational subjects.

The general-secondary school is designed to (1) further the general education started in elementary school and (2) prepare students for a vocation and/or college. Academic subjects include communication arts in English, communication arts in Pilipino, social studies, science, and mathematics. Practical arts are required the first year for at least two hours a week, and vocational courses are required for at least three hours a week for the next three years. (Revised Secondary Curriculum, 1973; Department Order No. 4–2, s, 1975.)

Over the past two decades two trends in curriculum revision have been of concern to educators and parents alike. The trends have been toward crowding many subjects into the basic curricula and making frequent changes in the curricula. Although the basic subject designations — reading, writing, arithmetic, science, social studies — have remained the same, the search for a happy mix in terms of time allotment and integration of subjects with practical courses (citizenship, vocational studies) has led to pendulum-like swings in curricula.

The latest thrust is "back to the basics" or "back to fundamentals." This move followed findings of a national survey on the outcomes of elementary education, a survey called Project SOUTELE (1976), which revealed that fifth-grade and sixth-grade pupils achieved at low levels in literacy and numeracy. The study further showed that teachers generally gave low assessments to the Continuous Progression Scheme (CPS), an innovation in evaluation and promotion that enables pupils to progress toward goals at their own rates and not in comparison to agemates. (Department of Education and Culture — EDPITAF, 1976.) The teachers' unfavorable reactions to the scheme can probably be traced to eight factors:

(1) A lack of understanding of the theory behind the CPS, that is, the theory of suiting schooling to individual differences in children's abilities and backgrounds.

(2) The Ministry's failure to provide teachers with adequate guidelines to implement the scheme.

(3) The increase in the teachers' workload that the scheme involved, since each child required individual attention and learning materials suited to his needs. Teachers resented this burden on top of their heavy teaching schedules and community activities.

(4) A lack of suitable instructional materials to meet children's individual needs.

(5) Demands of skill not possessed by the present crop of inservice teachers, because these teachers' preservice education did not provide training in psychological diagnosis, the preparation of materials for individualized instruction, the creation of behavioral objectives, and the like.

(6) A lack of inservice education to provide training in the necessary skills.

(7) Inadequate try-out of the scheme in a pilot project.

(8) A lack of changes in the organization of the school to suit the intention of continuous pupil progression. That is, graded classes continued on as usual.

In short, the Continuous Progression Scheme appeared to fail, not because the theory was wrong, but because implementation-planning was inadequate. A few school districts developed learning kits and/or individualized instructional materials, but by and large the individual teacher was responsible for the entire process — setting learning objectives, developing instructional materials, evaluating the child's progress vis-à-vis the child's ability and pace. To solve the problem, the Ministry is presently trying out "a continuum of basic and specific learning expectations expressed in behavioral outcomes" with a corresponding rating system prescribing the adoption of 75 percent mastery of the continuum as the criterion of learning success as determined on cumulative paper–pencil tests.

In summary, educational planners in the Philippines maintain permanent centers for curriculum revision and tryout, and the improvement of learning methods and materials is a continuing process.

Evaluating, Promoting, and Certifying Students

Student progress from one grade level to the next on the educational ladder depends mainly on individual teacher evaluations of student performance, evaluations generally based on teacher-made paper–pencil quizzes and examinations in combination with such other measures as performance tests, projects, reports, and participation in class activities. Intermittently — but far too seldom — a national assessment of pupil achievement of curricular objectives is conducted by the Ministry of Education and Culture to determine how adequately the school system is performing.

Prior to the adoption of the Continuous Progression Scheme in 1971–1972, elementary schools followed a grading system based on norm-referenced measures that evaluated a student's performance against a common, set standard. Pupils scoring below the standard received a failing mark, which in some schools was a percentage (75 percent) and in others was a number in a 1-to-5 system or a letter in an A-to-E scheme.

(Number or letter grades are found in private schools.) Such a pass—fail system was discarded in public elementary schools and replaced by the Continuous Progression Scheme in 1971—1972. (Department of Education and Culture *Memo No. 12, 1971.*) As noted earlier, the scheme is based on the assumption that every child is unique and capable of advancing at his own rate. It is a promotion plan calculated to reduce dropout rates and eliminate failure, since it is intended to enable every child to progress from grade to grade "without needless repetition." Standards are set for each grade level, but they are "considered as goals toward which each child is helped to grow at his own pace and not as a basis of promotion." (Soriano, 1971a, p. 5.) In effect, the scheme is not, strictly speaking, a "grading scheme." It is more a diagnostic and descriptive reporting of the strengths and weaknesses of the individual student in relation to the child's ability as determined by the teacher in assessing the child's progress toward curricular objectives set up by the Ministry. Regardless of how well the child performs, he is automatically moved to the next higher grade at the close of the school year.

Private elementary schools and all secondary institutions continue to follow the traditional practice of evaluating student performance against set standards that all must meet in order to be promoted. There has been a suggestion to extend the Continuous Progression Scheme to public secondary schools, but this had not yet been implemented by the close of the 1970s.

Hence, the grading and promotion practices of Philippine schools have been undergoing recent major revisions at the public-elementary-school level, and such changes are likely to influence such practices in secondary and private-elementary schools as well in the near future.

Supplying Teachers for the Schools

The Spanish colonial government had set up a normal school for men in 1863, an institution that graduated 1,813 teachers and 324 teaching assistants between 1865 and 1896 so that education could increasingly be transferred from the clergy to laymen. In addition, the first such institution for women was set up in 1875 (the Normal School for Women Teachers of Primary Instruction of Nueva Caceres), followed in 1892 by a higher normal school for women called the Municipal School of Manila. (Alzona, 1932, p. 73.)

However, the roots of modern-day preservice education of teachers are traced back to the Philippine Normal School, established in Manila in 1901 by Americans who, a year later, set up branches of the institution in six other provinces — Nueva Caceres (now Camarines Sur), Cebu, Iloilo, Vigan, Cagayan, and Misamis. For some time all were staffed by Americans, and for many years this series of schools was the only source of teachers for the country's elementary schools. (Alzona, 1932.)

A course to prepare secondary-school teachers was opened in 1913 at the University of the Philippines, which had been established in 1908 as the country's first state university. In 1918, the university organized its College of Education, the sole source of secondary-school teachers for the public schools for many years (Cortes, 1978.)

At the start, normal-school education was modest in amount, simply two years' long and part of the regular high-school program. With the American colonial government's ambition to provide universal elementary schooling, the demand for teachers soared so that by 1925 there were twenty-two of these high-school-level normal schools. (Swanson, 1960.) The rapidly expanding enrollment at the primary and intermediate levels made it increasingly difficult for the government to expand its financial commitment beyond the elementary school. As a consequence, education at the secondary level began to fall more and more into the hands of the private sector. Thus, teacher education which had begun as a purely public enterprise in 1901 had, 70 years later, become dominated by private educational institutions. Of 391 schools offering teacher-training courses in 1969, only 38 were government schools. The government schools included both normal schools and colleges of education in state universities and colleges. (Presidential Commission to Survey Philippine Education, 1970b.)

The prestige of a college degree and the traditional view of higher education as a privilege of the elite — plus the fact that teacher education is the college program most accessible throughout the nation — have resulted in ever-growing enrollments in teacher education. In 1958, of the 1,642 college courses authorized by the Department of Education 532 or 32 percent were in education. (Carson, 1961, p. 124.)

As early as 1960, the imbalance between a great quantity of teacher-education graduates and low quality of preparation became apparent when Department of Education records showed that of the 11,000 to 14,000 teachers graduated annually from both public and private institutions, only about 6,000 were passing the qualifying examinations given by the Department. (Swanson, 1960.) A caveat was then offered — that unless the quantity and quality of teacher graduates were regulated, there would be an oversupply of inadequately prepared teachers in succeeding years. This prediction became a shocking reality when the PCSPE revealed that from 1961 to 1968 there were 110,886 elementary-school teacher graduates and 5,924 secondary-school teacher graduates in excess of the actual demand for teachers. (Presidential Commission to Survey Philippine Education, 1970b.) A strategy calculated to cut down the production of teachers was strongly indicated. Accordingly, the PCSPE recommended raising quality through (1) accreditation of schools, (2) selective admission, and (3) collection and dissemination of information on the labor and education markets.

As a result of such concerns, the government has taken steps to deal with the problems of teacher supply, encouraging able teachers to remain in the profession, and improving their social status. One measure has been to raise the salary of public-school teachers and to require private schools to give their teachers a thirteenth month of pay. In addition, a new salary structure for public-school personnel was approved by the government, providing a parallel salary scale for school administrators and classroom teachers so that now a classroom teacher can earn as much as a school principal. Furthermore, scholarships in teacher-education institutions are being established in cooperation with agencies of the government as well as private sources to encourage able students to take up teaching as a career. To better ensure the high quality of students enrolling in a four-year college course leading to a bachelor's degree in education, applicants are required to pass the National College Entrance Examination. Some teacher-education institutions, such as the College of Education of the University of the Philippines, require both a standard in high-school grade-point average and an acceptable score on the College Admission Test for admission. In 1977, the government also approved the licensing of teachers. Starting in 1978, no one can be hired as a classroom teacher to fill a vacancy in either an elementary or secondary school without passing the Professional Board Examination for Teachers, and by 1980 no one shall be allowed to teach unless professionally licensed.

171

Hence, with the problem of the quantity of teachers more than solved, the Philippines government is taking strong measures to improve the quality of its teaching force.

Today all undergraduate programs in teacher education are four-year courses. The shift to four years of preservice education for elementary teachers did not begin until the early 1950s, a quarter century after the Monroe Survey of 1925 recommended such a practice. As mentioned earlier, teacher education started in the early 1900s as a two-year course after elementary education. Following 1925, the program was extended to two years' further study for graduates of a four-year high school. By the 1950s, teacher-education institutions became four-year degree-granting colleges. Five varieties of the bachelor-of-science degree in education are now offered — one for elementary education, another for secondary education's academic subjects, and three more for specializations in agricultural, technical, and commercial education. In addition, some institutions offer graduate study leading to a master's or a doctor's degree in education. In 1971, over 50 percent of the nation's graduate programs were in teacher education. (Higher Education Research Council, Senate of the Philippines, 1971.)

Currently the chief problems faced by teacher-education leaders are those of imbalance in types of teachers produced and of quality of graduates. Although the last half-decade of the 1970s witnessed a downward trend in teacher-education enrollment, the present stock of graduates remains substantial. The problem, then, is an oversupply of teachers in general, but an undersupply in such specializations as physics, mathematics, chemistry, and music. In addition, there is the age-old problem of the quality of teacher graduates. The low salary and low prestige associated with teaching do not help attract the better students into teacher-education courses. Teacher-preparation institutions find themselves in a dilemma. Should they institute selective-admissions policies in face of a diminishing pool of applicants, or should they open admissions so that many low-ability students enter the programs? These are the major problems of teacher education in the Philippines today.

The Future of Schooling in the Philippines – Plans and Problems

In the coming years the education system is expected to become

increasingly effective in terms of contributing to the nation's economic, social, cultural, and political goals. As noted earlier, the government's series of five-year development plans is directed toward "the attainment and sustenance of an improved quality of life for all Filipinos." This overall aim has been specified as seven subgoals to which every sector of society, including the education system, should contribute:
(1) Promote social justice and economic development through the creation of employment opportunities, reduction of income disparities, improvement of living standards of the poor, and enrichment of social and cultural values.
(2) Self-sufficiency in agriculture and other basic commodities.
(3) Attainment of high and sustained economic growth.
(4) Domestic resource mobilization and improvement of the country's balance-of-payments position.
(5) Development of depressed regions through infrastructure support, selective incentives, and other measures to disperse industry.
(6) Improvement of environmental management.
(7) Promotion of internal security and harmonious international relations.

The overall strategy for attaining these objectives suggests the vital role education is expected to assume, that of "creating conditions for more equitable access to social development opportunities and fuller utilization of human resources in national development efforts." (NEDA, 1977, Chap. 10.)

Education in the plans is viewed as a means of human resource development and hence an *investment* in progress rather than as an item of *consumption*. This investment is intended to improve the capacity of the population to produce and to enjoy the benefits accruing from increased productivity.

Within the overall national-development setting, educational planners have identified their own goals for the future. Most of the goals are derived from the 1972 Educational Development Act, the 1973 Constitution, and the National Economic and Development Authority's national plan of 1977–1982. The Constitution included a commitment to "a complete, adequate, and integrated system of education relevant to the goals of national development." (Art. XV, Sec. 8,1.) The Act of 1972 established an array of educational projects in the areas of: (1) establishing and up-

173

grading technical institutes, skills-training centers, and other nonformal training programs, (2) curriculum and staff development, (3) textbook production for basic education, (4) expansion of agricultural education, and (5) the improvement of physical facilities of selected educational institutions. The Educational Project Implementing Task Force was organized by the Minister of Education and Culture to monitor these projects.

Government priorities in education for the next two decades have been described in the national plan for 1977–1982 as:

> ... the educational system will be progressively reoriented towards equalizing educational opportunities, achieving universal literacy, and promoting the economic, social, cultural, and political goals of the country. Education, in the context of the Plan, will not be confined within the time-bound traditional type of formal education, but will enhance all learning processes and life activities. Formal, nonformal, and informal education will have specific roles while maintaining close linkages. (NEDA, 1977, Chap. 10.)

What, then, are the key problems educational planners face in seeking to achieve these aims?

A first challenge is to increase access to educational opportunities so as to ensure suitable participation of the entire populace in the development process. This challenge takes on increased significance when one considers its quantitative and qualitative dimensions. For example, the projected enrollment in schools based on medium population-growth assumptions for the 1977–1982 period are given in Table 4.4.

TABLE 4.4
Projected Enrollment (In Thousands)

Level	1978–79	1979–80	1980–81	1981–82
Elementary	7,925	7,985	8,065	8,160
Secondary	2,482	2,607	2,698	2,777
Tertiary	888	929	970	1,011

Percent of Each Age Group Expected to be in School 1978–1983

Elementary (7–12 years old)	98%
Secondary (13–16 years old)	60%
Tertiary (17–21 years old)	19%

(Source: NEDA, 1977, Chap. 10)

In addition to the task of accommodating the burgeoning school enrollment, there is the problem of providing education to the out-of-school youths who numbered approximately 4.5 million in 1978. Furthermore, a substantial group of adults had little or no schooling. The increasing social demand for education and the rising educational costs on the one hand as opposed to the limits on resources available for educational purposes on the other hand are likely to create serious problems of attaining quality education while widening the access to learning opportunities.

Qualitatively a principal drive of the school system today is to make the curricula relevant to the needs of Philippine society, specifically to such social and economic problems as population growth, poverty, unemployment, low productivity, malnutrition, and environmental degradation. In order to maintain the balance between the outputs of the education system and the manpower requirements of the various sectors of the economy, a system of channelling students away from the traditionally preferred college courses leading to white-collar professions has been instituted in the form of the National College Entrance Examination. This screening device is designed to regulate the flow of students into four-year college-degree courses which in the past have absorbed almost three-fourths of the collegiate enrollment, such as in business, commercial, teacher-education, law, humanities, and medical courses. The intention of the examination is to steer high-school graduates into the two- and three-year trade and technical courses. It appears, however, that acquiring a college diploma remains the one great ambition of every young Filipino — a value that has its origins in the country's historic past and which has continually been reinforced by the employment opportunities and the reward system of Philippine society. Unless equivalent social supports are instituted for the "blue collar" occupations, going to college and acquiring a diploma will continue to be the supreme aspiration of every Filipino.

Quality education is inextricably linked with quality teachers. There are more than 400 teacher-education institutions in the nation whose preservice education programs can stand rigid scrutiny in light of the rapidly changing views about education, learning, teaching, types of schools, and target clienteles in the Philippines. The recruitment and education of teachers for the future are now becoming a major concern for development planners, because there has been a sharp decline in the enrollment in teacher-preparation institutions in the latter 1970s, and

TABLE 4.5
National Government Expenditures for Education
(In Philippine Pesos)

Year	Total Budget for Education (in millions)	Total National Budget (in millions)	% of National Budget Furnished for Education
1948	120.4	1,509.7	7.98
1960	307.0	1,903.0	16.14
1962	437.0	1,383.0	31.60
1964	540.0	2,102.0	25.69
1966	691.0	2,074.0	33.32
1968	836.0	2,905.0	28.78
1976	3,170.5	21,275.4	14.90
1978	4,368.0 (estimate)	33,951.9	12.87

Sources: Data for 1948 from Philippine President's Budget for Fiscal Year 1948. Data for 1961 to 1968 from Presidential Commission to Survey Philippine Education, 1970a, pp. 47 and 128; and for 1976, 1978 from Budget Commission, 1978, p. 48.)

students pursuing teacher education are observed to be relatively poorer in ability than those of previous years.

Rising educational costs in the face of a decreasing share of the national budget (Table 4.5) spent on education call for a departure from the traditional approaches to the delivery of educational services and from traditional teaching-learning strategies. Already innovations in the delivery system are being tried out in the formal educational realm. These include the continuous-progression scheme and the In-School-Off-School Approach (IS-OSA), which is an experiment similar to Project IMPACT, aimed at deinstitutionalizing the process of education by combining formal instruction and nonformal learning activities in the home or community. Such innovations require corresponding changes in the structural and operational aspects of the school system. However, the structural changes have been difficult to effect in a system that has a long history of institutionalized norms and values. There are strong indications, however, that a break away from the system's dysfunctional characteristics is gradually taking place, motivated by a continuing clamor from the populace and the government for educational approaches more responsive to the nation's needs.

Conclusion

Over the past three decades, Philippine education has undergone a long, slow process of weaning itself away from its strong American orientation and from rather conservative views and misconceptions about education. In the process, the education system has moved toward a more Philippine-based and more practical approach to learning. In its search for roots in the Philippine social and cultural milieu, the school system has continually grappled with the problems of quantity versus quality, academic versus vocational orientation, basic-education versus higher-education priorities, and regional versus national problems of education. These issues are far from resolved, but the issues posed by these pairs of competing interests are being met head-on in current educational reforms. In this sense, the future of Philippine education holds great promise of improved performance.

References

ABELLA, DOMINGO (1965) State of Higher Education in the Philippine Historical Reappraisal, *Philippine Historical Review*, 1, No. 1.

ALZONA, ENCARNACION (1932) *A History of Education in the Philippines, 1865–1930*, University of the Philippines Press, Manila.

Budget Commission (1978) *The 1978 Philippine Budget Profile, Staff Papers*, Budget Commission, Manila.

Bureau of the Census and Statistics (1972) *Special Report No. 3. Population, Land Area and Density: 1948, 1960 and 1970*, BCS, Manila.

CARSON, ARTHUR (1961) *Higher Education in the Philippines*, U.S. Government Printing Office, Washington, D.C.

CHEETHAM, R. J. and HAWKINS, E. (1976) *The Philippines, Priorities and Prospects for Development*, IBRD and World Bank, Washington, D.C.

CONCEPCION, MERCEDES (1978) "Population" in *The Philippines Into the Twenty-First Century*, (manuscript), University of the Philippines, Quezon City.

CORPUZ, ONOFRE D. (1965) *The Philippines*, Prentice-Hall, New Jersey.

CORTES, JOSEFINA R. (1978) The UP College of Education and National Development, *Education Quarterly*, 24, No. 4, April–June 1978.

Daily Express (September 14, 1978) Daily Express Pub., Manila.

Department of Education and Culture (1903 to 1970) *Annual Reports*. DEC, Manila.

Department of Education and Culture (1971) *Memo No. 12*, (mimeographed), DEC, Manila.

Department of Education and Culture – EDPITAF (1976) *Report on the Survey of Outcomes of Elementary Education*, (Project SOUTELE) DEC, Makati, Rizal.

Department Order No. 4, s. 1975, (mimeographed), Department of Education and Culture, Manila.

Schooling in the ASEAN Region

Development Academy of the Philippines (1975) *Measuring the Quality of Life, Philippines* Social Indicators, DAP, Manila.

FERNANDO, ENRIQUE M. (1977) "1935 Constitution of the Philippines" in *The Constitution of the Philippines*, (2nd ed.) pp. 829–856, Phoenix Press, Quezon City.

FERNANDO, ENRIQUE M. (1977) "1973 Constitution of the Philippines" in *The Constitution of the Philippines*, (2nd ed.) pp. 775–828, Phoenix Press, Quezon City.

HAYDEN, JOHN RALSTON (1950) *The Philippines, A Study in National Development*, MacMillan, New York.

Higher Education Research Council, Senate of the Philippines, *Higher Education in the Philippines, Its Relevance to National Development*, (manuscript), HERC, Manila.

MANUEL, JUAN L. (1977) "Education Challenges for National Progress" in *The Fookien Times Philippine Yearbook, 1927–1977*. Fookien Times Yearbook Publishing Co, Manila.

MANUEL, JUAN L. (1978) "Non-Formal Education" *The 1978 Fookien Times Year-book*. Fookien Times Yearbook Publishing Co., Manila.

Metro Manila Philippines (1976) *A Framework Plan for the Nation, International Conference on the Survival of Human Kind: The Phil-Experiments*, MMP, Manila.

Ministry of Education and Culture (1978) *Order No. 25*, (mimeographed), MEC, Manila.

National Board of Education (1974) *Educational Statistics, School Year 1971–1972*, Vol. 17 (mimeographed), NBE, Manila.

NCSO (1975) *Integrated Census of the Population and Its Economic Activities: Population of the Philippines. May 1, 1975*, (Preliminary), NCSO, Manila.

NCSO (undated) *Social Indicators*, Vol. 2, NCSO, Manila.

NEDA (1974) *Statistical Yearbook*, NEDA, Manila.

NEDA (1976) *Statistical Yearbook of the Philippines*, NEDA, Manila.

NEDA (1977) *The Five-Year Philippine Development Plan, 1977–1982*, (manuscript), Chap. 10, NEDA Production Unit, Manila.

NEDA–NCSO (1972) *Journal of Philippine Statistics*, 2, Second Quarter. NEDA–NCSO, Manila.

NEDA–NCSO (1977) *Philippine Yearbook*, NEDA–NCSO, Manila.

NEDA–POPCOM–NCSO (1978) *Population Dimension of Planning: Population Projection for the Philippines by Province, 1979–2000*, Vol. 2, NEDA–POPCOM–NCSO, Manila.

Office of Non-Formal Education – DEC (1977) *Non-Formal Education, A Primer*, Department of Education and Culture, Manila.

PERFECTO, WALDO (1977) "Future Directions in Philippine Education" in *The Fookien Times Philippine Yearbook, 1927–1977*, Fookien Times Yearbook Publishing Co., Manila.

Philippine Almanac Printers (1977) *Philippine Almanac and Handbook of Facts*, Philippine Almanac Printers, Quezon City.

Presidential Commission on Reorganization (1973) *The Reorganization of the Executive Branch of the Philippine Government*, Vols. 1 and 2, Lawin Publishing House, Manila.

Presidential Commission to Survey Philippine Education (1970 a) *Education for National Development, New Patterns, New Directions*, PCSPE, Manila.

Presidential Commission to Survey Philippine Education (1970 b) *Teacher Education in the Philippines: Status and Prospect* (by the Area Group for Teacher Education), (manuscript), PCSPE, Makati, Rizal.

Revised Secondary Curriculum 1973 (1973), (mimeographed), Department of Education and Culture, Manila.

SHAHANI, LETICIA RAMOS (1970) *The.Philippines, The Land and People,* National Bookstore Press, Manila.

SICAT, G. (1978) "Review of Implemented Policies and Programs 1972–1977 and Major Development Thrusts in the Next Ten Years" in *The 1978 Fookien Times Yearbook,* pp. 154–158, 169, Fookien Times Yearbook Publishing Co., Manila.

SINCO, VICENTE G. (1962) *Philippine Political Law, Principles and Concepts,* Community Publication, Manila.

SORIANO, LICERIA (1971 a) *The Scheme of Continuous Progression,* p. 5, Bureau of Public Schools, Manila.

SORIANO, LICERIA (1971 b) Continuous Progression and Accountability, *Education Quarterly,* 19, Nos. 1 & 2, July–December 1971, pp. 12–18.

SWANSON, CHESTER J. (1960) *A Survey of the Public Schools of the Philippines,* Carmelo–Bauermann, Manila.

Task Force on Human Settlements (1975) *Social Services Development in the Philippines, Technical Report, Part I: Education,* DAP, Quezon City.

The Board of Educational Survey (1925) *A Survey of the Educational System of the Philippine Islands,* (Monroe Survey), Bureau of Printing, Manila.

The Philippine President's Budget for Fiscal Year 1948, (mimeographed), Government of the Philippines, Manila.

UNESCO–Philippine American Education Foundation (1953) *Fifty Years of Education for Freedom,* National Printing Co., Manila.

UP Law Center (1977) "Act No. 74 – 1901" in *Philippine Laws in Education, A Compilation,* Vol. I, (manuscript), UP Law Center, Quezon City.

UP Law Center (1977) "Act No. 447 – 1902" in *Philippine Laws in Education, A Compilation,* Vol.˙I. (manuscript), UP Law Center, Quezon City.

UP Law Center (1977) "Act No. 1870 – 1908" in *Philippine Laws in Education, A Compilation,* Vol. I. (manuscript), UP Law Center, Quezon City.

UP Law Center (1977) "Presidential Decree No. 6-A – 1972" in *Philippine Laws in Education, A Compilation,* Vol. IV, (manuscript), UP Law Center, Quezon City.

UP Law Center (1977) "Republic Act No. 74 – 1946" in *Philippine Laws in Education, A Compilation,* Vol. III, (manuscript), UP Law Center, Quezon City.

UP Law Center (1977) "Republic Act No. 896 – 1953" in *Philippine Laws in Education, A Compilation,* Vol. III, (manuscript), UP Law Center, Quezon City.

UP Law Center (1977) "Republic Act No. 1124" in *Philippine Laws in Education, A Compilation,* Vol. III, (manuscript), UP Law Center, Quezon City.

UP Law Center (1979) *Proposed Education Code of the Philippines,* Published by the Fund for Assistance to Private Education, UP Law Center, Manila.

US–Philippine Commission Report (1918) (microfilm).

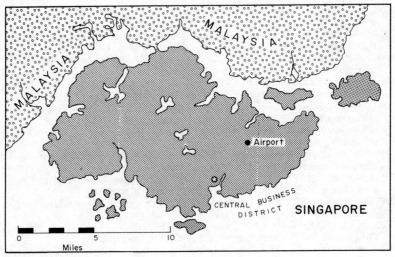

Map 5 Singapore

子曰﹁溫故而知新,可以為師矣﹂

If a man keeps cherishing his old
knowledge, so as continually to be
acquiring new, he may be a teacher of
others.

CONFUCIUS

5

Singapore

R. Murray Thomas, Goh Kim Leong, and R. W. Mosbergen

AMONG ASEAN countries, Singapore is unique in several ways that have strongly influenced educational development.

In the first place, Singapore is by far the smallest of the nations geographically. It consists of a central island at the tip of the Malay Peninsula and a few tiny offshore islands, making a total land area of only 597 square kilometers. In contrast, Malaysia is two hundred times larger and Indonesia twelve hundred times larger. This means that nearly all of Singapore's schools are less than an hour's drive from the central Ministry of Education, thus greatly simplifying the tasks of communicating with staff members throughout the school system, of delivering supplies, and of supervising administrators and teachers.

Singapore also has the smallest population – an estimated 2.4 million by 1980 – while Malaysia has nearly six times more people (13.7 million by 1980) and Indonesia over sixty times more (145 million). Furthermore, Singapore's population is growing at a slower rate than her neighbors' – at 1.2 percent annually compared to Malaysia's 2.9 percent and Indonesia's 2.7 percent in the late 1970s. (*Yearbook of Statistics, 1977/78*, 1978.) Hence, the magnitude of Singapore's educational task has been considerably smaller than that facing the other countries. Not so many new schools or teachers are needed nor at such a rapid pace as in the rest of the ASEAN nations.

Living conditions for the great majority of Singapore's citizens are also unique for the ASEAN region. Whereas most Southeast Asians live in rural settings and follow occupations in agriculture and fishing, Singaporeans are urban dwellers. They live clustered together at a density of over 4,000 people per square mile. About half of Singapore's population live in high-rise apartment buildings in housing estates, the products of the Housing and Development Board's public housing effort that began in 1960 and resulted in the construction of over 300,000 living units by 1978. (*Annual Report 1977/78, Ministry of National Development,* 1978, p. 2.) As a result of these housing estates in the new towns, most pupils do not have to travel far to their schools.

Another unique feature is Singapore's lack of natural resources. With little agricultural land and no mineral deposits, the city-state has had to build its economy by taking advantage of its strategic location and by making use of the resourcefulness of its hard-working people. The city sits at the pivot of the Southeast Asian sea routes; northeastward are China, Japan, and the Pacific, and westward are India and the Mideast. Singapore's economy is built on trade and manufacturing. Therefore, economic planners have assigned the education system the task of producing apt and willing workers for clerical, managerial, semiskilled- and skilled-labor jobs in the service, manufacturing, commerce, transport, and construction sectors. In the mid-1970s over 31 percent of the total labor force were in service occupations, 26 percent in manufacturing, 23 percent in commerce, 12 percent in transport and communications, but only 2 percent in agriculture and fishing. (*Europa Year Book,* 1977, p. 1449.)

The sorts of industrial areas for which workers were most needed in the latter 1970s are suggested by the sample of industries and the numbers of employees listed in Table 5.1.

Such is the structure of the present-day Singapore economic enterprise, and it is obviously not the structure typically associated with the term "under-developed country". It is clearly a "modern" and rapidly developing socioeconomic system. A variety of indices attest to its growing prosperity. Between 1965 and 1974 the gross domestic product grew at least 10 percent a year. At the same time, the government's population-

TABLE 5.1
Numbers of Workers in Largest Industries – 1977

Industry	Workers
Machinery, including electronic components and consumer electronics	67,457
Shipbuilding and repairing	28,218
Wearing apparel, including footwear	24,747
Sawmills, plywood; and wood products, including furniture	12,261
Fabricated metal products	12,253
Textiles	10,537
Printing and publishing	9,808
Plastic and rubber products	7,948
Chemicals and chemical products	5,128
Paper products	3,604

(Source: *Report on the Genesis of Industrial Production*, 1977)

control program lowered the growth rate of the population from 2.5 percent annually to 1.4 percent, with the result that the gross-domestic-product per capita in 1974 was nearly 250 percent greater than in 1964. (Skolnik, 1976, p. 13.) Over the ten-year period of 1966–1976 bank assets increased more than six-fold. Large ships docking in Singapore increased from 12,000 to 20,000, and cargo loaded or discharged doubled. Buildings under construction tripled in number (19,322 to 60,548). In the seven-year interval 1969–1976 the number of visitors to the city more than tripled. (*Yearbook of Statistics, 1977/78*, pp. 93, 126, 127, 152.)

Not only was the nation's progress over the 1960s and 1970s "the envy of other developing countries in the region" but prospects for the 1980s looked bright as well. A late-1978 survey of foreign investors conducted by Business International of New York "placed this city-state first worldwide as an investment site, on the basis of its skilled and disciplined work force and its highly developed transportation and communications infrastructure." (Weintraub, 1978, p. S1.)

Singapore's success clearly has not been achieved by luck or by permitting the economy freely to find its own way. Rather, the country's progress has been due to carefully managed political and socioeconomic development plans, put into operation and monitored, then redesigned in light of internal and international events. At each step in the planning, the education sector has played its assigned part.

More than any of its ASEAN neighbors, Singapore has been able to alter institutions and redirect people to suit the requirements of the times. In order to illustrate this point, we need to step back a few decades and see how these requirements have periodically changed. But before taking this historical excursion, we should note that of all the ASEAN countries, Singapore has the least margin for mistakes available to it. While the other four ASEAN nations can commit substantial errors of planning and execution without suffering complete disaster, Singapore cannot. The economies of the other four include large agricultural and fishing components. Thus, even if marked mistakes are made in the central planning agencies, most people in the country have jobs to go to and they can provide their own food and housing. They can subsist. But Singapore depends so heavily on trade and manufacturing that planning or management errors of any magnitude can bring immediate disaster. Much of the food and all the raw materials for the city-state's manufacturing establishment are imported. Any serious disruption of imports and exports leaves the populace without food and precipitates widespread unemployment.

Singapore's citizenry is well aware of their narrow margin for error. They recognize the necessity for managing their affairs well, avoiding political and social disorder. It is apparently for this reason that the populace has generally supported a style of government that Skolnik claims "is best called 'paternalistic authoritarianism'." He further describes the ruling People's Action Party and the government it operates as "honest, efficient, highly organized, prudish, vehemently anticommunist, and convinced of its own superiority." (Skolnik, 1976, p. 10.)

With this brief appraisal of Singapore's present-day political condition in mind, we turn now to earlier times in order to identify historical events that account for the island's current ethnic, socioeconomic, political, and educational make-up.

Raffles and British Colonialism

In the early 1800s Singapore (a name meaning "City of the Lion") was an isolated island of granite and marshes, inhabited by only a few fishing families, and connected to the peninsular Sultanate of Johore by a narrow strait. Then in 1819 a forward-looking official of the British East India trading company, Thomas Stamford Raffles, persuaded the Sultan of Johore to cede the seemingly useless Singapore island to the British. Over the following decades Raffles and his successors developed Singapore into the most important British trade center in Southeast Asia.

When the city of Singapore was first established, the British controlled only small, unconnected portions of the Malay Peninsula, such as the port of Malacca and the island of Penang. But by gradual steps over the next 90 years they acquired the entire area that now falls within the borders of Malaysia and Singapore. During these decades they guided the development of plantations, where rubber trees flourished, and of tin mining along with other commercial enterprises. Since the Malays who were indigenous to the area were too few to operate all the British-directed establishments, and since they often wished to continue pursuing their own livelihoods, the British colonial authorities encouraged the immigration of large numbers of Chinese and Indians, the latter mostly Tamils from Southern India. Likewise, Arab traders and peoples of Malay stock from the Indonesian archipelago settled on the Malay Peninsula. As a result, by the early decades of the 20th century, both Singapore and the Malay States were inhabited by a diversity of ethnic groups.

The large migrant community of Singapore at the turn of the present century consisted mostly of hard-pressed peasants who had left their homeland in China, India, or Indonesia in search of a better life. Newcomers usually felt most secure when they settled in the section of the city occupied by earlier arrivals who spoke their same language and followed the same religion and customs. As a result, the colony from its earliest days displayed a multiracial mix, with different sections of the city identified with particular ethnic strains. The resulting cosmopolitan flavor still exists in the Republic today.

Since English was the language of government, the use of English was regarded as a mark of prestige. The few inhabitants of the island who were privileged to learn English had an edge over the others in the realms of government and commerce, for it was from this English-speaking minority that colonial authorities and business houses drew personnel to staff the lower positions of clerks and store-keepers in their establishments.

However, the facilities for learning English were extremely limited, since it was never the intention of the colonial government to provide universal schooling. Only enough education would be needed to supply the lower-level staff members in government offices, commercial houses, and banks. The majority of the population continued to speak their native Oriental languages.

As the middle of the 20th century approached, Singapore continued to serve as one of the key trading centers of the British Empire. Then in February 1942, early in the Pacific war, Japanese forces attacked the city, avoiding the heavily fortified sea front in order to capture the island from the rear, approaching down the peninsula. With the end of the war three years later, British military administrators returned to govern Singapore until a Malayan Union was established under the British in 1946 to rule the Malay States, and Singapore was made a British crown colony in April that year. Plans for a more independent status for both the Malay States and Singapore evolved over the next decade. In May 1959, the People's Action Party in Singapore took the general elections by a wide margin, and Lee Kuan Yew was installed as the first Prime Minister of Singapore, a position he still held twenty years later.

Over the next three years the heads of government in Singapore, the Federation of Malaya on the peninsula, and Sabah and Sarawak in North Borneo met with British authorities to form the plans for a new nation to be called Malaysia. In mid-1963, the Malaysian Agreement was ratified by the separate governments, and they became a united nation.

However, the union did not last long. There were serious disagreements between the dominantly Malay leadership of the Malay States in Kuala Lumpur and the dominantly Chinese leadership in Singapore. The upshot of the disagreement was that in August 1965 Singapore separated from the Malaysian union and established an independent republic. It has continued in that state ever since.

Earlier we noted that Singapore's political-economic leadership has displayed a remarkable talent for adjusting development plans to changing external and internal conditions. Each such adjustment has required changes as well in the roles assigned to the education sector. This ready adaptability of the society is illustrated in a comparison of economic-growth plans before and after Singapore left the Malaysian federation in 1965.

186

As Singapore started toward self rule after 1959, the initial economic plans stressed industrialization for import substitution. This was a viable approach so long as the city was associated with the Malay States which provided a domestic market for goods produced in Singapore. But when Singapore was separated from Malaysia in 1965, the import-substitution tack was no longer appropriate, since Malaysia was now creating its own import-substitution industries aimed at reducing the nation's dependence on outside sources for items of daily use. Thus Singapore's economic planners looked ahead at the size of the labor force that their population growth-rate would produce in the coming years, and they established a different approach, one which has enabled the republic to prosper over the past decade-and-a-half. The new departure emphasized labor-intensive export industries designed to further "continued economic development through increased investment in skill-intensive high technology industries and the transformation of Singapore into an international centre for banking and finance and consultancy services." (Skolnik, 1976, p. 11.) Multinational industries were successfully encouraged to establish branches in Singapore so that by the final years of the 1970s the nation's prospects for growth were judged by outside observers as "more than fair". (Weintraub, 1978, p. S1.)

With the foregoing sketch of Singapore's geographical and political—economic situation as a base, we are prepared to review the evolution of the nation's schools.

The Origins of the Education System

Prior to the arrival of the British, education on the Malay Peninsula was apparently of two varieties. The first was the informal socialization of the young through the traditional child-rearing practices of the family and village. Children learned not only the language and customs of their tribe but also the vocational roles they would play in life, primarily roles in agriculture, fishing, and homemaking.

The second variety was a more formal kind of Islamic religious school-ing that developed gradually after the arrival of Islam in the 15th and 16th centuries from the Indonesian island of Sumatra. Youths would gather around a Moslem scholar at the mosque, in a prayer house, or in his home for instruction in Islamic tradition and in how properly to intone passages of the Koran in Arabic. They learned to chant the Arabic script, usually without understanding its meaning unless they followed advanced studies with the religious teacher. By the 19th century, when Raffles and his fellow British colonialists arrived, students in these Koran schools often studied a bit of Malay reading and writing after they had pursued the oral reading of the Koran and the memorization of principal Islamic prayers.

The 20th-century descendant of the Koran school is called a *pondok* and is still composed of a collection of pupils living oftentimes in a complex of rustic dormitories attached to the home of the religious scholar who, today as in the past, is called *Haji* or *Ustaz* if he is of Malay stock and called *Sheikh* or *Syed* if of Arabic origin. In the traditional pondok there was no set length of school term and no ladder of successive "grades" or "standards" up which pupils ascended year by year. Instead, pupils entered at any time to start their studies, and they left whenever they felt they had accomplished enough. They often repaid the Haji by working his rice fields, tending his livestock, or bringing gifts of food and clothing.

In summary, the early Islamic schools on the Malay peninsula focused on the Koran in the Arabic language, and only incidentally would some Malay-language reading and writing be taught.

To understand the development of Singapore's schools after these earliest times, it is best to take an ethnic and language perspective, since the school system which evolved into the mid-20th century was distinguished by four language streams – English, Malay, Tamil, and Chinese.

The desire of British colonial officials to maintain an ethnically segregated society in Singapore was clear from the beginning. In establishing the settlement, Raffles had issued a plan to section the city into residential districts, each intended for one of the major ethnic types. Part of the reason such a plan succeeded over the century was that it suited the inclinations of the new immigrants that continually flowed into and through the city. Newcomers found it far more comfortable to settle into an area where others spoke their language, followed their religion, and practiced their customs than to move in with neighbors they could not understand or readily accept. The ethnic segregation of these districts was faithfully maintained throughout the 19th century. Not until well into the 20th did the district borders become blurred by rapid population growth that spilled across the traditional district lines. Even today the areas of the original concentration of ethnic clusters are recognizable. Not only was differential treatment of ethnic groups by the British evidenced in the residential plan but in other matters as well, including educational policies. As time passed it became increasingly clear that the greatest favors were bestowed on schools conducted in the English language. Schools in the Malay vernacular were "protected" with a type of paternalistic support. A smaller stream of Tamil-language schools was "accepted" by British authorities. Chinese-language schools grew regularly and in the early 1900s flourished as an increasingly strong movement to form a fourth stream that was essentially neglected by colonial officials. We shall consider the development of each stream in some detail.

ENGLISH SCHOOLS – THE FAVORED STREAM

The first formal teaching in English, with a curriculum like that of British schools, was in the Singapore Free School, opened by an Anglican clergyman in 1834. It was later renamed the Raffles Institution, honoring the foresight of Sir Thomas Stamford Raffles who in 1819 had first proposed establishing a school in the Singapore settlement. Although the building to house the institution Raffles planned was erected in the early 1820s, it was not put to use immediately because he fell ill and had to return to England, and his successor as governor felt the funds to support such a project could better be used other ways. However, Raffles' intention was fulfilled in a sense when the Free School moved into his original building in 1837.

Throughout the 19th century additional English-language schools were set up, not by the government but by Britishers acting as private groups or by such religious organizations as the London Missionary Society, Roman Catholics, and American Methodists. Children of all races and religions were accommodated in these institutions. Although these schools were not set up by the government, they were officially encouraged by means of government grants-in-aid.

As the 19th century advanced, so did the desirability of the English schools among those Chinese, Indians, and Malays who were anxious to rise in the economic and social worlds, for opportunities in secondary and tertiary education lay chiefly in the English stream. To enable non-English-speaking pupils to transfer into the English stream from primary schools conducted in vernacular languages, the government in 1872 appointed a director of education for the three Straits Settlements of Singapore, Malacca, and Penang. The director established "branch schools" designed to furnish non-English-speaking students with three years of English-language study taught through the medium of their native tongue. However, after the Cambridge Local Examination system was adopted in the 1890s, the branch schools gradually eliminated the native medium and gave instruction in English only so as to improve students' chances of succeeding in the examination. Thereafter, additional schools established by the government were exclusively English. (Arumugam, 1975, p. 56.)

A further impetus for students to enroll in the English stream was the introduction of opportunities for higher education that required fluency in English. In the 1890s, the Queen's Scholarships were established, enabling apt graduates of Singapore's secondary schools to follow university studies in England. The local higher-learning institutions set up in the settlement, such as the King Edward VII Medical School in 1905 and Raffles College in 1928 (which were combined in 1949 to form the nucleus of the University of Malaya in Singapore), were conducted solely in English.

Up to the outbreak of World War II in the Pacific in late 1941, both primary and secondary schooling were designed chiefly to suit the needs of the British colonial administration. But by 1933 the English-language schools were over-producing, for it was noted that "the supply of pupils from English schools was beginning to exceed the demand for clerks." (Doraisamy, 1969, p. 42.) The government was clearly not interested in furnishing more opportunities for an English-language education than the demand for clerks warranted. If parents wanted to send their children to school, they would need to send them to private institutions.

In 1940, of the population of school-age children of 200,000, hardly more than one-third were in school, and most of these were not in the English-language stream. That is, of the total of 72,000 pupils, only 27,000 or around 37 percent attended English-language schools. The rest were in Chinese schools (38,000), Malay schools (5,800), and Tamil schools (1,000). (Doraisamy, 1969, p. 38.) The teachers in Government English schools and in private English-language schools aided by the

Government included some recruited from abroad, but most teachers were Singaporeans from all classes of society.

MALAY SCHOOLS – THE PROTECTED STREAM

We noted earlier that some simple reading and writing in the Malay language was found in certain Koran schools which the British found in operation when they arrived. However, the first formal school-instruction in Malay apparently was in the Malay section of the Singapore Free School established in 1834. Subsequently the colonial government began to set up additional primary schools in Malay throughout the Straits Settlements and in other sectors of the Malay Peninsula as the British gained gradual control of the region.

The government's financing of Malay-language schools was one of the measures reflecting the paternalistic, protective policy that the colonial government adopted toward the indigenous population, a policy not extended to the thousands of Chinese and Indian laborers imported into the colony over the years. To protect the Malay lands from exploitation, the British also discouraged immigrants from owning farm land, a policy that tended to keep Malays on the land, tilling small holdings, while the Chinese and Indians either worked in the tin mines and on rubber plantations or became shopkeepers in villages and in cities like Singapore.

As a result of both this policy and natural societal forces, Malays did not troop to the cities in large numbers during the century or more of British rule. Today the proportion of Malays living in Singapore is 15 percent of the population. However, a large number of these are the second or third generation offspring of immigrants from the Indonesian islands of Java and Sumatra. They are not immigrants from rural areas of the Malay Peninsula itself.

Thus, the British protectionist policy served to keep Malays in their original socioeconomic condition while it inadvertently encouraged ambitious Chinese and Indians to acquire the skills and goals better suited to the development of a modern industrialized, commercial society. This disparity between the Malays and the Chinese, caused partially by educational opportunities of the past, was a significant factor in Singapore's splitting away from the original Malaysian federation in 1965. Singapore was a Chinese-dominated (75 percent of the citizens are Chinese), urban, commercial society led by Western-oriented, English-speaking technocrats. The Malay Peninsula beyond Singapore Island was chiefly rural, with the Malays slightly in the majority. However, since the British had ruled the peninsula through the indigenous Malay sultans and aristocrats, political leadership of the Malay states was Malay. The Malay population was generally made up of farm families with a relatively low level of schooling, and even that had been exclusively in the Malay tongue, not well suited to commerce with the broader world or with acquiring the knowledge leading to modernization.

In effect, Malay schools in Singapore were supported by the colonial government. However, they have been of little significance in determining the fate of the society, since Malays over the past century have made up only a small proportion of the city-state's population. Furthermore, schooling in the Malay language has been more a liability than an aid in an individual's pursuit of higher education and a leadership role in the society.

TAMIL SCHOOLS – A WEAK, ACCEPTED STREAM

Like English and Malay, the first formal instruction in Tamil apparently was that offered to Indian children in a Tamil section of the Singapore Free School in 1834. (Wong and Gwee, 1972, p. 9.) However, over the next century Tamil schools did not expand at the rate of English and Chinese schools. One reason was that the number of Indians in Singapore was relatively small. Today, Indians make up only seven percent of the Singapore population. Another reason was that a significant proportion of Indian parents wanted their children to have the advantages of an English education, so they enrolled their sons and daughters in English-language schools.

Nevertheless, the numbers of parents who desired a traditional education in their native tongue was always large enough to maintain a series of Tamil-language schools in the city. Over the past two decades, however, most of these have closed, so that only 321 pupils were enrolled in Tamil schools in 1978.

CHINESE SCHOOLS – A STRONG, NEGLECTED STREAM

When the Singapore Free School opened in 1834 there were already at least three Chinese-language schools in the city, one conducted in the Hokkien dialect and two in Cantonese.

Singapore's Chinese community of the past and present could better be described as a cluster of communities, for the Chinese of the city have come from different parts of China where different dialects are spoken. In addition, two broad groupings evolved over the decades in the city – the English-speaking Chinese who gradually adopted more Western ways and dropped Chinese traditions, and the Chinese-speaking people who held more closely to traditional ways. There has been some intermixture between these two clusters, but essentially they are different. For example, 1970 census data showed that among the literate Chinese population over age ten, 54 percent were literate only in Chinese, 32 percent literate only in English, and only 12 percent literate in both languages. (Arumugam, 1975, p. 55.)

But despite the differences among the language groupings, all Chinese appear to feel the common bond of tracing their origins to the world's largest nation and to one of the most historically notable civilizations. This pride in their cultural traditions has periodically stimulated great interest in supporting private Chinese-language schools in Singapore. Such a surge of interest was noted early in the 20th century at the time of the revolution in China under Sun Yat Sen. It appeared again after World War II with the rise of China under Mao Tse-Tung. A second factor stimulating the growth of Chinese schools was the insurge of immigrants to operate the tin mines of Malaya after 1870 and to work in the rubber plantations between 1910 and 1930. Malaya became the supplier of half of the world's tin and rubber by the mid-1900s, and it was Chinese and Indian laborers, funneled through Singapore into the Malay States, that provided the workers for the mines and plantations. Some of the immigrants remained in Singapore and had children whom they enrolled in schools conducted in their native language.

Although the British did not purposely oppose the establishment of Chinese schools, colonial authorities did little to encourage or support them. Moreover, by favoring English-language secondary and tertiary education, the colonial government effectively frustrated the educational progress of youths whose lower-school training had been exclusively in the Chinese language. Prior to World War II, it was usually necessary for students from the Chinese stream to go to China for higher education.

While English, Malay, and Tamil schools enjoyed the patronage and financial backing of the colonial government, no such support was provided for Chinese-language schools. Chinese education was left to the initiative of private groups, with British authorities neither encouraging nor opposing them. The large enrollment of children in Chinese schools by 1940 was the result of the strong Chinese cultural tradition of respect for education, a tradition that stimulated the island's Chinese business community to provide the financial support to establish increasing numbers of Chinese-language institutions.

From the early years of the 20th century, Singapore's Chinese-language schools were suffused with a strong political spirit which, in the 1950s and early 1960s, would precipitate far-reaching public disorders. The revolution in China under Sun Yat Sen in 1911 disseminated a revolutionary fervor to overseas Chinese, including those in Singapore, and motivated the island's growing Chinese community to establish schools at an accelerating pace. Not only did the number of schools increase as a consequence of this ferment, but the products of such an education were better equipped for a life of activism in China than for a career in the British colony of Singapore. The strong China bias might be expected, since both textbooks and teachers for most of the schools were imported from China.

One effect of the political bent of the Chinese-language schools was to stimulate British authorities in the early 1920s to abandon their traditional laissez-faire, neutral attitude toward Chinese education. The government passed legislation ordering the registration of all schools, teachers, and members of school-management committees. Chinese-school personnel regarded such legislation as an insidious attempt to control Chinese-language education, so many of them resigned their positions and numbers of schools were forced to close for lack of staff. In what then appeared to be a move to soften the blow, grants-in-aid were made available to all Chinese schools beginning in 1923. Previously, such grants were given only to Chinese-language institutions run by Christian missionary groups. Despite the government offer, many Chinese-language schools refused the grants in order to maintain their independence from government supervision.

Singapore

By 1941, there were 370 Chinese registered schools in Singapore with a combined enrollment of about 38,000 pupils, of which about one-third were girls.

In sum, over the century leading to World War II, the Chinese-language schools were neglected by the British colonial government, so they had to depend upon the initiative of the non-English-oriented segment of the Chinese community for their support.

The Modern School System (1959–1979) – Goals and Structure

The foregoing brief history of the four language streams defines one of the two main problems of Singapore's present-day education system – that of integrating diverse schooling channels so as to produce increasing unity in the island-nation's society. The second main problem is to furnish the particular mixture of curricula and school levels that will provide the types of manpower needed for the economy and simultaneously satisfy the aspirations of the nation's citizens. We shall consider each of these problems or goals in turn.

PROMOTING POLITICAL AND CULTURAL UNITY

As British authorities in 1947 planned with Singaporeans toward the independence of Singapore over the next decade or so, they issued a Ten-Year Programme for Education Policy which set forth guidelines for future action: (*Ten-Year Programme,* 1949)
(1) There was to be universal, free primary education for six years.
(2) Education in Malay, Chinese, and Tamil schools was to continue in the mother tongue, with English as a second language.
(3) There would be freedom for parents to choose the kind of education they wanted for their children.
(4) The system of grants-in-aid was to continue for "mission" schools as well as for Chinese and Tamil schools. The registration of private schools would also continue as had been required prior to World War II.
(5) The administrative and professional staff of the Ministry of Education was to be expanded to improve supervision and inspection of all government and government-aided schools.

Along with the ten-year plan, a Supplementary Five-Year Plan was also implemented to accelerate the pace of educational development. The Supplementary Plan embodied measures that were intended to restore prewar schools as efficiently functioning institutions and to provide school places for the backlog of youths whose education was interrupted by the war. The Five-Year Plan also revived teacher-training programs, outlined the establishment of a Teachers' Training College, and improved salaries for teachers.

THE 1957 ALL-PARTY COMMITTEE ON CHINESE EDUCATION

Despite these provisions for improving educational opportunities, schooling in the early 1950s did not progress without difficulties. The post-war industrial unrest, growing unemployment, shortages of commodities, and inadequate housing all produced a political atmosphere ripe for exploitation by the Malayan Communist Party (MCP). During the wartime Japanese occupation of 1942–1945, the Party had acquired a high level of prestige for leading the armed resistance to occupation forces. Immediately after the war, the party established in Singapore and British Malaya a vast network of Communist-front organizations in the form of trade unions, cultural groups, cooperatives, and associations for women, farmers, students, and out-of-school youths. In 1948, following the outbreak of Communist-led violence in Malaya, the Party was banned by British colonial authorities. Many of the Communist-front organizations were closed down and their leaders arrested or banished to Kuomintang China. Other leaders went underground and reestablished the front organizations under new names.

Teachers and pupils in the Chinese schools were soon drawn into the conflict. In China, the status of the Kuomintang government was declining while the power and prestige of the Chinese Communist Party steadily increased. As a consequence, among many Singapore Chinese, pro-Communist sympathies grew. The Malayan Communist Party, from behind the scenes, took advantage of this increasingly sympathetic atmosphere to step up the activity of their front organizations. Before long, many Chinese language schools were controlled by underground MCP cadres that organized pupils to demonstrate against the colonial government and to foment political and industrial disorder under the pretext of promoting the struggle for independence from British imperialism. In 1955 and 1956, students and trade unionists played leading roles in riots that caused great loss of life and property.

Student participation in the riots was not simply irrational behavior. In other words, the student had not merely been duped into mass action by the underground MCP. Rather, the students had serious grievances of their own which the MCP exploited. In the mid-1950s the career prospects for graduates of Chinese-language schools were dismal. Not only was unemployment high in the private sector of the economy, but jobs with the government required a command of English which students from Chinese schools did not possess. In effect, students pictured themselves as supporters of agitation to overthrow a social order they considered manifestly unjust.

As a step toward correcting objectionable aspects of the colony's educational enterprise, a Legislative Assembly appointed an eight-member All-Party Committee on Chinese Education chaired by the minister of education. The Committee's terms of reference included the charge to prepare "recommendations for the improvement and strengthening of Chinese education and orderly progress toward self-government and ultimate independence." The Committee report in 1956, aimed at curing the deep malaise afflicting Chinese education, recommended:

(1) Equal treatment for all the four language streams in Malay, Chinese, Tamil, and English.

(2) Equality of grants, conditions of service and salary for all government and government-aided schools.

(3) Implementation of common curricula and subject syllabuses (including ethics) in all schools.

(4) Encouragement of the intermingling of students from the various language streams in the field of sports to build greater unity within the multiracial society.

(5) Introduction of bilingual education in primary schools and trilingual education in secondary schools. (*Report of the All-Party Committee,* 1956.)

To implement the recommendations, the Assembly passed the 1957 Education Ordinance that outlined a new set of school-registration, inspection, supervision, and financial-management procedures which, with a few revisions, continue in effect today. However, in the late 1950s implementation of the Ordinance proved difficult because of unending political unrest punctuated by riots, general strikes, the closure of schools caused by student sit-ins, and public demonstrations. (Clutterbuck, 1973.)

Not until the People's Action Party (PAP) took over firm control of the government in 1959 did a new decade of vigorous change take place in the education system. Under the PAP the goal of equality of opportunity was promoted by the erection of more public schools and the awarding of grants-in-aid to private schools so that by the latter 1960s free primary education was available for each child of school age. Universal elementary schooling had become a reality. New syllabuses in all basic school subjects were prepared for all four language streams. A uniform set of examinations in the four languages was developed for school leavers. The loan of free textbooks to pupils, a practice formerly found in only the English stream, was extended to all schools. Every new school was coeducational, with boys and girls attending the same classes and with women and men teachers on the same salary scales. At the same time, secondary-school facilities were expanded, with admission to secondary education based strictly on pupils' record of performance in elementary school and on the primary-school leaving examination. (Wong, 1974, pp. 8–10.)

THE SCHOOL SYSTEM UNDER STRAIN

To make good the 1959 election promise of free, universal primary education, the government embarked on an accelerated school building

TABLE 5.2
New Schools Constructed 1959–1967

	Government Schools	Government-Aided Schools	Total
Primary	57	27	84
Secondary	44	3	47
Total	101	30	131

(Source: *Age of School Buildings,* 1977, unpublished document, Ministry of Education, Singapore.)

TABLE 5.3
Primary and Secondary School Enrollment 1959–1978

Year	Enrollment	Year	Enrollment
1959	315,348	1969	514,862
1960	343,946	1970	509,258
1961	369,927	1971	511,458
1962	390,951	1972	516,119
1963	420,081	1973	518,393
1964	447,759	1974	511,993
1965	471,811	1975	504,625
1966	496,935	1976	494,257
1967	513,102	1977	484,535
1968	522,611	1978	476,913

(Source: *Trends in Education,* 1979, unpublished document, Ministry of Education, Singapore.)

program. In the nine years from 1959 through 1967, nearly 72 million dollars (Singapore $) were spent building 101 new government schools, and over three million dollars more were provided as grants to 30 government-aided schools for new buildings (Table 5.2).

Even this accelerated building program, however, could not cope with the increase in numbers brought about by the population boom of the late 1950s. For this reason, a double-session system was introduced to maximize the use of limited resources. This meant that a single school building was used by two sets of pupils. One set occupied the premises during the morning session from 7.30 to 12.55 p.m. Another set used the buildings in the afternoon from one o'clock until 6.30 p.m. Simultaneously, the government used its influence to induce the remaining privately run Chinese schools to accept grants-in-aid to improve their facilities and operation.

Patterns of enrollments illustrated in Table 5.3 show that the number of pupils accommodated in school between 1959 and 1968 grew by 20,000 to 30,000 a year until the goal of free, universal primary schooling had been achieved. Over the decade following the peak enrollment year of 1968, attendance declined nearly every year, due primarily to the successful family-planning campaign of the early 1960s that markedly reduced the nation's birthrate.

The vast increase in numbers of schools and pupils produced a crop of problems. One of the most serious was that of the uneven quality of

199

education between the best schools and the poorest ones. Some of the older government and mission schools which enjoyed good reputations continued to attract pupils from educationally and economically advantaged homes. These schools were staffed by more experienced, proven teachers than were the newly established ones which drew a large proportion of their pupils from families whose culture did not suit children well for succeeding in an academic program, whether the program was in English or in Mandarin Chinese. Many of the pupils in the newer schools were taught in languages they never heard at home. Most of Singapore's Chinese families have used one of the Southern China dialects in daily discourse — Hokkien, Teochew, Cantonese, or Hainanese. In school, the pupils would be taught Mandarin as a first language in the Chinese stream and as a second language in the English stream. Although there is some resemblance between Mandarin and the several dialects in terms of grammar and sentence structure, the pronunciation of words is entirely different. For such children, learning Mandarin was a sufficient challenge. But far more difficult was the task of learning English as well, since English was neither spoken nor even highly regarded in many homes. And the teachers of English in the newer Chinese-stream schools were often far from being masters of English. Under these conditions, only the most talented and dedicated children could progress satisfactorily.

The discrepancy between the higher-quality older schools and the lower-quality newer ones was more apparent at the secondary than at the primary level. Nevertheless, at both levels the difference in quality had a demoralizing effect on staff members, on pupils, and on parents in the less favored schools.

To staff the new primary schools, the government launched crash teacher-education programs. At the time that the Teachers' Training College was established in 1950, it had concentrated on offering full-time courses to produce teachers for the English-language schools. It succeeded rather well with this assignment over the first decade of its operation. However, in 1959 when the government pledged to furnish a suitable education for every child of primary-school age, it was obvious that training facilities would be needed for teachers of the Chinese, Malay, and Tamil streams as well. The Training College thus had to expand its facilities immediately to accommodate all the candidates needed to staff the new primary schools. Full-time courses were replaced by part-time courses, and a uniform curriculum was designed for teachers of all media. When the teacher-education students were not attending lectures at the College, they were gaining practical experience as staff members in the new primary schools. Hence, the strategy of part-time study and part-time work helped solve the teacher shortage by providing schools with the immediate services of teachers-in-training. However, officials responsible for the program concluded that the quality of instruction provided by such inexperienced, part-time candidates was lower than that furnished by experienced, full-time teachers. The quality of instruction for schools was further diluted by the fact that the Teachers' Training College had lowered its entrance standards in order to attract the large quantity of candidates which the primary-school staffing scheme required. Between 1960 and 1965, the student population at the Training College doubled from 2,500 to over 5,000.

During these years the College not only had to satisfy the demand for primary-school teachers but also had to meet the needs of an expanding secondary-school system. Students who held Higher School Certificates or university-degree qualifications were admitted for professional training as secondary-school instructors. In 1968, the College added a further program for training instructors to man the technical-education workshops in secondary schools.

In summary, the government's commitment to provide universal primary education and extensive secondary education after 1959 stimulated the nation's sole teacher-training institution to expand its enrollment in order to prepare teachers for all four language streams at both primary and secondary levels.

CULTURAL INTEGRATION

While the goals of furnishing universal six-year primary schooling and of equal opportunity for entering secondary schools on the basis of test scores were attained rather soon, the aim of achieving cultural unity has proved more difficult. A first step toward integrating the language streams in the 1960s consisted of locating two or three language groups in newly constructed schools, chiefly in government rather than government-aided schools. For example, the number of government secondary schools increased from 28 to 68 between 1960 and 1972. Of the 28 in 1960, only two were integrated (meaning the inclusion of more than one language stream), while by 1972 a total of 49 of the 68 schools were integrated. In effect, language-stream integration increased from 7 to 72 percent. In contrast, none of the 52 government-aided schools existing in 1960 was integrated, and only one of the 45 remaining government-aided schools in 1972 had adopted the multiple-language-stream plan. At the primary level no public or private schools had two language streams in 1960. By 1972, over 29 percent of the 197 government primary schools were integrated, while less than 3 percent of the 241 government-aided schools had more than one language stream. (*Trends in Education,* 1979.)

The intention of this school-integration program was not simply to house pupils of different ethnic backgrounds in the same building but to promote the government's bilingual policy which aimed at producing true cultural unity within the nation. The hope was that each student would become literate and orally fluent in at least two of the country's four official tongues – English, Malay, Tamil, and Chinese (Mandarin). In pursuing this policy, educational planners faced the problem of determining which combination of languages a pupil should seek to master. During the 1959–1965 period before Singapore separated from the Malaysian federation, bilingualism was to mean fluency in Malay plus one other language. Malay was to be the national language in Malaysia, so it would need to be the unifying language in Singapore as well. Throughout the 1960s and into the 1970s, Malay continued to be called the national language of Singapore. However, in actual practice it was not. Official business continued to be conducted chiefly in English within the government, and higher education at the University of Singapore (which had been called the University of Malaya in former times) was in English. Furthermore, the school-integration scheme which pressed for incorporating two or more language streams in each school usually took the form of English plus one of the other languages. Hence, schools would be English/ Chinese or English/Malay or English/Tamil. English provided the medium for interaction among the different ethnic groups and for Singapore's communication with the international community. The vernacular language of the child's ethnic origin provided the means of maintaining his cultural traditions.

The problems of implementing the bilingual policy have been considerable. The technique mentioned above for encouraging bilingualism — that of locating children from two language streams in the same school — has run into difficulties apparently not foreseen clearly by educational planners. Arumugam (1975, p. 64) reports that for the sake of convenience the pupils from the different streams have been located in separate sections of the school, thus making interaction among language groups difficult. A lack of fluency in more than one language on the part of staff members and students alike has inhibited communication among the language streams.

A further problem is that of producing fluency in a second language in the amount of time dedicated to second-language study. It is usually considered a demanding task to bring children up to an acceptable level of skill in one language. It is more than doubly difficult to educate the average student to an acceptable level in speaking and reading a second language that is studied simply as one subject among many in the curriculum. In effect, the lack of success pupils have experienced in pursuing a second language has been a considerable disappointment to the government.

It is true that the abler children have benefited from a full, concentrated program in English — enough to produce fluency — and at the same time have been able to study their own mother tongue as their second language. As a consequence, they have approximated the goal of true bilingualism by the end of secondary school. However, children who have been less apt and less motivated have not succeeded in the English stream and thus have failed to become literate in either English or their own vernacular.

Over the two decades of 1959–1979 there has been a consistent, strong tendency for parents to enroll more and more children in the English stream. Table 5.4 shows that in 1959 only 47 percent of children entering the first grade of the elementary school — the level called Primary One — were in the English stream, and nearly as many (46 percent) were in the Chinese stream. By 1979, the English stream enrolled 91 percent of all Primary One children, with only 9 percent in the Chinese stream and a negligible number in the Tamil and Malay language sections.

The distribution of students at both primary and secondary levels in 1976 is shown in Table 5.5. By that year, 74 percent of pupils in the primary grades were in the English stream, while 66 percent at the secon-

TABLE 5.4
Trends in Primary-One Enrollment 1959–1979

Year	Total Primary-One Enrollment	English Stream N	%	Chinese Stream N	%	Malay/Tamil Streams N	%
1959	59,362	28,118	47	27,223	46	4,021	7
1962	59,056	31,580	53	22,669	38	4,807	8
1965	59,130	36,269	61	17,735	30	5,126	9
1968	56,170	34,090	61	18,827	34	3,153	6
1971	54,177	37,505	69	15,731	29	941	2
1974	47,393	36,834	78	10,263	22	296	1
1977	47,325	40,622	86	6,590	14	113	—
1979	49,390	44,770	91	4,540	9	80	—

(Source: *Trends in Education*, 1979, unpublished document, Ministry of Education, Singapore.)

TABLE 5.5
Enrollment by Language Stream in Singapore Schools – 1976

Language Stream	Primary Students			Secondary Students		
	Boys	Girls	Total	Boys	Girls	Total
Government schools						
English stream	105,678	92,741	198,419	44,712	47,282	91,994
Chinese stream	6,492	5,634	12,126	16,849	13,511	30,360
Malay stream	1,055	1,512	2,567	1,736	4,058	5,794
Tamil stream	13	24	37			
Private schools with government aid						
English stream	17,867	18,211	36,078	11,263	13,195	24,458
Chinese stream	35,296	31,201	66,497	11,279	11,950	23,229
Tamil stream	101	148	249	134	201	335
Unaided private schools						
English stream	119	84	203	571	923	1,494
Chinese stream	57	32	89	187	141	328
Total	166,678	149,587	316,265	86,731	91,261	177,992

(Source: *Yearbook of Statistics*, 1977, pp. 195, 199.)

dary level studied English as their primary instructional language. But with the trends illustrated for Primary One enrollments by 1979 (Table 5.4), it is clear that in the 1980s and beyond, the main language streams other than English will be virtually wiped out.

As Table 5.5 also shows, there were more boys (53 percent) than girls (47 percent) in primary schools in 1976, but in the secondary schools girls (51 percent) were in slightly larger numbers than boys (49 percent). This shift apparently occurred as the result of more girls scoring higher than boys on the Primary School Leaving Examination that serves as the filter for entrance into secondary education.

The dramatic drift of pupils from the Chinese-stream schools to the English stream has been in response to the economic-development patterns of the nation over the past two decades. The success of the country's industrialization drive has created a demand for technologists and skilled workers. Educational institutions training such people conduct their courses in English. Over this same 20-year period, tourism has grown more important, and the language spoken by most tourists has been English. Thus the major hotels and other support services have used English as their language of business. Increasing external trade and the growing role of Singapore as a key financial center for Asia have further stimulated the need for employees fluent in English. And public administration continues to be carried out in English. Hence, parents have become more and more convinced that their children's vocational futures are heavily dependent on English-language competence, offering better career opportunities than will an education in Chinese, Malay, or Tamil.

While the rapidly increasing popularity of English-language schooling promises greater communication among ethnic groups in the future and likely promotes cultural unity, it has created some vexing problems for educational planners. The first problem is that the quality of learning in the English stream has decreased. Two surveys conducted by the Ministry of Education in 1975 showed that at least a third of the primary pupils in the English stream did not meet the minimum level of literacy set for their grade levels (*Attainment of Basic Numeracy and Literacy,* 1975, and *Ability of Primary 4 Pupils to Follow Oral and Written Instructions,* 1975). The decline in quality has been attributed to several factors. One is the lack of English language in the children's home environments. Another is the lowering of the quality of the average teacher in the English stream, a condition caused by the need to train so many new English-language instructors in so short a time. A third is the increase in class size, so that as many as 44 pupils are in a single class.

A second major problem is the fear of many Chinese parents that Chinese cultural values will be lost in the shift of so many pupils into the English-language stream. Parents are afraid that Chinese education will soon be a thing of the past, as all Chinese schools will likely close down for lack of pupils in the near future. Realizing the great cultural loss if the non-English-medium schools were to disappear altogether, the government in 1979 introduced two schemes to arrest the decline of enrollment in the better Chinese-medium track by raising the standard of English in them to meet parents' demand for a higher level of English instruction.

The first scheme is a preprimary program instituted in 67 Chinese-stream primary schools, a program which exposes pupils to equal amounts of English and Mandarin. In the year following the preprimary exposure, pupils are admitted to Primary One to follow both English and Chinese at the "first-language" level, that is, using both languages as the media for instruction. The intention is to give pupils the proficiency in English necessary for career advancement along with the exposure to Chinese language and culture that will enable them to maintain their ethnic traditions.

The second scheme consists of a special-assistance plan aimed at developing nine high-quality Chinese-stream secondary schools into bilingual institutions. Students use both English and Chinese as media of instruction. The assistance involves providing better teaching facilities and more proficient teachers as well as opportunities to attend regular classes part-time in English medium schools.

The response to the first scheme was more enthusiastic than the reaction to the second. Nearly all places in the preprimary program were filled, and plans were laid to expand the program as more teachers could be trained and facilities provided. But the reaction to the secondary-school special-assistance plan was more subdued. Pupils who scored in the top eight percent on the primary-school leaving examination were given the opportunity to enter the English-Chinese program. However, only half of those invited accepted the offer. While 90 percent of the eligible Chinese-medium candidates accepted, only 25 percent of the English-medium pupils chose to follow the program, apparently because their parents preferred to have them in a concentrated English stream. (Goh, 1979, pp. 2–4.)

In summary, recent years have witnessed a strong shift from Chinese, Malay, and Tamil medium schools into the English stream, with educational planners and parents concerned about the effect this shift will exert on maintaining the cultural roots of the ethnic groups that make up Singapore's multiracial mix. Language unity may soon be achieved, but probably at the expense of cultural traditions.

PRODUCING CAPABLE WORKERS

Singapore has been more successful than its ASEAN neighbors in suiting the pattern of the educational system to the manpower needs of the evolving industrial and commercial economy. This success has been achieved through close cooperation between the government and the private commercial sector.

The Singapore government in recent years has attempted a sophisticated, systematic method of determining future manpower needs and of orienting both schools and other educational institutions toward meeting these needs. Data for estimating manpower requirements are gathered by means of annual surveys of the labor force, of regular surveys of the stock of specific kinds of manpower, and of studies tracing the employment patterns of school leavers. Because educational planning and administration is highly centralized, and industry cooperates closely with government vocational-education programs, the government is able to alter the patterns of educational institutions in a relatively short time to match upcoming needs in the job market.

This use of manpower-requirement studies as the principal tool for fashioning the shape of Singapore's educational system is of quite recent origin, chiefly a product of the 1970s. Skolnik (1976, pp. 37–38) has concluded that:

> Although most Singaporeans agree with government as to the proper functions of the learning system, there is some fear that a technical determination of manpower and educational needs may lead to mistakes in policy that will be very costly in a nation with such a small labour force. Some would suggest that educational policy should be less deterministic, and more flexible and responsive to market signals. Others are simply uncertain of an approach that has only recently been attempted. In any case it is now too early to assess

the Singaporean experience with formalized manpower planning of the type discussed above.

In terms of manpower production, the role of the six-year primary school is to teach the basic skills of literacy and numeracy and to inculcate such work habits as diligence, promptness, and preciseness. At the end of Primary 6, pupils write four test papers in the Primary School Leaving Examination, papers treating the first language, the second language, mathematics, and science. In recent years (1975–1977), about 80 percent of the Primary 1 enrollees passed this examination six years later and moved into secondary school. (Goh, 1979, p. 6.)

During the first two years of secondary school, all pupils follow a common curriculum comprising academic subjects (first and second language, history, geography, science, mathematics) and either workshop practice or home economics. All boys enroll in technical drawing and workshop practice, while girls take either technical drawing and workshop or home economics.

During the next two years of secondary school, pupils follow a core curriculum comprised of the first language, the second language, mathematics, a science subject, an arts subject, and three electives. The electives can be subjects in the arts, science, commercial studies, or technical studies. At the end of the fourth year of secondary school, students sit for the Cambridge General Certificate of Education "O" Level Examination. Those who score high can enter the preuniversity course, at the end of which they sit for the Cambridge "A" Level Examination which is the chief filter for admission to the universities. Other pupils who have passed the "O" levels may enter Singapore Polytechnic, Ngee Ann Technical College, and the Institute of Education, to pursue certificate and diploma courses.

Pupils who drop out of the school system below the tertiary level may avail themselves of opportunities in the nonformal-education sector.

The Contributions of Nonformal Education

In contrast to the formal school system, Singapore's educational structure features a variety of nonformal programs aimed chiefly at training the labor force required for the island-state's progress. By *non-*

formal we mean such learning arrangements as apprenticeship training, on-the-job training, evening and weekend classes, and instruction via radio and television. Many of the country's nonformal programs are at the post-secondary level and thus are not of central concern in this chapter. However, others are attended by students who have not completed secondary education and hence properly fall within our purview.

The most important sponsor of nonformal learning has been the Vocational and Industrial Training Board, a body recently formed by the amalgamation of the Industrial Training Board and the Adult Education Board. The two sectors of the Board's program that are of greatest significance for manpower production among primary-school leavers are those offering general education and vocational preparation.

The general-education courses are the equivalents of those in the formal secondary-school and preuniversity system, designed for pupils who either failed school-leaving examinations or dropped out of secondary school before earning a certificate. Completing these courses entitles pupils to sit for "O" and "A" level examinations and, upon passing the examinations, to receive formal certification. Thus, the Board provides an alternate route to higher education for people who have not made it through the formal secondary system. Other courses, for example, language studies and further-education classes (such as Chinese cooking), are also available. In 1977, nearly 12,000 pupils were enrolled in general-education classes, while another 17,000 were in language studies, further-education classes, and auto-driving courses. (*Annual Report, 1977–78, Adult Education Board,* 1978.)

The vocational-preparation courses sponsored by the Board range from artisan classes in such areas as bricklaying and plastering to offerings in such highly skilled fields as applied electronics. Commercial courses in bookkeeping and typing and ones in auto maintenance are also available. Some courses are part of the Board's permanent offerings. Others are organized on a one-time basis at the request of an industrial or commercial organization that wishes to upgrade the skills of a segment of its personnel, such as bus or truck drivers or beauty-shop operators. By 1977, the Industrial Training Board, prior to its integration with the Adult Education Board, offered vocational studies to over 11,000 pupils. (*Annual Report, 1977–78, Industrial Training Board,* 1978.) In the same year, the Adult Education Board was organizing commercial and technical courses for nearly 12,000 pupils. (*Annual Report, 1977–78, Adult Education Board,* 1978.)

Vocational studies at a less advanced level are sponsored by the People's Association, an adjunct of the government that conducts social-service activities at centers throughout the city. In the mid-1970s, over 7,000 Singapore citizens attended these nonformal education courses in electronics repair, dressmaking, carpentry, and similar skills.

A variety of other nonformal vocational programs is offered by labor unions and industrial groups, especially courses focusing on skills specific to particular jobs and that upgrade workers' present skills.

In all of these endeavors, close coordination is maintained through the Ministry of Education between formal and nonformal programs, enabling Singapore to relate the education system more closely to the world-of-work than is true in any of the other ASEAN countries.

Administrative Efficiency

It should be apparent from our discussion so far that Singapore has been remarkably successful in pursuing its educational goals. Universal primary schooling was achieved before the close of the 1960s, even under the awkward condition of requiring four separate sets of curricula and teaching staffs to serve the four language streams. Furthermore, opportunities for secondary schooling were extended to far more pupils. For example, enrollment in secondary education increased by 35 percent between 1966 and 1976 (from 132,088 to 177,992). With these successes in meeting quantitative goals in the 1960s, the nation's educational planners could focus attention in the 1970s on improving the quality of education in both the formal and nonformal sectors.

Much of this success was due to administrative efficiency, which itself was the result of several key factors. One obvious factor is the size of the nation. As noted earlier, Singapore is the smallest in population and most compact in area of the ASEAN countries. Data needed for wise planning are relatively easy to collect, and communication to all parts of the island-state is quick and sure. A second factor is the stability of the government. The People's Action Party has been able to maintain tight control of the government for two decades, with its position virtually uncontested after the early 1960s. The Party's community-service centers throughout the city function as listening posts to inform the leadership of the people's moods and needs and also to act as agencies through which individuals' wants can be served. When the government has adopted a policy, it has been able to move with a sure hand to carry the policy into action.

An example of the administrative implementation of such policy is the nation's family-planning program. In 1966, the government set up the Family Planning and Population Board which was charged with responsibility for conducting a vigorous population-education and family-services program enabling the nation to achieve a stable zero-population growth within the foreseeable future. With the motto "Girl or boy, two is enough", the Board sponsored a widespread publicity campaign, offered sterilization services to parents, provided for legalized abortions, furnished family-planning counseling to a large number of mothers and fathers, and raised taxes of parents who produced large families. The more children, the higher the tax. Through these measures, the nation reduced its annual growth rate between 1965 and 1970 from 2.5 to 1.8 percent, and by 1977 it was down to 1.2 percent. (*Eleventh Annual Report,* 1976, p. 6.) By the latter 1970s, these measures had affected the primary school population by reducing the number of children of primary-school age by about 15 percent. (*Yearbook of Statistics,* 1978, p. 194.) Hence, with a smaller number of pupils to serve, the school system required a smaller operating budget at the primary level and could reroute funds and energies to improving the quality of instruction and to expanding secondary schools.

The government's arm for coordinating all sectors of the nationwide learning system, public and private, is the Ministry of Education. It is headed by a minister, who is the body's main political figure, and staffed by division directors and their professional personnel who are the career educators that make the system run smoothly. The Ministry traces its origin back to 1872 when a colonial Department of Education was established for the Straits Settlements. It was converted from a Department to a Ministry in 1956. However, its basic role as the central controlling agency for all of education has remained the same over the decades. From time to time, the administrative framework of the Ministry has been altered to suit the envisioned direction of the city-state in coming years.

For instance, in 1968 the Ministry was divided into two major departments, one in charge of general education and the other responsible for
technical and vocational education. This reorganization gave additional
stress to developing the sorts of manpower training programs that would
serve the needs of the changing economy quickly and precisely.

To bolster its expertise, the Ministry frequently sets up special committees whose members are selected not only from the Ministry's own
staff but also from the schools, the country's higher-education institutions, other governmental bodies, and the private industrial and commercial sectors. Like the broader Singapore government, the Ministry has
sought to keep up with the times in terms of utilizing modern technology,
such as computers, and organizational practices, such as systems approaches,
in performing its work.

Approaches to Curriculum Development

While such nations as Indonesia and Malaysia have assigned curriculum
development to a permanent agency in the Ministry, in Singapore curriculum planning has been conducted chiefly through committees appointed
periodically for the task. Two successive committees in the 1960s reorganized syllabuses in the various subject-matter areas so they were uniform
for the four language streams, and they reviewed the contents of textbooks adopted in the schools. However, according to Wong (1974, p. 43)
the sort of analysis that might result in fundamental improvement in
instruction was not performed.

> The actual "development" of the content took the form of a listing of topics
> considered to be suitable for teaching in local classrooms. The preliminary
> work of examining and analysing various objectives of teaching and learning
> was generally lacking. Where a set of objectives was given, the operational
> definitions were either unannounced or unclear.

To increase the effectiveness of curriculum development, the Minister
of Education in 1970 constituted a new Advisory Committee on Curriculum
Development which met once a month to deliberate on all issues related to
the current curricula and formulate plans for improvements. The Committee served as an overseer and policy guide to subcommittees working
in such subject-matter fields as mathematics, science, beginning reading,

213

and others. Projects initiated or supported by the Committee drew their participants from a wide range of personnel outside the Ministry, such as school principals, teachers, and subject-matter experts at the university level. Seminars and workshops for principals and teachers were conducted at the implementation stage of a new curriculum project, guided by the motto: "If everyone, parents and children, administrators and teachers have a share in the educational enterprise, the gains will be better assured." (Wong, 1974, p. 49.)

This mode of broad-scale participation of people in curriculum improvement, in contrast to the limited approach of syllabuses and textbook revision by small groups in the 1960s, encountered numerous difficulties in implementation. But by the mid-1970s it was judged informally to be an improvement over past approaches. (Wong, 1974, p. 53.)

Teacher Education

During British colonial times each of the four language streams had its own source of teachers. For a half century after the founding of Singapore, teachers for the Malay stream were recruited from among the Islamic Hajis who were experienced in teaching the Koran in the village mosques and prayer houses. Then, in 1878, the colonial Department of Education converted the Malay High School in Singapore into a training college for Malay teachers. The English stream drew teachers from among the mission workers who sponsored many of the English schools. From time to time in the early 1900s attempts were made to start an English teachers college for men in Singapore, but there were too few applicants to make the project feasible. In 1928, when Raffles College was established, it served as the source of graduate English teachers until the University of Malaya in Singapore was opened in 1948. Most teachers for Tamil schools were imported from India. Chinese teachers in the main were recruited from China, though some instructors for the primary grades were trained in Normal Classes affiliated with Chinese-language high schools in Singapore. (Wong and Gwee, 1972, pp. 12–14.)

From the 1950s into the 1970s, the official bodies responsible for teacher education in Singapore were the University of Malaya (now known as the University of Singapore) in its School of Education and the Ministry's

Teachers' Training College, both started in 1950. The University offered a one-year diploma course to students who already held a university degree in a subject-matter discipline. Until the latter 1960s, the Training College offered programs for both primary and secondary teachers, mostly on a part-time, inservice basis because the pressures of furnishing enough teachers to achieve universal-schooling goals were too great to free most candidates for full-time preservice study.

Dissatisfaction with the bifurcated nature of teacher education caused the government in April 1973 to establish the Institute of Education, incorporating the responsibilities previously assigned to both the University and Training College. Since that date all teacher education and a substantial amount of the research and development activities associated with teaching have been centered in the Institute. With the reduction in the number of teachers needed under a low population-growth-rate, the Institute has focused its efforts on the improvement of the quality of teaching rather than graduating large quantities of teachers. This has meant raising standards of preservice training and conducting intensive programs of inservice upgrading. In terms of standards, applicants for the Certificate of Education program that qualifies them as primary-grade teachers must now have passed "A" Level examinations from the Higher Secondary School in order to gain admission. In earlier years, a lower level of educational preparation was acceptable. Applicants for the Diploma in Education course must hold a university degree. Those applying for post-graduate study must hold advanced diplomas.

To promote educational experimentation and the demonstration of new teaching methods, the Institute has adopted a series of experimental schools throughout the city. These are primary and secondary schools typical of those in the island-state, but they serve as centers of research and innovation.

The sort of modern approaches to teacher education practiced by the Institute staff can be illustrated with an inservice course in evaluation designed to improve the skills in assessing pupils' progress of more than 3,000 primary-school teachers. The six-month course was offered each semester over the period 1975–1978.

> In order to train such large numbers, a team-teaching approach using closed-circuit television is used to transmit 12 key video-taped lectures. These lecture sessions are followed up with weekly workshops which provide the oppor-

tunity for discussion and clarification of difficult concepts and for learning by doing. The workshop sessions are conducted in Chinese, English, Malay, and Tamil to cater to the teachers of the four languages. (Chin, 1976, pp. 239–240.)

Thus, teacher education in Singapore today features sophisticated instructional techniques that focus on the preparation of a limited number of highly skilled teachers rather than on large numbers of less-qualified instructors to meet the needs of a rapidly expanding school population, as is the case in the larger ASEAN countries.

Problems and Prospects for the Future

The education system conducted over the 1959–1979 period was essentially a system designed for the brightest pupils. For example, secondary pupils were expected to sit for the Cambridge General Certificate of Education "O" Level Examination after only four years of secondary schooling compared to five years taken by students in Britain. Yet all pupils, regardless of their ability, were expected to learn at this fast pace. Although in theory the weaker pupils could be retained at any grade level if they failed to achieve minimum standards, in practice teachers were reluctant to hold pupils back. Many of the weaker pupils were given virtually automatic promotion to the next higher level regardless of their lack of skill in coping with the present grade's work. The result was that many pupils advanced up the academic ladder, understanding less and less at each level until they either dropped out on reaching maximum schooling age or else they failed the terminal examination.

Pupils also faced the additional burden of trying to master two languages, neither of which was their native tongue. By 1979, nearly all pupils were in English-stream or Chinese-stream schools. However, over 85 percent of them spoke neither English nor Mandarin at home. (Goh Keng Swee, 1979, p. 1:1.) As a result, many could neither read nor write either language. Over 60 percent who sat for the two language tests in the common examinations at the end of primary and secondary schooling failed one or both tests. The Ministry of Defense reported that many young men enlisted in the Singapore Armed Forces were unable to communicate in either English or Mandarin, despite eight years of schooling. (Goh, 1979, pp. 3–4.)

TABLE 5.6
Enrollment Attrition Rate 1978

School level	Entered	Percentage of age group that	
		Dropped out or failed final exam	Graduated but did not continue to higher level
Primary (6 yrs)	100	29	0
Junior Secondary (4 yrs)	71	36	21
Senior Secondary (2 yrs)			
(Pre-University Course)	14	5	4
Tertiary	9	–	–

(Source: Goh Keng Swee, *Report on the Ministry of Education, 1978*, Ministry of Education, 1979, Singapore.)

In an attempt to remedy the problem of pupil failure in the primary school, the government in 1977 introduced a basic course for pupils who had failed in the primary grades at least three times. The objective was to arm them with some literacy and numeracy before they sought employment as unskilled or semiskilled workers. However, since the level of literacy designed for such pupils was quite low, the participants in the program quickly regressed to illiteracy after leaving the course. Even further courses for these pupils to parallel employment in the job market did little to improve their literacy.

The strain imposed on pupils in Singapore's single-track system of education, requiring the study of two "foreign" languages at a fast pace, resulted in the high attrition rates reflected in Table 5.6.

In an effort to identify reasons for problems in the education system and to suggest solutions, Prime Minister Lee Kuan Yew in August 1978 asked the Deputy Prime Minister, Goh Keng Swee, to lead a team assigned to study the current condition of the nation's schooling enterprise. Seven months later the team issued its *Report on the Ministry of Education, 1978*, highlighting the problems discussed above and recommending a new system for primary and secondary schooling. (Goh, 1979.)

The old single-track system of primary education is being replaced by three subtracks catering to pupils of different ability levels. Above-average pupils who can pass the Primary School Leaving Examination without having failed any year in the primary school course are placed in the bilingual stream. They study both English and their mother tongue (Malay,

Chinese, or Tamil) on a first-language basis and sit for the Primary School Leaving Examination at the end of six years of primary education. In the course of their education, they may study a third language as well.

Average pupils are ones who will pass the Primary School Leaving Examination, but only after seven or eight years of primary education in the "extended bilingual stream". They follow the same syllabuses as the above-average students, doing English and their mother tongue. However, the pace in the extended stream is slower than that in the above-average stream.

Educational planners now consider "bilingualism" for the weakest pupils to mean virtual illiteracy in both languages. Pupils not academically inclined but potentially successful in vocational courses are channeled into a monolingual stream, concentrating on one language (written and spoken) and offering only some oral skills in a second language. Those pupils from Chinese-dialect homes learn Mandarin plus some oral English. Those from English-speaking homes or Malay or Tamil families learn English and some oral skills in their mother tongue. At the end of eight years of primary education, these pupils join the Vocational and Industrial Training Board's program for vocational preparation.

In the primary grades, children are not placed in ability streams until after three or four years of school, that is, until after·a careful assessment of their likely potential has been made. To permit any errors in channeling to be corrected and to allow late developers to take advantage of their potential, lateral transfers between the subtracks are allowed. Pupils who have done especially well in a stream can be promoted to a more demanding one, and those who suffer difficulties in a more advanced stream can be transfered to a slower one.

At the secondary-school level, pupils are located in separate streams chiefly on the basis of their scores on the Primary School Leaving Examination. The brightest are placed in a four-year Special Bilingual Stream where they study English and their mother tongue on a first-language level. Such pupils should be able to pass their Cambridge "O" Level Examination after four years, then pass the "A" Level Examination after two more.

Above-average pupils are channeled into the Normal Bilingual Stream where they study English as a first language and the mother-tongue as a second. They are expected to finish secondary schooling in four years and pass their Cambridge "A" Level Examination after another two or three years.

Average pupils, unable to pass the Cambridge "O" Level Examination at the end of four years, are permitted to take five years before sitting for the test.

In response to critics who claim such multiple-stream plans are unkind and undemocratic, the study team that devised the new system has written: (Goh, 1979)

> Educationists and others who oppose streaming of children according to their ability to absorb instruction often forget that the final result could be even more cruel to the children who do not make the grade and suffer repeated failures. The end product would have lost self-confidence, self-esteem, and developed a host of character defects produced by feelings of inadequacy. It is far better that these children leave school literate in one language. Since they are not exposed to competition from brighter children in classes, there is less danger of loss of self-esteem.

In addition to providing multiple learning tracks, the new system places strong emphasis on moral education. Unlike the practice of the 1970s, when the study of civics and ethics concentrated on information and exhortation, the new approach stresses the teaching of simple moral precepts through stories of great men, folk tales, and legends.

The foregoing plan, then, is the program inaugurated in primary schools in 1979 and in secondary schools in 1980.

As for the future, we would estimate that no marked changes in the nation's political-economic development are in the offing, so it is likely that the goals of achieving greater social unity and a proper balance of manpower production will continue to be paramount as guidelines for educational planners.

The chief barrier in Singapore to social and cultural unity continues to be language diversity. Until Singaporeans can all communicate with each other directly within both work and social settings, they are still likely to feel estranged from ethnic groups other than their own. Hence, the coming decades will witness further efforts to ensure that everyone gains a working knowledge of a common language, with the most reasonable choice being English rather than Malay, which was the language adopted as the national tongue when Singapore was still in the Malaysian federation in the early 1960s. The nation can also be expected to continue subscribing to bilingualism. Not only should all citizens command a language in common, but each one should be fluent in the traditional tongue of his ethnic group. The logical instruments for promoting national unity through a common language will continue to be integrated schools, extra-curricular activities in the areas of athletics and social events, and the nation's mass-communication media — television, radio, and the press.

The new multiple-stream learning program introduced in 1979 is intended to reduce educational wastage that occurs when pupils are placed in school programs unsuited to their talents and interests, wastage marked by disappointment for the learners and by improper preparation of the workers required for efficient functioning of the society. The government views the new system as only the first of many needed improvements. One of the most pressing current problems is that of raising the quality of teachers, particularly language teachers. Recruiting large numbers of talented teachers in a society that already has full employment and many job opportunities for people of skill is proving to be a most difficult task. Other problems are those of improving the system of curriculum development, of enabling children from one ability stream to transfer into a more appropriate stream if their performance warrants transfer, and of maintaining valued aspects of traditional ethnic cultures in face of the drive for national unity.

Educational planners in Singapore face these assignments while, at the same time, concerning themselves in the SEAMEO structure with helping ASEAN neighbors achieve some of the schooling gains attained by Singapore over the past two decades.

References

Ability of Primary-Four Pupils to Follow Oral and Written Instruction (1975) unpublished report, Ministry of Education, Singapore.
Age of School Buildings (1977) unpublished report, Ministry of Education, Singapore.
Annual Report, 1977–78, Adult Education Board (1978) Adult Education Board, Singapore.
Annual Report, 1977–78, Industrial Training Board (1978) Industrial Training Board, Singapore.
Annual Report, July 1974–July 1975 (1975) Institute of Education, Singapore.
Annual Report 1977/78, Ministry of National Development (1978) Ministry of National Development, Singapore.
ARUMUGAM, RAJA SEGARAN (1975) "Education and Integration in Singapore" in Wu Teh-yao (ed.) *Political and Social Change in Singapore,* Institute of Southeast Asian Studies, Singapore.

Attainment of Basic Numeracy and Literacy (1975) unpublished report, Ministry of Education, Singapore.

BUCHANAN, IAIN (1972) *Singapore in Southeast Asia,* Bell, London.

CHIN LONG FAY (1976) "Innovations in Teacher Education" in *Exploring New Directions in Teacher Education,* UNESCO Regional Office for Education in Asia, Bangkok.

CLUTTERBUCK, RICHARD, (1973) *Riot and Revolution in Singapore and Malaya 1945–1963,* Faber & Faber, London.

DORAISAMY, T. R. (ed.) (1969) *150 Years of Education in Singapore,* Teacher Training College, Singapore.

Education in Singapore (1972) 2nd edition, Ministry of Education, Singapore.

Educational Building and Facilities in the Asian Region (1976) Unesco Regional Office in Asia, Bulletin 17, Bangkok.

Eleventh Annual Report (1976) Family Planning and Population Board, Singapore.

Europa Year Book (1977) Europa Publication, London.

GOH KENG SWEE (1979) *Report on the Ministry of Education, 1978,* Ministry of Education, Singapore.

Population Projections for Singapore 1970–2070 (1974) National Statistical Commission, Singapore.

Prospectus 1977 (1977) Institute of Education, Singapore.

Report of the All-Party Committee of the Singapore Legislative Assembly on Chinese Education (1956) Government Printer, Singapore.

SINGH, P. HARBANS (1975) *Centralized Workshops in Singapore,* UNESCO Regional Office in Asia, Bangkok.

SKOLNIK, RICHARD L. (1976) *The Nation-wide Learning System of Singapore,* Institute of Southeast Asian Studies, Singapore.

Statistical Yearbook – Unesco, 1976 (1977) UNESCO, Paris.

Teacher Education in Singapore (1974) Institute of Education, Singapore.

Ten-Year Programme – Data and Interim Proposals (1949) Department of Education, Singapore.

WEINTRAUB, PETER (December 1978) Growth Prospects Judged to Be 'More Than Fair', *International Herald Tribune,* Paris.

WONG, FRANCIS H. K. and GWEE YEE HEAN (1972) *The Development of Education in Malaysia and Singapore,* Heinemann, Kuala Lumpur.

WONG, RUTH H. K. (1974) *Educational Innovation in Singapore,* UNESCO, Paris.

Yearbook of Statistics, Singapore, 1976/1977 (1977) Department of Statistics, Singapore.

Yearbook of Statistics, Singapore, 1977/1978 (1978) Department of Statistics, Singapore.

Map 6 Thailand

Meua Noi Rian Wicha,
Hai Ha Sin Meua Yai

Earn knowledge when young.
Earn wealth when grown.
THAI PROVERB

6

Thailand

Chalio Buripakdi and Pratern Mahakhan

FROM ancient times until the recent past, the chief purpose of education in Thailand has been to study the virtuous life and how to attain
it. Such an education has involved teaching youths to read and write
and how to shape their characters according to Buddhist moral precepts.
However, in a series of five-year national-development programs that have
guided the nation's destiny over the past two decades, a new prime purpose has been fashioned. This new aim pictures education as a key instrument for achieving socioeconomic and political progress in a complex
modern world. Thus Thailand's educational planners face the task of
reforming educational practices in a way that suits both national-
development goals and the traditions of a society which has prized good-
ness over material wealth and has regarded knowledge as a desirable end
in itself rather than as a vocational tool.

To understand the assignment confronting Thai educators, one first
should know something of the land and the people, of the economy, the
dominant religion, social-class structure, and traditional attitudes toward
life. These are the matters we review in some detail before considering
the history of the education system, its current condition, and problems
that will engage educational planners in the years ahead.

223

Land of the Free

Thailand — a word meaning "land of the free" — occupies an area of 514,000 square kilometers. It is shaped like an axe with a long handle, that extends down the peninsula to Malaysia. On the northeast the Mae Khong River separates Thailand from Laos. On the northwest a mountain range separates it from Burma. Across the southeast border is Kampuchea (Cambodia). The country extends from north to south 1,000 miles and east to west 500 miles, all within the tropical zone.

Geographically, the country is divided into four regions: Northern Thailand is mountainous with fertile valleys and plains suitable for growing rice and teak. Central Thailand is located in the fertile Chao Phraya basin and it is here that Bangkok (meaning 'city of angels') the capital is situated. The northeastern region is the driest part. Its long dry season and relatively scarce rainfall make it the least productive region in the country and the least modernized. Southern Thailand is moist and produces rubber, tropical crops, and tin.

In 1978, Thailand's population was about 44 millions, of which 80 percent live in rural areas. The crude birth rate is approximately 33 per thousand and the crude death rate is 9 per thousand, giving a population growth rate of 2.4 percent per year. At this rate, Thailand's population will double every thirty years, which poses a major problem for primary and secondary education.

The high birth rate can be traced back to the policy of earlier years when the size of the military force was the security of the nation. In 1911, the population of Thailand stood at about 8 million; with its natural resources, it was felt that the country should be able to accommodate a five- or even six-fold increase. As late as 1956, bonuses were still offered for large families (twelve children). In 1960, the national census indicated that the average family had five to six children. As a result of recommendations by groups of social scientists in Thailand and from international organizations, a new population policy was promulgated by the Government in March, 1970: (Sa-ngad Plenvanich, 1970, p. 87)

> The Thai government has the policy of supporting voluntary family planning in order to resolve various problems associated with the high rate of population growth, which constitutes an important obstacle to the socio-economic development of the nation.

TABLE 6.1
Estimated Population of Thailand in 1970, 1977, 1981
(in thousands)

Age Group	1970		1977		1981	
	Male	Female	Male	Female	Male	Female
0–4	3,243	3,113	3,428	3,309	3,357	3,237
5–9	2,746	3,664	3,257	3,145	3,349	3,242
10–14	2,316	2,235	2,904	2,805	3,179	3,068
15–19	2,003	1,935	2,450	2,377	2,787	2,701
20–24	1,702	1,631	2,071	2,002	2,334	2,266
25–29	1,279	1,248	1,772	1,712	1,981	1,922
30–34	985	1,013	1,418	1,371	1,685	1,627
35–39	892	935	1,049	1,055	1,305	1,271
40–44	770	798	867	913	972	994
45–49	649	676	776	821	827	880
50–54	493	518	644	680	715	764
55–59	402	428	498	538	577	624
60–64	303	327	366	404	421	469
65–69	215	241	269	306	298	345
70–upward	253	357	356	476	422	560
Total	18,251	18,119	22,125	21,914	24,209	23,970

(Source: Ministry of Education)

By the end of the 1970s there was evidence that the birth rate would be likely to decline, primarily because of the economic constraints of raising a large family. (Burpakdi, 1977, pp. 59–63.) Even with such a decline, the children already born and entering school are placing a great burden on the education budget. Table 6.1 presents a breakdown by age groups of the population of Thailand for the years 1970, 1977, and 1981. The high proportion of school-age children can be seen. A calculation shows that the education budget for the year 1980 will be 12,644 million baht, and in 1990 this will be 26,889 million baht, all at the fixed baht value (approximately 20 baht to 1 US$). Note that in 1970 the budget was only 4,604 million baht.

Several ethnic groups form the total population. The largest ethnic group, over 80 percent of the population, are Thais and Thai–Laos subgroups who are said to have migrated from southern China. The significant minority ethnic groups in Thailand are Chinese, Thai–Malay, and Vietnamese. The Chinese, comprising about 10 percent of the country's population, play an important role in Thailand's economy, especially in the commercial sector. The Chinese and the Thais are similar in many respects. The differences are in religion, customs, and language. If a Chinese masters the Thai language, and adopts a Thai name, he can become a Thai citizen. This is a common way for the Chinese to acquire his status in society. The Thai—Malays, a smaller group of about 4 percent, are mainly in the four southern provinces of Thailand. This group considers itself culturally akin to the Malay in Malaysia and holds to the religion of Islam. Different from the Chinese, the Thai—Malay in general prefers agriculture to commerce. The Vietnamese are refugees from their homeland and are mainly in the northeastern part of the country and in Chantaburi province. Other than these four major groups, there is a mere sprinkling of Cambodians, Indians, Pakistanis, and small tribal groups.

Buddhism is the national religion of Thailand. It is tremendously influential in ceremonies and all aspects of life. As of 1977, there were about 25,702 Buddhist monasteries in the country. Approximately 94 percent of Thais are Buddhist. The other religions are the Chinese religion, Islam, Christianity, and Hinduism.

Ethnic differences pose some practical problems for education but not serious ones. The fact that there is no segregation in schools cuts down most of the possible dissatisfaction concerning educational opportunity. Furthermore, there is also the legal provision that private schools may be run using a special curriculum provided by the Ministry of Education. The only problem felt in this aspect of ethnicity has to do with the comparability of standards and types of knowledge the pupils receive in each type of school.

The private schools are the Chinese schools and the Moslem schools or "pondoks". These are decreasing in number and may diminish in the future in favor of the official type of formal school.

SOCIOECONOMIC BACKGROUND

Thailand is basically an agricultural country of small villages growing rice, rubber, coconuts, and a variety of other crops. Thailand today is engaged in a steady process of diversifying its economy, advancing with increasing rapidity from a base of subsistence farming to a market economy with a growing capital-intensive sector. In comparison with other countries in the region, it has set out on this road with considerable advantages. While it has from time to time been obliged to struggle for its independence, Thailand is the only country in the region which has never known foreign rule. Despite provincial and other differences, it has maintained a fundamental but unaggressive sense of national identity and unity. By Asian standards, it has been relatively prosperous, with land and the current rate of economic growth sufficient to support its substantial population increase without great problems. But, as the following résumé will imply, Thailand will have to have social reorganization and reorientation in order to achieve and maintain significant material progress. Apart from efforts to ensure an appropriately trained supply of manpower for development and to take the slack out of underemployment in the agricultural sector, great care will be needed to prevent social change from exercising disintegrating pressures, and in the adaptation of positive values from the traditional culture to the needs of modern society. How far this can be done will, in large measure, depend on the evolving pattern and equality of education.

About 80 percent of the population is engaged in agricultural occupations, and lives in the village. Of the rest, 10 percent in Bangkok and about 10 percent resides in other towns with more than 5,000 inhabitants. Within as well as between these two sectors are a number of marked contrasts.

Bangkok, which includes Thonburi, is the only metropolitan area in Thailand, with about 10 percent of the population or 4.4 million people. The educated elite, many of whom have studied in the West, are concentrated here; the others residing in provincial capitals and district towns are mostly in government service and generally regard themselves as representatives (in exile) of the high society of Bangkok as well as of the central government. Most of the major educational institutions and industrial enterprises are concentrated in Bangkok. The striking contrasts of wealth and poverty seen in Bangkok are not evident in other towns. While there is a big gulf separating the life of the upper classes of Bangkok from even the life in villages very near Bangkok, upper-class members in other urban areas are much like their village brethren in the simplicity of their ways and wants. What sets the town apart from the surrounding villages is the presence of government officials who generally lead a life apart from the rest of the townpeople.

While Bangkok has influenced the pattern of society in towns, it is far more stratified, with its aristocracy, high government officials, business executives and the most successful of the professional people forming the summit of the society. The Chinese, whose concentration is in Bangkok, are fully accepted at this level in their role of businessmen, and it is not unusual for aristocrats to enter joint enterprises with them. High officials who are responsible for the security of the country consider this a reason for maintaining full control of the Chinese in Thailand who otherwise would form antigovernment power groups. However, in the middle class (constituting some 50 percent of the inhabitants in Bangkok) in which the Thais are mainly lower government officials and professional people, and the Chinese are merchants and small businessmen, there is little contact between the two groups. The lower middle class is comprised largely of craftsmen and skilled workers (mostly Chinese) and the lower ranks of government employees (mostly Thai); the rest of the population is composed of vendors, unskilled laborers, and domestic servants.

Government service, which in the days of absolute monarchy used to be the only means of entering the upper-status group for people not of noble birth, continues to exert a special attraction. In Bangkok, over 25 percent of the employed labor force is engaged in government service at various levels, including appointments at universities and schools.

In rural areas, the basic social structure and pattern of life varies little, but there are considerable differences in the standards of living, ranging from the rich central plain, the rubber plantations, and the tin-mining area of the southern peninsula, to the dry northeastern region. In the first two areas, the impact of the market economy and the growth of an acquisitive social order may be noted. Nevertheless, by and large, rural communities still remain remarkably free of a hierarchical class system. Generally, Thai farmers place little value on material goods beyond meeting the immediate needs of the family. Merit making (known as *tam-boon*) is considered high in their value system. This is done by giving goods and necessities, particularly to monks in the temples (*wats*), but also to other needy persons or animals. Merit can also be made by going to the temple on religious days and listening to the preaching of priests.*

*The concept of merit or "boon" may be interpreted as a good personality quality accumulated by individuals through thinking or saying or acting in a "good direction". Thus, listening to preaching and thinking about it is one way of merit making.

The spiritual aspect of life, which includes traits such as kindness, wisdom, broad-mindedness, and freedom of mind, is regarded as more important than physical material comforts.

Over 87 percent of the agricultural families own their own land, averaging about six acres (less than 10 percent own 84 acres or more) and live in hamlets (*muban*) of 100 to 150 households, which generally form part of larger village communities (*tambon*) of about 3,000 individuals. The family unit, too, is small, as couples usually establish their own household. This is often part of a larger family compound, and ties of kinship are strongly felt. Village life centers around the temples and religious festivals, while deference is shown to all elders and to officials as symbols of authority. The highest respect goes to the Buddhist monks, regarded as the most meritorious and power-embodied as well as the wisest members of the community. Possessing large land holdings and other marks of wealth do not confer a high status as such, except insofar as they may be felt to have resulted from merit earned earlier in the present life or in previous lives, and therefore a symbol of virtue. The villager is generally indifferent to social disparity even if it exists around him, and at most he employs the technique of evasion to avoid its undesirable effect on him. Individualism is high, which is a quality that often accompanies indifference and evasion. Such a pattern of interpersonal attitude has an equilibrium in itself and is therefore unconducive to change from within. Also, insofar as it is a generalized pattern of behavior it also provides resistance to change from outside. As is often the case, the farmer is not easily moved by the power of government regulations or directives. Law enforcement is a difficult thing to be achieved in rural areas, mainly due to the characteristics of the villager. However, there are other means of social (basically interpersonal) control of behavior, ranging from gossip, apportioning blame in someone's absence, punishment by holy spirits, to the use of physical power such as beating or killing. Institutional pressure is not rigid; the temple is flexible, group activity is unstructured, and the family is permissive. At the individual level, the villager is rather indulgent, free-minded, yet friendly, cooperative, trusting, and fun-loving. One can be surprised how the farmers combine work and fun in the loosely structured cooperative economic activity of group help (*long-khaek*) when planting or harvesting rice. For example, groups will often freely help on each other's plots with a lot of pleasure and efficiency.

Thailand has a national average of 80 percent of the over-15-years-old age group having at least four years of primary education. This is not far below the metropolitan Bangkok average of 90 percent. Marked differences appear only when one compares higher levels of educational attainment. The Bangkok population has 40 percent with more than four years of schooling, while the total population has only 12 percent. In the rural area only 6 percent of the population has this level of education. Graduates of higher education comprise 0.26 percent of the Bangkok population, 0.02 percent of the total population, and 0.01 percent of the rural population.

The Education System

HISTORICAL BACKGROUND

a. The Early Stage (1350–1850)

Thailand's social system of the past was centered around the institutions of the temples (wats) and the king's palace, in addition to the family. It is from these three institutions that the Thai system of education originated. The family was basically interested in the child's occupation, which in those days meant learning agricultural skills and social skills in the context of the extended family social norms. These two purposes were often combined in the popular practice of sending one's child to his uncles or aunts so that he learned a broader spectrum of occupational arts and gained a comprehension of ties among family relatives. That the child understood this family tie (or bondage) was important in those days, since it is within the context of this bondage that an individual was valuable and meaningful. And it was to these relatives and friends that he or his family could turn without a word of reproach in time of difficulty. The temple, being the community's sociocultural center and the place specialized in wisdom and spiritual study, was capable of providing a grown-up child with the broader framework of socialization than the family and of teaching him the intellectual-spiritual quality highly valued by the society. The temple-boy had abundant opportunity to provide and receive service from community members who were and were not family relatives, whom he had to treat impartially. Thus he learned how to live with others in society. He also studied reading, writing, and simple arithmetic in order to understand Buddhist principles when he entered monkhood at the age of twenty. The king's palace provided another kind of education more or less of a manpower oriented approach. The king and the royal family were responsible for the stability of the country, and therefore had to train people who were skilled in this important task.

As time went on, interest in organizing a more formal system of education, given the available resources, was a dominant activity at the king's palace and the temple, while the family continued its role on a limited basis. These two streams of education were later consolidated into what is the basis of the present system of Thai education. This occurred in the time of King Mongkut, Rama IV, and King Chulalongkorn, Rama V, in the second half of the 1800s.

b. The Initial Stage

King Mongkut, who reigned from 1851 to 1868, was a monk for about seventeen years before ascending to the throne. During his stay in the temple, he was a diligent Buddhist scholar and also studied English, Latin, science, geography, and astronomy with foreign missionaries, among whom was the well remembered Dr Bradley. After becoming king he engaged Western tutors for royal children. Among these was the English governess Anna Leonowens, whose story Margaret Landon related in her book *Anna and the King of Siam,* which later became the popular musical and film *The King and I.*

King Chulalongkorn, whose reign lasted from 1868 to 1910, opened the first school within the royal palace in 1871. The school was intended to be a training ground for future government officials who would probably have to work in contact with foreigners. Thus, much of the teaching was along Western lines, and the students were the sons of princes and high government officials. Soon after the setting up of the first school, the king commanded another school to be opened in the palace especially for the teaching of the English language. In 1884, another palace school was opened at Suan Kularb Palace, and several temple schools were also opened for common people with priests as teachers. In the following years, more temple schools of this type were opened. In addition to this, the king sent his own sons to Europe for further studies and encouraged the opening of private schools by foreign missionaries. This period marked the growth of public education in Thai history. In May of 1887, the Department of Education was set up. At that time, there were 34 schools under the department with 81 teachers and 1,994 pupils. From this small beginning, progress was rapid. In April 1892, the Department became the Ministry of Education, which brought about fast expansion in the educational system in the succeeding years. A provisional educational plan was set up in 1898. This provisional educational plan was used for 15 years and was succeeded by that of 1913 which laid a new stress on social objectives for education.

c. The Formal Stage

King Wachirawut, Rama VI, who reigned after his father, King Chulalongkorn, died, was very much interested in expanding the country's educational activities. He set up the country's first university, Chulalongkorn University, as the institution of higher learning in 1917. In 1918, the Private School Act was issued which brought privately sponsored schools under state registration and supervision. In 1921, he made four years of primary education compulsory for all Thai children, boys and girls. Girls who had had no direct participation in the education system now had a full role equal to boys. Following this royal decree, many free government schools were established. General secondary schools were highly popular and the number of schools of this type, both in Bangkok and in the provinces, increased as rapidly as the national budget permitted. The vocational secondary schools developed slowly and were not popular. Only a small number of schools were established in the area of commerce and arts and crafts.

In this same period higher education also expanded. Within Chulalongkorn University there were four faculties, namely Medical Science, Public Administration, Arts, and Science. Outside Chulalongkorn University there were a Teacher Training College, a College of Law, and a Medical College.

d. The Modern Stage

The change of government system from absolute monarchy to constitutional monarchy in 1932 placed a demand on primary education, since the constitutional government had promised to establish a fully elected parliament as soon as half of the population in each province had completed four years of primary education.

Qualitatively the education system after 1932 acquired a new tone, following the ideology of the People's Party. Education was more oriented towards political socialization in order to sustain the new type of government system. This system of education was much influenced by the English system, partly due to Great Britain's influence in Southeast Asia at that time and partly because many high-ranking Thai officials had had their training in England or under English influence.

Five levels of education were established: Pre-Primary, Primary, Lower Secondary, Higher Secondary, Pre-University and University Education.

Pre-Primary education was designed for children between 3½ and 7 years of age, and it was not compulsory.

Primary or elementary education was divided into four grades. This level was compulsory according to the Compulsory Primary Education Act, and no child between 7 and 14 years of age could leave school unless he had completed grade 4.

Secondary education was divided into two courses: lower secondary – grades 1–3, and higher secondary – grades 4–6. And, of course, there were two tracks within secondary education: academic/general education and vocational education.

The two year pre-university education covered grades 11 and 12 and basically prepared the student for university education, which required a high standard of academic background.

e. The Development-Planning Stage

The strong emphasis on national development came with Field Marshall Sarit Thanarat, who headed the coup d'etat of 1958. The First National Development (five-year) Plan was for the period of 1962–1966; the education-development plan was part of the National Development Plan, with specified targets in terms of inputs and outputs. Prior to this, Sarit had set up a committee to reform education. Upon completion of its task the committee was replaced by the National Education Council. The new scheme of education was implemented in 1960.

Education planning formed an integral part of each successive Economic and Social Development Plan; the second 1967—71, the third 1972—1976, and the fourth 1977—1981.

AN EVOLUTION OF POLICY

"Learn knowledge while young, earn wealth when grown-up." This is an old saying which was intended to guide the young to pay prime attention to seeking knowledge rather than seeking money. It also became a general principle followed by the government in organizing the system of education. Vocational education is seen as different from literacy education and is only given to those who have had enough of the latter, if it is to be given at all. Otherwise the individual enters an occupation to seek wealth after finishing literacy education. The growth of adult-education programs with the concept of "lifelong education" in recent years has been only a partial modification to this guideline, because of the social need to overcome illiteracy. Perhaps this has been a major reason for the split of vocational secondary education from general secondary education; and perhaps it was also true that in earlier days there was no need for vocational training.

Education, in its early days, started at two ends in society, with the sons of the royal family and high ranking officials who would form the ruling class and sons of the commoners who would form the moral and agriculturally productive citizens. There was no intention of making education a means for transforming sons of commoners into members of the ruling class. Nor was this the motive of individual farmers. It is of interest to note that the royal decree for compulsory primary education in 1921 was received by the people with fear rather than enthusiasm. This is understandable. Education (to get through it) is a burden and pressure. Farmers preferred to see their children enjoy a relaxed life on their land abundant with rice and fish.

After 1932, the new government realized that education was one of the basic ingredients needed for modernizing the country along the line of constitutional democracy. The general populace must have a certain level of literacy in order to participate in the polity. Communication and mobilization of the mass through the written word would become dominant, and this would require some level of reading and writing.

In the 1960s, Thailand was forced to associate itself with "nation development". The relationship between education and development did not appear distinctively clear by the time educational development was included in the First National Development Plan 1962–1966. Two concepts seemed to be implied: that education was something desired by the people and society (thus requiring targets to be achieved, like numbers of beds in hospitals to be provided and the amount of land to be irrigated) and that education was an important means for changing the knowledge, skills, and values of the people for future socioeconomic well-being.

This same dual relationship between education and nation development was reflected throughout the successive development plans.

In the Fourth Economic and Social Development Plan (1977–1981), the view of using education as an instrument for the nation's socioeconomic development became clearer, although there was still some "confusion" between taking education as the means or the end. This can be seen in the following policy statement taken from the fourth five-year plan:

> The objectives of educational development in the Plan are to make an intensive effort to develop every educational level and type appropriate to the nation's real social needs and for the general benefit of national development. It is accepted that education plays a role in the promotion of human quality and the solving of manpower problems. At the same time, education helps develop knowledge, skills, and attitudes in order to direct society toward a better future. Efforts will be made to organize the educational system effectively and efficiently.
>
> In order to meet the objectives, the educational development policy is as follows:
> (a) To organize the in-school education system into four levels: the Pre-compulsory Education level, the Primary Education level, the Secondary Education level, and the Higher Education level. The primary and secondary education system will also be changed from 4–3–3–2 (3) to 6–3–3.
> (b) To make better provision for educational opportunity. This will be met by providing compulsory education; the government will support the efforts to expand education in order to provide equal educational opportunity for people.
> (c) To improve the quality of every educational level in both urban and rural areas, and in both government and nongovernment organizations. Special emphasis will be given to the lower-quality sectors.

235

(d) To improve the educational system to be consistent with the national social and economic development plan, by organising the educational system appropriately to provincial conditions; and to make it more free and flexible. Also, to organize the in-school and out-of-school educational programs consistently and appropriately to the labor market.

(e) To improve and change the content and process in every level and type of the educational system, including the population education program, in order to make it appropriate to the reality of specific areas, and of the nation. To provide for the study of the theoretical along with the practical and to re-adjust the organization of educational content and educational processes in a way that will help create integration of moral, ethical, intellectual, and material development.

(f) To improve the teacher-training system so that it will meet the needs of the nation by improving the quality and quantity.

From the above review of education policies in different time periods, an observation may be made: just as the policy of the nation has been undergoing a struggle for transformation from absolute monarchy to self-sustained democracy, so the education policy has been evolving from king-sponsored to people-sponsored and from being sacred to being common. And this transformation of education policy has not been faster than that of the policy itself. For some people, education was generally associated with the temple and it was taken as something holy and mysterious. Old people, generally in rural areas, would consider the child who places books of any kind in the direction of his feet as seriously misbehaving, not to mention sitting on or stepping on his school books.

Present School Structure and Enrollment

FORMAL SCHOOL

The structure of the Thai school system from 1960 to 1977 was 7–5–4: seven years of elementary divided into a four-year lower cycle and a three-year upper cycle, five years of secondary divided into a three-year lower cycle and a two-year upper cycle, and four years for a first degree. In 1978, this changed to the 6–3–3 pattern. Table 6.2 depicts the present system.

The main differences between the two educational structures may be summarized as follows:

(1) The length of the primary cycle has been reduced from seven to six years. This is combined with an increase from 180 days to 200 days

TABLE 6.2.
Structure of Educational System in 1977

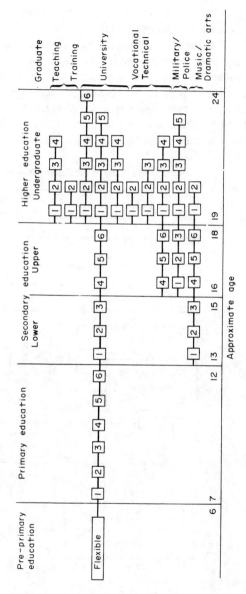

per school year. This results in about the same number of classroom hours as under the seven-year school system.

(2) The two streams of academic and vocational secondary education remain, with the academic-stream curriculum modified by providing elective subjects and vocational skills for students to choose. Vocational subjects at the lower-secondary level are provided for students to explore their ability and aptitude, whilst at the upper level the emphasis is on achievement for their future careers. This emphasis is intended to improve the transition from school to work.

TABLE 6.3
Articulation Chart of the School System

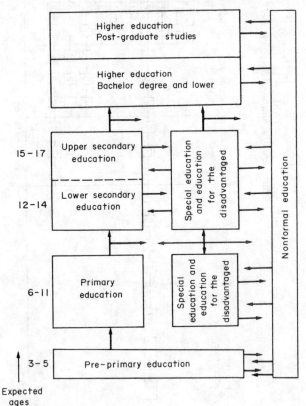

(3) The upper-secondary cycle is increased from two to three years, allowing students to master sufficient vocational skills to get a job or providing a sound academic basis for those who wish to pursue higher education.

(4) There is more flexibility throughout the system, with students being allowed to enter and leave school when they want and graduating when they have amassed a sufficient number of credits, which can be gained either through formal or nonformal education. This flexible articulation is shown in Table 6.3.

All educational management in Thailand is under the control and supervision of the state. Financial responsibility lies mainly with the government sector, assisted by the private sector. Thus, there are two types of school for every level of education, government and private.

(1) *Government schools* are set up and maintained by the government budget. The organization is the responsibility of ministries: the Ministry of Education, the Ministry of the Interior, and the Office of University Affairs. The division of responsibility among these three agencies will be shown later.

(2) *Private schools* are set up by individuals or groups of individuals from their own private funds or from fees. Some private schools are founded and funded by religious organizations. These schools have generally adopted the Western form of management.

Table 6.4 summarizes the enrollments in all formal schooling.

NONFORMAL EDUCATION

As stated in the National Educational Policy of the National Education Scheme 1977, the significance of nonformal education is as follows:

> The State shall endeavour to step up and promote various kinds of out-of-school education in order to make available life-long education to all, especially to those who missed initial formal schooling.

Since the out-of-school population makes up almost 80 percent of the total school-age population, an attempt was made to expand rapidly nonformal education. The central coordination system is at present under the National Committee on Nonformal Education, and the administrative

TABLE 6.4
Number and Percent Distribution of Students by Grade and level of Education, 1977

Level of education	Age group	Students	School-age population	Ratio of enrollments to school-age population	% of total enrollments
Kindergarten 1	4	92,438	1,420,060	6.51	1.07
Kindergarten 2	5	79,868	1,377,284	5.80	0.93
Pre-Primary	6	73,180	1,337,136	5.47	0.85
Kind. and Pre-Prim.	4−6	245,486	4,134,480	5.94	2.85
P. 1	7	1,527,737	1,296,800	117.81	17.72
P. 2	8	1,289,613	1,256,464	102.64	14.96
P. 3	9	1,262,049	1,201,495	105.04	14.63
P. 4	10	1,105,265	1,176,592	93.94	12.82
Lower Elem.	7−10	5,184,664	4,931,351	105.14	60.13
P. 5	11	702,799	1,130,239	62.18	8.15
P. 6	12	540,306	1,090,997	49.52	6.27
P. 7	13	448,278	1,060,698	42.26	5.20
Upper Elem. + Equiv	11−13	1,691,383	3,281,934	51.54	19.62
M.S. 1	14	337,340	1,024,522	32.93	3.91
M.S. 2	15	312,307	985,678	31.59	3.62
M.S. 3	16	278,599	950,022	29.33	3.23
Lower Sec. + Equiv	14−16	925,246	2,963,222	31.33	10.76
M.S. 4	17	199,556	916,602	21.77	2.32
M.S. 5	18	165,086	883,337	18.69	1.91
M.S. 6	19	53,173	855,928	6.21	0.62
Upper Sec. + Equiv	17−19	417,815	2,655,867	15.73	4.85
1st year	19	37,542	855,928	4.39	0.44
2nd year	20	49,178	831,028	5.92	0.57
3rd year	21	34,041	807,957	4.21	0.39
4th year	22	21,789	784,327	2.78	0.25
5th year	23	2,959	766,512	0.39	0.03
6th year	24	642	745,790	0.09	0.01
Higher Ed.	19−24	146,151	4,791,572	3.05	1.70
Higher cert.	−	404			
Master degrees	−	7,860			
Doctoral degrees	−	92			0.10
Total Higher Ed.	−	154,507	4,791,542	3.22	1.79
Total All Level		8,622,101	21,902,468	39.37	100.00

(Source: Educational Planning Division, Ministry of Education, 1977)

work is carried out by the Adult Education Division in the Department of General Education in the Ministry of Education.

After the Compulsory Education Act of 1921, there was a steady rise in the rate of literacy until the outbreak of the Second World War. In 1940, the Adult Education Division was set up in the Ministry of Education. In that year, the government adopted a policy requiring all illiterate adults to attend adult classes to learn how to read and write in Thai. Comparing the census data of 1947 and 1960, it appears that the rate of literacy increased from 52 percent to 68 percent, although the absolute number of illiterates remained more or less unchanged. In 1970, the literacy rate had increased to 82 percent. In 1978, this figure should have been something like 85 percent, although no definite figures are available.

Programs Under the Ministry of Education

The Ministry of Education which is responsible for nonformal education throughout the country operates a number of programs.

One of them is the *Functional Literacy Program* which started in 1970. In 1975, there were 17,807 adult learners enrolled in the program; the number decreased to 10,459 in 1977.

A second program which is well known among the people is the *School Equivalency Program* which provides an opportunity for those who need grade-level equivalency certificates for employment purposes. The enrollment was 138,163 in 1977.

The *Village Newspaper Reading Centers Project* is another program set up to provide the community with news and information, to promote literacy skills, and to prevent the people from relapsing into illiteracy. A village newspaper reading center is normally used not only as a place where people can read newspapers but also as the center for the dissemination of knowledge and as a clearing house for all information coming from various mass media channels. In 1977, there were 3,979 village newspaper reading centers in various parts of Thailand.

The Ministry of Education also runs a *Radio and Television Program* as a project of nonformal education. Since 71 percent of the total number of households in Thailand have radio sets, radio has an advantage over other mass media in that it can offer educational opportunities to the majority of the people at little expense. Television has been recognized as an effective tool of education, and the Center for Educational Technology and the Department of General Education, in cooperation with existing radio and television stations, is beginning to develop programs.

The *Interest Group Program* has been organized to provide training on request to any group on any subject arranged by the Adult Education Division. The topics for study are based on the problems, needs, and interests of the people so that what is studied can provide the knowledge and experience necessary to help the people and their community. At present, the duration of a group is limited to a minimum of 5 hours and a maximum of 30. The program was launched in 1973 and is now running in nearly every province in the country.

The *Mobile Vocational Training Program* provides short vocational skill training programs in various fields. Its main emphasis is on the provision of knowledge and skills for solving the people's problems in daily life and work and to upgrade their living conditions. A mobile unit will teach in one place until the needs are fulfilled and then move to another place. Typical vocations taught by the mobile training units are motorcycle-repairing, hair dressing, mushroom farming, and radio repairing. The courses are of 20–50 hours duration. If a farmer needs intensive training in order to take up a new profession, he may have to take a full length course of up to 100–200 hours. But for those who desire to brush up on their old skills or are interested only in certain components of the course, or who do not intend to move elsewhere for a new job, a short course of 20–30 hours will be sufficient. After completing the course the learner receives a certificate from the Ministry of Education.

Polytechnic Schools (organized by the Technical School Division Department of Vocational Education in the Ministry of Education) provide short courses for young people needing vocational training after their formal schooling.

Another type of nonformal education program, whose curriculum is under the control of the Ministry of Education although the program is run by private individuals, is the *Private Special Vocational Schools Program*. Private schools offer short and long courses in trade training such as dress-making, commerce, and typing. The enrollment is high in both Bangkok and the provinces.

Table 6.5 summarizes the enrollment in various schools under the control of the Ministry of Education in 1977.

Programs Outside the Ministry of Education

There are also many other nonformal education programs run by other government and private organizations:

(1) *Agricultural Training Centers* These centers are under the Ministry of Agriculture and Cooperatives and provide short preservice and inservice training courses in specific agricultural skills.

(2) *Summer Training Courses at Kasetsart University for interested people* This program makes use of the already existing facilities

TABLE 6.5
*Number of Students in Nonformal School System under the
Control of the Ministry of Education by type of Education,
1977*

Type of nonformal Education	Bangkok metropolitan area	Other regions	Total
Functional literacy	79	10,380	10,459
Adult education: general	35,775	102,388	138,163
Basic literacy	25	572	597
First & second level (P. 2, 4)	3,020	2,442	5,462
Third level (P. 7)	10,794	35,320	46,114
Fourth level (M.S. 3)	15,547	41,574	57,121
Fifth level (M.S. 4–5)	6,389	22,480	28,869
Adult vocational education	2,495	33,531	36,026
Skill training centers	2,495	7,158	9,653
Mobile trade training centers	0	5,042	5,042
Mobile trade training schools	0	21,331	21,331
Polytechnic schools	14,856	8,382	23,238
Private special vocational schools	47,638	54,538	102,176
Total	100,843	209,219	310,062

(Source: Educational Planning Division, Ministry of Education, 1977)

of the university. There are various courses of about 15–30 days in agricultural training.

(3) *Short Course in Cooperative Management* This type of training was provided by training centers with boarding accommodation lasting from a week to as long as six months. The Ministry of Agriculture and Cooperatives is responsible for this program.

(4) *Military Mobile Training Units* These units are organized by the Armed Forces. The training unit travels to where the clientele is and conducts the training course. After completion of a course or a series of courses of about 20–50 hours or 100–200 hours, the training unit moves to another site.

(5) *Yuwa Kasetakorn (Young Agriculturalist) or 4-H Youth Clubs of Thailand* This is a kind of youth club training which is given to young adults for the development of leadership skills in the area of agriculture.

In some cases, the above programs are run by one organization, and in other cases it is a joint operation of more than one agency. Indeed, it can be any combination of the following agencies: the municipalities, the University Women's Association, Kasetsart University, the Armed Forces, the Ministry of the Interior, the Ministry of Agriculture and Cooperatives, or the Thai Rural Reconstruction Movement (a nongovernmental agency).

Administrative Structure

A THREE-LEVEL SYSTEM OF ADMINISTRATION

Parallel to all other sectors of public administration in Thailand educational administration follows the three-level approach. This is the central (or national) level, the regional level, and the local level. Administrative bodies at the central level represent a top–down policy, those at the local level represent the bottom–up, and those at the regional level do both. This system provides flexibility for the coordination of the national need and the local need.

In the past, however, the bodies at the local level have not assumed strong roles, thus leaving the national bodies to play the dominant role. This makes the educational administration of this country look highly centralized. It is anticipated that, in future, when the organization and staff of the local bodies are stronger the trend will change to be of a more balanced nature.

The Central Level

Responsibility for the administration of education at the central level is divided among four government ministries: the Office of the Prime Minister, the Ministry of Education, the Ministry of the Interior, and the Office of State Universities. In general, it can be said that the Office of the Prime Minister is responsible for overall financial and staffing aspects of the whole educational system, the Ministry of the Interior for primary education, the Ministry of Education for secondary level education and the pedagogical aspects of primary and secondary education, whilst the Office of State Universities is in charge of education at the tertiary level. As there is often some overlapping of authority amongst these ministries, some further description of their different functions in education will be given.

Within the *Prime Minister's Office* there are some organizations solely concerned with administering education, and various other organizations part of whose function is related to the educational system. In the former category, there is the National Education Commission (NEC), and in the latter category there are the National Economic and Social Development Commission (NESDC), the Budget Bureau (BB), and the Civil Service Commission (CSC).

The NEC is the organization responsible for the overall coordination of planning and for ensuring that the activities in different parts of the education system are consistent with each other. In addition, it also carries out educational research of general interest usually at the request of other agencies. Finally, the NEC has to report to the Cabinet on serious educational problems and make recommendations on the reorganization of the educational system or on the development of new policies to solve these problems.

The functions of the NESDC, the BB, and the CSC deal with all matters of staff administration for education.

The *Ministry of the Interior* is responsible for the administration of most public primary education. During 1963 and 1966, the authority for most public primary education was transferred from the Ministry of Education to the municipal and local authorities. The local authorities are administratively under the Department of Local Administration in the Ministry of the Interior. The Ministry of Education, however, remains responsible for primary-school teacher training, curriculum development, textbook production, and the supervision of instruction.

The Ministry of the Interior's main function is to allocate subsidies to local authorities and municipalities for primary education, to approve new teaching posts and new facilities, and to enforce compulsory education.

The Ministry of Education is responsible for the pedagogical aspects of primary education and is fully responsible for all types of secondary education. Post-secondary programs in technical institutes, the College of Technology and Vocational Education, and teacher training colleges are also under the Ministry's responsibilities. Furthermore, there is a departmental-level committee, the Private Education Commission, looking after private education at primary and secondary levels.

The *Office of State Universities,* established in 1972, is responsible for the administration of government universities. The Office serves as coordinator between universities and the government. Top-level policy making and planning, setting the guidelines for curriculum and the administration of university personnel, as well as recommendations on budget allocations are among the functions of this Office.

The *Teacher Institute* is a central body with the dual function of representing the teachers' employers both in the government and private schools on the one hand, and representing the teachers as employees on the other hand. Thus the institute regulates the employer's requirements placed on the teachers as well as the welfare and benefits they receive. It also assists in the teacher's inservice training, a task which is mainly carried out by the Department of Teacher Training in the Ministry of Education. In addition, the Institute helps the teachers and the pupils they teach by providing books and educational material at low cost. This is perhaps unique when compared with the concept of Teacher Unions or Teacher Associations found in most other countries.

The Regional Level

Educational administration at the regional level consists of administrative bodies at three sublevels: the Regional Education Office, the Provincial Education Office, and the District Education Office.

Regional Office In order to improve the quantity and quality of education in the rural areas, the Ministry of Education decentralized its administration and grouped the seventy-two provinces of the country into twelve educational regions or *Khets* (see earlier map), each region having a Regional Office. The regional education staff serve as general supervisors, provide inservice training for teachers in the region, and implement the policy made by the central office.

Provincial Office Formally, the Provincial Governor is responsible for education in the province but, in practice, he allocates his *academic* authority to the Provincial Education Office which is part of the Ministry of Education, and he allocates his *administrative* authority for primary schools to the Organization of Provincial Administration. The Provincial Education Officer and his staff in turn give academic assistance to the Organization of Provincial Administration and municipalities through academic supervisors who are responsible for schools in the Province. Pre-primary and secondary schools, private schools, and adult schools are under the responsibility of the Provincial Education Office.

However, there are some kinds of educational institutions in the province that are directly controlled by the central office in Bangkok. They are the experimental schools, vocational schools, teacher colleges, agriculture colleges, universities, and the mobile trade-training centers.

District office The District Education Officer is assigned educational responsibilities by the Ampoe Officer or Sheriff. His duties are the same as the Provincial Educational Officer's, but at the District level.

The Local Level

For the community where there is a municipality, the municipality is responsible for local public primary schools in its area. It receives financial support from the Government through the Ministry of the Interior.

For other areas where there is no municipality, the Organization of Provincial Administration is the unit that is in charge of administering

247

public primary schools except for Bangkok where there is the Bangkok Metropolis in place of the Organization. However, the Ministry of Education through the Provincial and District Education Officer as well as the academic supervisors still controls academic aspects of public primary education.

FINANCE

The major source of educational finance in Thailand is the national budget. However, 6.5 percent of the educational budget comes from fees paid by students and a further 2 percent from gifts and properties.

Table 6.6 presents the per-pupil expenditure for different levels of education for 1972.

Thailand allocates slightly less than 4 percent of its Gross Domestic Product (GDP) for education. This comprises about 20 percent of the national budget. For the fiscal year 1978, the education budget was 16,168.2 million baht (about 808.4 million US dollars). Table 6.7 summarizes this financial record from 1967 to 1978.

As has been seen, Thailand has several agencies responsible for education. Table 6.8 below shows this proportion (1967 through 1978) of the education budget being allocated to the major agencies.

Given the increasing school-age population, there is a projected 20 percent increase in the educational budget between 1978 and 1981.

TABLE 6.6
*Estimate of per-pupil expenditure (including recurrent
and investment expenditure) for various levels of
education*

Type and Level of Education	Per-pupil Expenditure (baht) (~20 baht = US$ 1)
Primary	730
Secondary general	2,000
Secondary vocational	5,000
Teacher training	3,000
University	13,500

(Source: Report of the Educational Reform Committee, Watanapanich Press, Bangkok 1977, p. 281)

TABLE 6.7

Relationship between GDP, National Budget and Education Budget 1967–1978 (in baht).

years	GDP		National Budget			Education Budget			
	number	% ±	number	% of GDP	% ±	number	% of GDP	% of NB	% ±
1967	108,224.3	6.75	19,288.3	17.77	27.00	2,973.3	2.75	15.46	18.74
1968	116,770.0	7.89	21,262.0	18.21	10.58	3,363.9	2.88	15.82	13.14
1969	128,570.0	10.10	23,960.0	18.64	12.69	4,039.7	3.14	16.86	20.09
1970	135,940.0	5.73	27,299.8	20.08	13.94	4,604.8	3.39	16.87	13.99
1971	143,900.0	5.85	28,645.0	19.91	4.93	5,191.1	3.61	18.12	12.73
1972	162,100.0	12.65	29,000.0	17.89	1.24	5,543.5	3.42	19.12	6.79
1973	215,190.0	32.75	32,030.0	14.88	10.45	5,952.5	2.77	18.58	7.38
1974	279,010.0	25.47	39,027.6	14.45	21.85	7,023.3	2.60	17.99	17.99
1975	295,610.0	9.48	50,500.0	17.08	29.39	10,011.3	3.39	19.82	42.54
1976	325,900.0	10.25	62,650.0	19.22	24.06	12,982.2	3.98	20.72	29.68
1977	376,125.0	15.41	68,790.0	18.19	9.80	14,841.0	3.95	21.57	14.32
1978	426,900.0	13.50	81,000.0	18.97	17.75	16,168.2	3.79	19.96	8.94

(Source: Budget Bureau, Preview of Annual Budget, 1977–1978)

TABLE 6.8
The Educational Budget of the Ministry of Education, the National Educational Commission and the Office of State Universities, Local Authority, and others (in million baht).

Budget year	Ed. Budget (EB)	Ed. Budget of the Ministry of Education (% of EB)	Ed. Budget of the Nat. Ed. Comm. and Office of State University (% of EB)	Ed. Budget of Local Authority (% of EB)	Ed. Budget other (% of EB)
1967	2,973.3	79.69	15.91	–	4.38
1968	3,363.9	35.37	17.90	43.88	2.84
1969	4,039.7	32.83	14.99	45.51	6.66
1970	4,604.8	33.01	14.95	50.10	1.93
1971	5,191.1	32.75	14.99	50.08	2.18
1972	5,543.5	33.66	13.45	50.75	2.10
1973	5,952.5	34.30	12.50	50.36	1.84
1974	7,023.3	33.79	14.49	50.81	0.93
1975	10,011.3	33.84	13.67	50.72	1.61
1976	12,982.2	30.98	14.40	52.53	2.11
1977	14,841.2	33.45	13.01	51.71	1.82
1978	16,168.2	34.91	13.65	49.76	1.69

(Source: Budget Bureau, Preview of Annual Budget, 1967–1977.)

SUPERVISION

Supervision of education in Thailand is divided into two categories, supervision of administrative matters and supervision of academic matters. Administrative supervision is concerned with regulation and ordinance, placement and remuneration, physical and financial planning, and execution. Academic supervision involves the use of curriculum materials, instructional techniques and examinations.

For administrative matters each administrative agency (e.g. the Ministry of Education, the Organization of Provincial Administration, and the Ministry of the Interior) has an inspectorate system. The educational inspectors supervise and evaluate performance of educational personnel at various levels. This is done by regular visits to their offices and/or by remote operation through issued orders and directives.

On the academic side, each Department is responsible for school curriculum and instruction through its supervisory unit. The supervisors visit schools on the Department's schedule (and also at the invitation of the schools) to supervise their implementation of the curriculum through curriculum materials and classroom instruction. The Unit also provides free or inexpensive textbooks and supplementary readings for students in order to facilitate the teaching process. It also conducts research related to curriculum and instruction and disseminates the findings to the schools.

Curriculum

The development and administration of the primary and secondary school curriculum is the responsibility of the Department of Educational Techniques in the Ministry of Education. The Department has four specialized Centers working on different aspects of curriculum and instruction, in addition to its regular administrative divisions.

The Curriculum Development Center has the following functions:
(1) To identify and translate national needs and aspirations into curriculum specifications.
(2) To plan and develop curriculum programs aimed at continuous, systematic, and effective development in children's education.
(3) To develop and produce curriculum materials such as syllabuses, teacher guides, learning materials, evaluation instruments, audio-visual aids, and equipment needed in the teaching-learning situation.
(4) To disseminate information on curriculum changes to teachers in schools and other people in the community.
(5) To organize inservice teacher education in order to upgrade teachers for new developments in education.
(6) To survey and analyze significant world trends and developments in curriculum and instruction.

The Text Book Development Center, attached to the Department of Educational Techniques, is responsible for the production and distribution of educational materials (including teacher aids).

The Educational Technology Center is responsible for the production and distribution of teaching aids and gives guidance on their use. With the implementation of the 1977 curriculum, the Center has an increased amount of work with the production of certain textbooks and teacher's guides, teaching aids, and the organization of inservice programs for teachers.

The Institute for Promotion of Teaching Science and Technology is responsible for research and development in technology and science teaching in secondary schools. It also organizes inservice training courses for science and mathematics teachers, and disseminates information useful to science teachers and administrators throughout the country.

Some flavor should be given of the content of the new curricula. Some examples are, therefore, given below from primary and secondary school educational objectives.

PRIMARY-SCHOOL CURRICULUM (1977)

Primary education is considered to be the right and obligation of all boys and girls, and it is the responsibility of the government to see that this is so. This education is for the moral, physical, intellectual, and practical growth of pupils so that they become good citizens in the democratic society of Thailand. Primary Education must foster national unity, and at the same time, allow each region to add curriculum objectives appropriate to its local needs.

The primary-school curriculum emphasizes the following clusters of individual development:

(1) *Character* This includes unselfishness, group-benefits, self-discipline, perseverance, diligence, honesty, nationality, thinking, analysis, decision-making, tolerance of criticism and differences, sportsmanship, appreciation of others, working with others.

(2) *Knowledge for living* This includes physical and mental hygiene, language, mathematics, artistic appreciation and expression, law(s), economy, scientific process, science and technology, cooperative process, work, ecology, and seeking of knowledge.

(3) *Peaceful life* This includes adjustment to change, understanding of religion and the application of its principles, efficient use of time, useful creativity, accommodation of differences in thinking, peaceful problem solving.

(4) *Good citizenship* This includes belief in constitutional democracy, conservation of national heritage, awareness of right and wrong, understanding the importance of family and society, understanding of the interrelationships of regions in the world, collectivity for national security, understanding the value of freedom, and pride in being a Thai citizen.

The content of the primary school curriculum can also be divided into four clusters:

(1) *Basic Skills*: Thai language and mathematics.

(2) *Life Experience*: Social studies, science, and hygiene, to be taught in an integrated way rather than as separate subjects.

(3) *Good Habits*: Moral education (including religious studies and practices), physical education, fine arts, musical arts, and special activities, all aiming at building good values, tastes, and attitudes for the good life.

(4) *Work Preparation* includes such subjects as agriculture, crafts, and trades.

Foreign language is not compulsory in the primary school but may be offered as an elective.

SECONDARY-SCHOOL CURRICULUM (1975)

Secondary education is considered to be an education for individuals who are interested in further education and is, therefore, not compulsory. The state promotes this level of education to the extent that resources are available, and it encourages private organizations to participate in organizing this level of education under the control of the state. Secondary education aims at providing students with general knowledge and skills useful for earning a living, or to continue their studies at a higher level if they so desire.

The secondary curriculum in the lower-secondary school (Grades 7–9) emphasizes the encouragement and development of the following:

(1) General development of abilities and aptitudes.

(2) Habits of searching for knowledge, analytical skills, and creative thinking.

(3) Good attitudes toward all honest occupations, work discipline, industriousness, perseverance, economy, and beneficial use of time.

(4) Honesty, self-discipline, respect for the law and social rules, responsibility for oneself, family and society.

(5) Awareness of rights and duties, team work, group affiliation, self-sacrifice for collective benefit, peaceful problem-solving.

(6) Basic knowledge and skills for improving family life, for entering an occupation, or furthering studies.

(7) Good physical and mental health, and how to improve community hygiene.

(8) Love for and wish to remain in a native area and improve surroundings for development of the community and promoting Thai cultural heritage.

(9) Pride of being a Thai; loyalty to nation, religion, and king; knowing and following the constitutional-monarchical form of government; and having a collective spirit to protect the security of the country.

(10) Good understanding of Thailand and of peaceful mutual living.

The general aims of education at the higher-secondary level (Grades 10–12) are the same as at the lower level with the addition of:

(1) knowing how to think and make rational decisions; learning how to use time beneficially and how to think creatively.

(2) understanding political problems, economic problems, and sociocultural problems of the country today.

The content breakdown for lower-secondary education (Grades 7—9) is as follows:

| Subject cluster | Periods per week | | | | | |
| | Grade 7 | | Grade 8 | | Grade 9 | |
	Compulsory	Elective (up to)	Compulsory	Elective (up to)	Compulsory	Elective (up to)
Language Thai	4	–	4	2	4	4
Foreign	–	6	–	6	–	8
Science-Math						
Science	4	–	4	–	4	–
Math	4	–	4	–	–	6
Social Studies	5	–	5	–	5	4
Personality Development						
Physical Education	3	2	3	2	3	4
Art Education	2	2	2	4	–	6
Activities	3–5	–	2–5	–	3–5	–
Work and Occupation	4	6	4	6	4	12
Total	35		35		35	

For higher-secondary education (Grades 10—12) in 1978 (a transitional stage) the total semester credits required were approximately 150:

Compulsory subjects (approximately 50 semester credits)

Thai language	*c.* 18 credits
Social studies	*c.* 18 credits
Science	*c.* 9 credits
Physical education	*c.* 5 credits
Subtotal:	*c.* 50 credits

Elective Subjects (approximately 100 semester credits)

Thai language	up to 24 credits
Social studies	up to 24 credits
Sciences	up to 66 credits
Mathematic	up to 36 credits

Vocational subjects*	up to 84 credits
Physical education	up to 18 credits
English	up to 60 credits
Another language	up to 24 credits
Art education	up to 18 credits
Other subjects	up to 12 credits
Special·activities	up to 6 credits
Subtotal:	up to 100 credits
Grand total	150 semester credits

It should be also noted that the secondary-school curriculum as shown above is the type geared toward vocationalization which is different from what used to be offered earlier.

Since 1978, the academic stream has had six years — three lower and three higher — but the pattern of curriculum remains much the same. Up until 1965, all the academic-stream schools concentrated on academic subjects, while practical vocational training was left to secondary vocational schools. In 1966, it was decided that this would not satisfy the country's need for trained middle-level manpower. Rather, the academic secondary schools should be transformed into "comprehensive schools" using an academic/vocational combination, and the secondary vocational curriculum for grades 8–10 was phased out. The notion of this more balanced academic/vocational curriculum is slowly being introduced into the upper academic secondary schools, although at this level there are still separate vocational schools.

SECONDARY VOCATIONAL SCHOOL CURRICULUM (1978),
(COURSE OF 3 YEARS, GRADES 10–12)

Vocational education includes training in professional subjects and technical skills. The aim is to supply manpower needed for the development of the national economy, particularly in the fields of agriculture, industry, commerce, and home economics.

Vocational education is provided at four levels:

(1) Semiskilled labor to produce workers for specialized fields of work in a short time and with a flexible approach.

*Note that the vocational subjects presently comprise six areas. These are (1) Fine and practical Arts, (2) Agriculture, (3) Home Economics, (4) Commerce, (5) Crafts, (6) Industrial Arts. Thus with one additional program on general education for those preparing to enter university, the school can possibly offer seven specialized programs.

(2) Skilled labor, to produce workers with sufficient knowledge and skills needed for the jobs requiring some degree of problem-solving.

(3) Semiprofessional level, to produce technicians and laboratory assistants.

(4) Professional level, to produce administrators, planners, and managers.

It should be noted, however, that the vocational subjects provided in the comprehensive secondary schools are intended to be occupationally oriented rather than to be occupational training. This latter is the task of the vocational school.

The general objectives of the secondary vocational schools are similar to those for the ordinary secondary school but, of course, with a vocational bias.

The content consists of general subjects, all compulsory, worth 45 semester credits. Of the occupational subjects, 55 credits are compulsory and 40 credits elective. For illustrative purposes an example of Level 2 agriculture is given:

The general subjects include Thai language, social studies, physical education, English, science and mathematics.

The occupational subjects include plants, animal husbandry, agricultural arts, agricultural business, agricultural industry, principles of agriculture, and practicum and seminar in agricultural occupations.

Examinations

Examinations in the early days focused on skills in language and arithmetic and on the memorization of materials which had been read. In 1950, the idea of also evaluating the emotional, social, physical and intellectual development was introduced. The administration of examinations was highly centralized and confined to selected groups of educators so that classroom teachers had limited roles to play. A major revision of methods of measurement and evaluation in schools took place in 1967. Broader aspects of pupils' development were taken into account, and working forms were provided to facilitate teachers' assessment procedures. Examinations were not only used for evaluating students, but also for evaluating the effectiveness of the teaching—learning process. The classroom teacher who is close to his pupil has thus become more involved in the process. It is the Ministry of Education, in collaboration with the

College of Education, that has been making attempts to improve the evaluation system in Thailand.

The most recent guidelines issued by the Testing Bureau of the Ministry of Education for student assessment include such statements as:

(1) The grading system is used in all schools. Passing grades are: 1 – satisfactory or pass, 2 – fair, 3 – good and 4 – very good. Unsatisfactory or failed is 0.

(2) For graduation, a student must earn or pass at least 100 units of which 34 are required and the rest are elective. School attendance is at least 4 regular semesters (Grades 11 and 12).

(3) The Ministry of Education has agreed that student assessments are internally done by schools. It is up to the school authority to certify and confer diplomas on students or award transcripts.

Prior to this new law examinations at the terminal grades were partially centralized in order to establish regional comparability. This was done at different levels at administrative authority or province or at the national level (by the Ministry of Education). At each level, committees were formed to set examination questions on each subject and to score the answers.

Examinations in primary-school grades are conducted solely by the school, with the exception of the examination at the terminal grade (Grade 6) in rural schools which standardize by the "school group" of the area. A school group normally involves 3–10 schools joining together in setting examination papers and scoring them. This practice helps maintain the standard of education in each school of the group.

Teacher Preparation

Thailand has given special attention to the preparation of teachers in the past twenty years.

Nowadays, experienced educators inside and outside the country agree that the decision to expand teacher education made twenty years ago was only a little late. It did not merely produce teachers to man the increasing number of classrooms, but also provided them with new technical knowhow. Furthermore, it produced far-sighted educational planners and administrators capable of navigating the education system of this country without an imperative need for expatriate staff. Some teacher-training institutions were raised to university status.

The concept of teacher training in Thailand is based on the trilogy of learning: general subjects, a specialized subject as a major or minor, and professional subjects which include methods of teaching, educational psychology, guidance, and school administration. Prospective teachers are trained in an integrated manner to be able to teach both primary and secondary classes. The courses are divided into three levels:

(1) *The Lower Certificate in Education* Students who have graduated from secondary Grade 3 may sit for an entrance examination to a teacher-training college. After two years of training, they are awarded the Lower Certificate in Education, which qualifies them to teach in the seven grades of primary school. This will be phased out by 1982.

(2) *The Higher Certificate in Education* Students are recruited from among the graduates of Grade 12 or from among those who have obtained the Lower Certificate in Education. They follow another two-years course at a teacher-training college which enables them to teach in classes up to Grade 10.

(3) *Degree Courses in Education* There are two types of courses leading to a B.Ed. degree. These are:

(a) A four-year course after the Lower Certificate or after Grade 12.

(b) A two-year course after the Higher Certificate.

These courses are offered at twenty-five out of the thirty-six teacher-training colleges as well as at faculties of education in various universities, including Srinakharinwirot University (formerly the College of Education). It is only at Srinakharinwirot University that two further types of pre-service education take place:

(1) A one-year course after B.Ed. leading to a Higher Certificate for Specialized Teaching.

(2) A two-year course after B.Ed. leading to an M.Ed. degree.

Though, in recent years, teacher training has been the fastest growing sector of the education system, this is now being reduced. In 1975, there were about 145,000 persons studying in day and evening classes for the Teacher's Certificate and Higher Teacher's Certificate, but by 1977 this had reduced to about 110,000 persons. There are indications that by the end of the 1970s supply and demand were nearly in balance.

By 1982, all teacher-training will be at the post-secondary or degree level. The effort to produce academically better qualified teachers has developed well and in 1978 there were some 3,000 teachers graduating with a B.Ed. degree.

The expansion of evening classes and the annual examination given to self-studying working teachers were introduced into the system as measures for the inservice training of teachers so that they could become better qualified. Later, however, these classes were also open for nonteaching persons who said they wished to become teachers. Perhaps the major reason for this was the demand for education at this level among Thai youth whereby they entered any college where they could get a place. Now with the provision of broader opportunities for a college education, such as that provided at Ramkamhaeng University, the demand for evening-class education has decreased somewhat.

Although the plethora of evening courses, summer courses, correspondence courses as well as day courses (it was once said that there were about thirty-two combinations of ways to become a qualified teacher in Thailand) has solved the problem of shortage of qualified teachers in urban areas, there is still a reluctance on the part of teachers to teach in rural areas.

The Department of Teacher Training has recently adopted a policy of training teachers to be competent for working in rural areas. Student teachers are encouraged to do their teacher practice during their training in needy areas so that they grasp the acuteness of the teacher-shortage problem in rural areas. The aims are also to make them familiar with the educational situation and hope that they will be prepared to teach in rural communities after their training. The employment system also provides special remuneration for teachers who take posts in remote areas.

The success in the training of teachers has been noteworthy.

Problems and Priorities

DEVELOPMENT NEEDS OF THE COUNTRY

An education system, although being a complete functional unit on its own, is but a subsystem of the country to which it belongs. An evaluation of a subsystem like this can only be made in relation to the larger system. For no matter how good the subsystem is — its inputs, its outputs, or its efficiency – this is meaningless unless it fits the nature of the larger system. In the same way, for an education system to be good it must suit the conditions prevailing in the country. The inputs it draws from the society must be appropriate, the working techniques it employs must be appropriate to the culture and the outputs it produces must be desirable in relation to the development needs and goals of the country. In other words the discussion of problems and priorities of the Thai education system is valid only in the context of Thailand's development needs and goals. Thus this section begins by analyzing the development needs of Thailand, specifically in the areas which require maximum contribution from education, as a basis for discussing necessary adjustments to the education system.

In 1979, Thailand's development needs (in the areas of prime interest to the education system) may be summarized as follows:

Literacy

Knowing how to read and write at least one language, preferably the national language of one's country, may be taken as a human right in the modern world. It is important for the individual and society. Functionally, illiterate citizens are handicapped in communicating with society and particularly the government. Socially, language which is a cultural thread binding society's members into a social group cannot be effective with illiterate members. One interesting fact about this problem is that although the percentage of people who are literate is constant or even slightly decreasing in developing countries, the absolute numbers of illiterate people is increasing due to population increase.

In Thailand only about 15 percent of the people beyond the age of 10 are illiterate. However, in number this is 6.6 million. In addition, it should be noted that in this statistic 10-year-old children in Grade 3 are counted as literate, while in reality about 40 percent of them leave school upon completing Grade 4 or even before that, after which a great number of them living in remote areas lapse into illiteracy before long. Therefore it is likely that the illiteracy rate in Thailand is higher than indicated by the statistics.

Literacy is, therefore, among the prime development needs of Thailand.

If Thailand is to progress to the next stage of development, as many as possible of the 6.6 million or more citizens must be made literate. Education must respond to this need in a more effective and efficient way than hithertofore.

Knowledge of Environment

Man lives his life in his physical and social environment. Life is bound to be difficult at the individual level and the societal level, if man does not understand the nature of what surrounds him, or if he holds wrong ideas or concepts about it. Literacy may have some effect in removing such ignorance.

Many Thai people, especially peasant farmers, are either ignorant or misinformed about much of their physical or social environment. Unfortunately, it sometimes occurs that knowledgeable people, instead of helping to enlighten this group of people, take the opportunity of capitalizing on their ignorance and abusing them. The country has to depend heavily on its education system for improving knowledge among the people. Education must emphasize scientific theories and principles more than in the past and must foster self-learning. In addition, it must create among knowledgeable people a desire to enlighten ignorant people and not exploit them.

Perseverance to Achieve

The quality of our life, individual or collective, is fundamentally determined by what we achieve in its materialistic and spiritual aspects. Despite the stereotype of the Thai philosophy of "contentment with what exists", the Thais are not happy to accept the low level of living which results from their previous contentment. Therefore, contentment is not the true life philosophy of the Thais; rather it is a psychological mechanism one employs to console oneself when one can see no hope for improvement. There is nothing wrong in employing this mechanism; indeed, it is very good and inexpensive mental hygiene. But one must recognize that it is just a temporary mechanism and not mistake it for the true life-philosophy.

Schooling in the ASEAN Region

If this is a correct analysis, Thailand will have to persuade its people to improve their "perseverance to achieve" in areas important to their quality of life. Such a demand will be readily understood by the Thais, since it is generally accepted that Thai people have less perseverance than the peoples of some other countries or even some other ethnic groups living in Thailand. It is the education system which should attempt to bring about this improvement.

Sense of Nation Building

A nation is more than a group of people living in a given area of land. It also implies belongingness and contribution. A group made up of highly achieving and progressive individuals may not necessarily make any national progress, if each of those individuals possesses no spirit for collective progress and is not ready to contribute to the achievement of national goals. In the long run, each person seeks his own way to personal well-being or that of his own clique or clan; this could result in national collapse rather than progress.

Under the dedicated leadership of its various monarchs, Thailand has been quite successful in getting the people to exhibit a spirit of national concern; however, it is not clear whether they do so because of loyalty to the king or because of their felt need for collective progress. Whichever it is, the approach of waiting for the king's dictum before beginning to do anything is not sufficient, since the problems and needs of the society are now so complicated and diversified that it is impossible to expect the king or even the government to see them all. The people must participate in formulating national goals for progress, since otherwise it could turn out to be a selfish social abuse for personal benefit. Such an attitude has to be built up in the minds of individuals from a young age; and education must give a strong helping hand.

Righteousness

For a group of persons to be involved in a collective pursuit (such as that discussed above) each individual member needs to trust others and must himself be trustworthy. The fact that there is large scale corruption in Thailand is a major factor preventing people from participating in the setting of and contributing to the achievement of national goals. It is urgent that the country build up the quality of honesty among its people and particularly among government officials. Corruption must be wiped out as soon as possible. Here also the education system has an important role to play.

Health

Health standards in Thailand are quite low. The level of disease is generally high, medical services are inadequate, especially in rural areas; environmental cleanliness is substandard, hygienic habits are lacking among most people, and air and water pollution are at dangerous levels in many places. Food and nutrition in Thailand should theoretically not be a problem since Thailand is agriculturally rich. Unfortunately, this is not the case. The problem is neither with the quality nor the quantity of food products. Rather it has to do with the economy and with eating habits. According to an estimate of the Ministry of Public Health, more than 60,000 children of primary-school age in 1978 died directly or indirectly because of insufficient food — basically the poverty-stricken group of the population who cannot afford proper food. The Ministry has also reported that many Thai people, regardless of their socioeconomic status, have diseases of the digestive system, basically due to eating unclean food, uncooked food, and too spicy food. The gross mortality rate, infant mortality rate, and life expectancy rate, another set of health indicators, are not too bad (9 percent, 15 percent, and 56 years respectively in 1978) but could be much improved.

Health as a national-development goal cannot be accomplished through education alone. Economic and sociopolitical measures play an important role. But education can do a great deal, especially in the domain of knowledge about and attitudes toward eating habits. Most food habits are learned in childhood and are difficult to change, and this will be a great challenge to education to help in changing these habits.

Employment

According to the Labor Department, about 1.6 million people were unemployed in 1977, i.e. 3.8 percent of the population or about 8 percent of the labor force. Although compared with other countries this figure is not high, it is, nevertheless, a serious matter for the Thai economy because the rest who are "employed" are in fact underemployed because of the unmodernized agriculture sector. The production of the "employed" group can barely support the unemployed. This is one main cause of theft and crimes. From the experience of working in close contact with the Penitentiary Department, the authors estimate that 57 percent of all crimes committed in 1977 were stealing and robbing for monetary purposes.

The combination of the subdividing of land for inheritance purposes in large families and the nonmodernization of farming techniques resulted in increasing underemployment in the agricultural sector. The surplus labor spilled into towns and cities. These rural youths lack the knowledge, skills, and attitudes for town jobs. No serious attempt has been made to transform this surplus manpower into useful human capital for production purposes. The provision of vocational education has been to serve the interest at the individual level without manpower forecasts and planned enrollments. Students receive little career guidance; those from rural areas do not have much idea of what city jobs require and often make uninformed decisions. And even if a rural student were to do well academically, the situation in Thailand is such that an employer lays much more weight when selecting employees on personal recommendation rather than academic qualifications. Thus, the nature of the labor market leaves only a small door open for graduates who have come from rural areas. This exacerbates unemployment.

It would seem that the present situation of vocational training should be changed so that both the educational system and the employers become responsible for such training. Apprenticeship during training should decrease (or even eradicate) the problem of distrust or lack of confidence on the part of the employer and uncertainty on the part of the trainees. For underemployment which is mainly in the agricultural sector due to the peak and nonpeak nature of the work, formal and nonformal education can monitor the labor utilization of the farmers to make it more productive. Second-cropping or alternate cropping may be introduced and supervised during nonpeak seasons.

Production

The need for higher production in Thailand is seen from two indicators: the per capita gross national product of approximately 318 US dollars, and the international trade deficit of more than 1,000 million US dollars per year. 13.3 percent of the 1978 national budget is for debt-paying. To live at par, Thai people will have to produce at least 13.3 percent more than they do now, assuming that there is no increase in the consumption rate.

The international trade deficit indicates that Thai people consume more of other countries' products than they produce for other countries. The residual is mainly due to the import of oil, heavy machinery and industrial products. If Thailand wishes to eliminate this trade deficit, it has either to cut down the consumption of such products or produce them at home.

In both cases — of low productivity and lack of production in certain lines — the educational system can help. Training and research must be directed at increased productivity in already established occupations and at the establishment of new industrial production that would replace imports.

Social Equity

The major source of social disparity in Thailand is the very skewed distribution of wealth. This is a free society where wealth implies educational and occupational opportunities. In turn, education and occupation lead to further wealth, thus increasing the disparity in wealth among the socioeconomic groups in the society.

Of the many theories advanced for this state of affairs, one is worth noting here. It asserts that the spirit of hard work for self advancement tends to be low in a highly differentiated society because the high group thinks that it is now sufficiently high and there is no further need to work hard and the low group sees no way to reach the level enjoyed by the high group and hence ceases to work hard, leaving only the middle group to try to match the high. But the middle group, too, resorts to working less hard than it would since no one else is working hard. As a result, if this theory holds true, we have a society of underworking people.

The education system has an important role to play in solving this problem. First, it could make education free for all, or at least not dependent on differential wealth. Second, it should inculcate knowledge of and a receptive attitude towards egalitarian living and provide the corresponding environment in the school itself.

ADJUSTMENTS TO THE EDUCATION SYSTEM

If the country creates a policy of fulfilling its development needs and education is to be part of this process, then certain adjustments in the educational system are necessary. Possible adjustments of some of the major components of the education system are discussed below.

The *aims of education* are what people in the society assume to be desirable and worthy of their efforts. At present, students and parents generally regard education as a means for achieving a higher status in the social structure and, at the same time, they regard the social structure as unalterable. Thus schooling is not seen as an opportunity for self-development and growing up to be a self-actualized individual and a useful member of the society. As a result of this approach, learning itself is not so important as the receiving of a certificate, since the latter is the passport to a higher status.

The State, on the other hand, has not provided clearly and adequately conceptualized goals. The statement of aims of education in the various National Education Decrees do not deal with the overall aims of the educational subsystem (in relation to the other subsystems of the society) but simply lists a number of characteristics it expects young Thais to learn, such as morality, honesty, occupational skills and attitudes, health, etc. From the authors' point of view, these are more appropriately stated as curriculum objectives in specific subject areas. An unpublished survey of opinion conducted by one of the authors among members of the Education Society of Thailand in 1974 (most of whom hold postgraduate degrees in education with more than ten years of experience) showed that the aims of education in Thailand were not clear to them nor did they think that the aims were clear to the teachers.

These present statements provide guidelines for teachers' work and curriculum development but neglect other components of the system, such as enrollment, the meeting of manpower needs, administration, financial allocation, etc.

An education system in the future needs to be clear in its aims, and the aims must be worthy of the input it requires. Education will become a big industry consuming something like 20 percent of the national revenue and cannot be allowed to run on the basis of unclear aims or aims not worthy of the financial input. The aims of education in Thailand need reconceptualizing, if they are to be clear and worthy of support. The statement of new aims must appear in the form that serves both the learners and the society in a synchronized way. Various studies should be undertaken to ascertain the needs of individuals and the needs of the society. Such studies should be undertaken systematically and continuously to ensure that education is relevant to both sets of needs.

Two major issues in *enrollment* are what programs of training should be offered and who should be enrolled in these programs. It has been seen, earlier in this chapter, that after compulsory schooling there is the comprehensive secondary school (with academic and vocational subjects) and then a multiplicity of vocational courses in the vocational secondary school. In addition, courses and programs are offered within the non-formal educational system.

One major problem in enrollment has to do with the lack of reliable manpower forecasts. Each program sets its enrollment number for each year based on the capacity of the existing facilities. In some cases, it produces an under-supply, and in other cases an over-supply, of graduates to the corresponding labor market. To solve this problem, Thailand would need an additional agency established in the educational sector to be in charge of meshing the educational output to the labor market. It would feed its forecasts to the educational planning office of the education system so that enrollment could be adjusted to these needs. This agency could also undertake two additional tasks. It could coordinate preservice and inservice training in selected skills with assistance from firms, and it could also place graduates from the educational sector into jobs with the assistance of the Labor Department. Preferably the agency would be controlled by a board in which the Labor Department, the Ministry of Industry, and the private sector participated. An example of such an agency is the Industrial Training Board (ITB) of Singapore, which works very effectively.

Another major problem of enrollment in Thailand concerns the geographic and socioeconomic distribution of opportunity. Education beyond the primary level in Thailand is not easily accessible for children from low-income families and from rural areas. The low-income parent either has to save the child's labor for earning a living or cannot afford the school fees. The rural dweller, who is also typically low-income, still has one more barrier — the distance to the nearest secondary school. The temples in towns and cities are the only places where parents can lodge their sons while attending secondary schools. But due to economic factors, the temple, too, has become less available for this purpose today. The selection examination for secondary school also tends to ask questions more to do with town life and culture, thus placing rural children at a cultural disadvantage.

Thailand needs a reform of enrollment and of lodging facilities for government secondary schools. An enrollment capacity should be set for each year, and the quota given to each and every hamlet based on some justifiable index. The secondary school responsible for each area should enroll that quota of students without entrance examination and board and lodge them at the government's expense.

Two major drawbacks in the area of the *administration of education* are low achievement and low morale, which are themselves interrelated and related to other factors. Low achievement is a function of a number of things, such as unclear work objectives, unclear areas of responsibility or job descriptions, lack of competence to achieve the objectives (even when they are clear), or lack of commitment. These should be relatively easy to put in order.

Perhaps it should be emphasized that the improvement of organizational administration in Thailand must be attacked as a low-achievement problem rather than a low-morale problem. It is a low achievement that causes low morale in most organizations which are expected to achieve highly but do not do so. In organizations which have low achievement, it is possible to have high morale. Why is achievement in organizations in Thailand generally low? This has to do with the culture. Thais are basically farmers and are not competent in office work. In the case of educational administration, another factor makes this worse, namely that most administrators have been promoted from successful classroom teachers and not originally trained as administrators. Too often such an administrator does not see the whole picture of what is to be achieved, but perceives his role only in terms of control over people and resources. This is a phenomenon which underlies the low achievement in most Thai government organizations.

The *curriculum* (specific objectives in particular subject areas at particular grade-levels) is derived from the national aims of education dealt with above. It is on the basis of these specific objectives that the textbooks and other learning materials are written. A major criticism of the existing textbooks and learning materials is that they emphasize factual learning, impart in some cases unproven assumptions and neglect teaching scientific principles. Even worse is the neglect of teaching the need for critical questioning of facts, reasons, and assumptions.

The present teaching—learning process generally fosters passivity on the part of the learner rather than activity. The learner normally sits still in class and listens to the teacher or reads books, not having much opportunity to act out what is being learned. For instance, the class studies the lesson on cooperation without attempting to apply what they have learned to solve the problem of lack of cooperation in the class. The content of the lesson also encourages the passive mind rather than the active one. As an example, it forbids the pupil to smoke or to drink alcohol but gives no guidance on what to do if friends attempt to persuade him to do so. As a result, the pupil tends to withdraw from being active in general spheres of life when he grows up.

It is expected that the work currently being undertaken by the newly established Curriculum Center and other curriculum groups will help solve these types of problems, but it will clearly take some time for the curriculum development cycle and the teacher training to achieve this.

The *study of education* by those responsible for administering the educational system has, in general, not included courses on the role of education (or a specific subsector of it) in fostering the achievement of certain national-development goals, on manpower forecasts for educational enrollments, etc. Rather, they have studied the teaching of specific subject areas, evaluation, curriculum development, or primary-school

269

education. As a result, the educators are specialized in various subareas of educational development and consider this to be the ultimate aim of their service in this profession. Very few educators consider "education for nation development" as the approach to take in their service. In fact, when this concept was introduced in a proposed doctoral program in "development education" in 1973 most educators thought that it was a misnomer for "educational development". Fortunately, the program was approved and has been in operation since 1974, but the confusion still remains among many people. Efforts must be made to overcome this problem.

Educational research is another area that needs more impetus and better direction than in the past. Parallel to the study of education mentioned above, educational research conducted in Thailand has not focused on policy-relevant issues such as what should be the role of the educational system in helping the country achieve its development goals; what should be the aims of education in relation to the need of the individual and the society; what specific type of political and economic attitudes need to be taught to present-day pupils and whether those attitudes are now sufficiently taught; what irrelevant materials or unobjective information are there in the present curriculum and whether they should be removed. Research on educational forecasts, which has been undertaken has mostly been by foreign experts and not Thai graduate students and Thai researchers, pertains to the detailed aspects of curriculum and instruction, such as how to teach a given subject for better results, what psychological characteristics relate to what. Such research is good in itself, but insufficient for policy planning. A wider spectrum of research would seem to be desirable.

Conclusion

Thailand is a fortunate country to be situated in an area fertile for agriculture, so that the supply of food for its people is not a serious problem. More fortunate even is the fact that it has a system of government that protects the easy life of its people, and frustrated individuals can always find rest for their psyche in religion. Even with a series of socioeconomic and political turmoils here and there over the world during the past century, the Thai people have never experienced a very difficult time when they have had to struggle hard. This results in the Thai people having a relaxed life style, being easy going and friendly, mixing freely with foreigners, and occasionally being rather extravagant.

The Thai system of education is a reflection of the above socioeconomic and political background. A broad-minded and long-sighted monarch initiated education for his subjects, and it was well received. Later the government built up the momentum of the educational system into something that now receives an input of some 20 percent of the government's budget, enrolling some 40 percent of the country's school-age population. It is an open system accessible to people of all social classes, although socioeconomic—demographic factors do play a role in the practical implementation.

This review of the Thai primary and secondary education system has found no serious fault with it. The review has, however, identified several drawbacks which, if adjusted, would make it a more powerful instrument for achieving national-development goals. The drawbacks identified have been in the area of awareness of national-development goals in the educational aims, and the response to such goals through enrollment patterns, the administration, the curriculum, and the study of the subject of education. In most cases, better practices have been suggested for each of these drawbacks.

In the world of today, when all countries over the planet, developed and developing alike, are facing the problems of rising expectations and diminishing resources, Thailand too must face this phenomenon realistically. Its education system, capable of transforming the people's attitudes and habits, must commit itself to serving the nation's needs. It must make appropriate adjustments for better efficiency and effectiveness. With such conditions met, Thailand too can promise a bright future for its people.

References

ABHAI CHANTAWIMOL (1959) *Education in Thailand,* Ministry of Education, Bangkok.

ADAMS, DON (1970) *Education and Modernization in Asia,* Addison-Wesley, Menlo Park, Cal.

AMNUAY TAPINGKAE and SETTI, LOUIS J. (eds.) (1973) *Education in Thailand:*

Schooling in the ASEAN Region

Some Thai Perspectives, U.S. Department of Health, Education, and Welfare, Washington, D.C.

ATTAGARA BHUNTKIN; TAMBOONTECK, R.; and TUNSIRI VICHAI (1976) Teacher Education in Thailand, *Teacher Education in ASEAN,* (WONG, FRANCIS (ed.)) Heinemann, Singapore.

BURIPAKDI, CHALIO (1977) *The Value of Children,* Vol. 4, East–West Center, Honolulu.

DARLING, FRANK C., and DARLING, ANN B. (1971) *Thailand: The Modern Kingdom,* Asia Pacific, Singapore.

EDMUNDS, I. G. (1972) *Thailand: The Golden Land,* Bobbs-Merrill, New York.

Education for Life and Society (1975) Educational Administrator Association of Thailand (in Thai), Bangkok.

Education in Thailand: A Century of Experience (1969) Department of Elementary and Adult Education, Bangkok.

MEYER, ADOLPH E. (1949) *The Development of Education in the Twentieth Century,* 2nd ed, Prentice-Hall, Englewood Cliffs, N.J.

MILLER, T. W. G. (ed.) (1968) *Education in South-East Asia,* Ian Novak, Sydney.

National Development Scheme 1977 (1977) Ministry of Education, Bangkok.

NUECHTERLEIN, DONALD E. (1965) *Thailand and the Struggle for Southeast Asia,* Cornell University, Ithaca, N.Y.

Planning Office (1977) *Educational Statistics 1977,* (in Thai), Ministry of Education, Bangkok.

PRA WORRARAJMUNI (1975) *Thai Educational Philosophy,* (in Thai), Kled Thai Publishing, Bangkok.

Research Division, Department of Educational Techniques (1958) *Educational Development in Thailand 1949–1958,* Ministry of Education, Bangkok.

SA-NGAD PLENVANICH (1970) *A History of the Development of Population and Family Planning in Thailand,* (lecture published in Thai), Ministry of Public Health, Bangkok.

SEIDENFADEN, ERIK (1967) *The Thai Peoples,* The Siam Society, Bangkok.

SWAT SUKONTARANGSI (1967) *Development of Thai Educational Bureaucracy,* National Institute of Development Administration, Bangkok.

Thailand: Past and Present (1957) Ninth Pacific Science Congress, Bangkok.

WRONSKY, STANLEY P., and KAW SAWASDI PANICH (1966) *Secondary Education, Manpower and Educational Planning in Thailand,* Thai Watana Panich, Bangkok.

Bertambah keras pergerakan rakyat
menghendaki watak den pekerti, sabar
dan ketetapan hati.

The increasing magnitude of the
people's movement requires
character and a strong nature,
patience and a steadfast heart.

MOHAMMAD HATTA,
Indonesia's first vice-president

7

The Future

T. Neville Postlethwaite and R. Murray Thomas

The foregoing chapters have shown that all ASEAN education systems by the end of the 1970s had achieved marked progress in elementary and secondary schooling. However, the task the five nations had set for themselves had obviously not been completed. So at the outset of the 1980s educational leaders face challenges that the final decades of the century bring in terms of (1) expanding elementary and secondary education, (2) improving the quality of learning, (3) achieving a more effective structure for education, (4) increasing administrative efficiency, and (5) improving the teacher-supply system. In addition, (6) the nations are seeking to promote more satisfactory intercountry cooperation.

In Chapter 7, we inspect these six areas by first identifying the general goal ASEAN leaders appear to hold for each. We then consider those conditions that influence achievement of the goal, we identify methods for pursuing the goal, and we speculate about what sort of progress may be expected over the next decade or two.

Expanding Elementary and Secondary Education

THE GOALS

The central quantitative objective to which all five nations are committed is that of universal primary education. This means entering 100 percent of six- or seven-year-olds in school and ensuring that all of these children progress through the primary-school system of five to seven years in length. Singapore has already achieved this goal, and the Philippines and Malaysia are making good progress toward it. Indonesia and Thailand have yet a long way to go.

In addition, all five nations are attempting to expand their secondary-education enrollments. However, what proportion of teenage youths the nations' leaders intend to educate and to what grade level is difficult to identify from official documentation.

CONDITIONS INFLUENCING EXPANSION

The stark, shattering statistics which leap to the eye from the previous chapters is that, with the exception of Singapore, the population growth rate in the ASEAN region ranges from 2.4 percent annually in Thailand to 2.9 percent in Malaysia. The current population estimates place Malaysia at 13 million, the Philippines at 42 million, Thailand at 44 million, and Indonesia at 145 million. At a 2.4 percent growth rate, Thailand's population will double in 30 years. Indonesia's, at 2.7 percent, will exceed 240 million by the year 2000. Again with the exception of Singapore, 60 percent of ASEAN populations are under age 19, and between 70 and 90 percent of the people live in rural areas.

In general, about one-fifth of the gross domestic product of the region is being spent on the total educational budget, with the universities often receiving a disproportionately large part of the budget from the standpoint of the number of students served. In effect, in recent years education has been a costly business in the ASEAN countries, and still the largest of the nations are short of the goal of universal basic schooling.

Educators in Southeast Asia have expressed the hope that the population growth rate will decline in the near future, but there is a serious question about how realistic this hope is. Clearly enormous efforts by educators and the populace alike and larger amounts of money will be required if the goal of universal primary schooling is to be achieved. And even greater efforts will be needed to expand secondary education significantly. Indeed, with the populations growing so rapidly one wonders if it is even possible to keep constant the present proportion of each age group now in school.

Along with population increases there has been an accelerating social demand for education. And with increased industrialization urged in the nations' economic-development programs, there is every reason to expect an ever-rising demand from industry for more vocational and technical education, thus further extending the variety of schooling each country will be asked to provide. Hence, we can expect continued pressures to serve more pupils with a greater array of educational services.

A further condition affecting quantitative expansion is the dropout problem and the causes lying behind it. Particularly for the larger countries, the problem of children leaving the primary school before finishing the six-year course continues to be serious. For instance, in 1975 the national assessment of achievement in sixth grades in Indonesia showed that 57 percent of six-year-olds entered the first grade of the primary school, but only 38 percent reached Grade 6. In the middle and late 1970s, Indonesia exerted an all-out effort to construct more schools and train more teachers in order to reach the goal of enrolling at least 85 percent of all six-year-olds in first grade by 1980. However, consider the actual number of children that this plan endeavored to accommodate. If 57 percent of the nation's estimated 4 million six-year-olds were enrolled in 1975, then about 2.28 million were in school and 1.72 million were not. By 1980, with the high population growth rate there would be an estimated 4.6 million six-year-olds. If Indonesia was to enroll 85 percent or 3.91 million of these children, the country would have to increase school facilities and teachers to accommodate 1.63 million more children than there were spaces for five years earlier in 1975. To expect that this magnitude of growth in the school system could be accomplished in the five-year span of 1975–1980 would seem unreasonable. The spirit displayed by the Indonesian government in setting such a goal is noble indeed, but in face of such rapid population growth it is too great to accomplish. And this is only for the first grade. If the nation sought to reduce the dropout problem in subsequent grades at the same time, the number of pupils that needed spaces in school would be far greater. In sum, the chief enemy of the educational planner is rapid population increase.

Except for Singapore, the other ASEAN nations' problem in trying to catch run-away population growth is the same as Indonesia's in kind, though of less magnitude, because of smaller initial populations.

With the passing years, the five nations' gross national product has been increasing so that the countries' ability to finance schooling is progressively greater. However, in none of the larger ASEAN countries is the GNP increasing at the rate required to make the additional expenditures the educational budget requires to make universal schooling a reality in the near future.

ACTION BEING TAKEN

In terms of the proportion of an age group entering and progressing through primary education, only Singapore and Malaysia can be said to have achieved universal primary education. In Thailand and Indonesia, there are high dropout rates throughout primary education, with the Philippines lying somewhere between a relatively small proportion reaching sixth grade and 85 percent or more reaching that level. (UNESCO, 1974.) And, with the exception of Singapore, rural children in the ASEAN region have higher dropout rates than urban children.

On the other hand, in terms of meeting quotas set in the latest development plans, each of the countries has done rather well in establishing school-building programs, albeit with some delays. However, in their haste to set up new schools, educational planners have tended to hold to one or two school styles throughout the nation or a region, and in doing so they have sometimes not suited the building or its equipment to the setting or the pupils who are enrolled. In other cases, schools have not been placed properly in rural areas, so that there is not a good match between school size and the number of students within easy transportation distance from the institution. However, progress in solving these sorts of problems can be expected in the future as planners gain additional experience with school design and school mapping.

In recent years, there has been a mixed picture in teacher-preparation programs. Thailand has cut back on its teacher production, although a large influx of children seeking to enter schools can be expected with the population increase in the 1980s. Indonesia in the late 1960s stopped hiring teachers on the government payroll in order to reduce the size of a swollen corps of civil servants. At the same time, there was some reduction in the preparation of teachers. But recently enrollment in teacher-training schools increased, and emergency post-secondary, short-term courses to prepare junior-high teachers were reinstituted to fill the shortage of teachers at the junior-secondary level.

Inservice education has been accelerated in the ASEAN nations for teachers who need upgrading in order to handle larger numbers of students effectively and to be oriented about curriculum revisions.

Of particular interest in the latter 1970s have been the nonformal-education programs in the Philippines and in Indonesia to accommodate children who either have dropped out of primary school or else never have had a chance to attend. In mid-1979 Indonesia began its open junior-secondary-school experiment to provide a junior-high education via radio and self-instructional modules for children who have finished the primary grades but can find no room in the crowded junior-secondary schools. The next two decades should see more such experiments with nonformal methods of furnishing learning opportunities to the masses of children and youths.

PROSPECTS FOR THE FUTURE

As implied above, we are somewhat pessimistic about the chances of the largest ASEAN countries achieving universal primary education in the foreseeable future. With careful planning in both population-control programs and in the expansion of educational facilities, and with increasing the gross national product in the economic sphere, it is conceivable that the target might be achieved sometime in the 1990s. But census data which planners need are not always accurate, and the process of designing plans and administering them in developing countries is usually difficult to manage efficiently. Furthermore, the economic growth rate in the larger nations may well be insufficient to cover the costs of expanding educational opportunities.

Many of the development projects in nonformal education and in technical/vocational programs are still in the trial stage, so their impact is yet unknown. Systematic formative evaluation has not been built into many of the projects. Hence, those people in charge of the projects have not been able to monitor the progress of their activities in order to correct errors and strengthen weaknesses and thereby keep the projects on target. However, in recent years there has been an encouraging increase in effective evaluation, with results used for the improvement of the components of the programs. More such careful assessment can be expected in the future as larger numbers of educators acquire the requisite skills.

Despite the above qualifications, we have been greatly impressed by the way the ASEAN countries have met the challenges they have faced over the past two decades and by the ingenious innovations they are attempting. It is our estimate that the ASEAN countries lead the world's developing nations in the example they are setting in attacking the problem of offering universal schooling. As noted earlier, how closely they will approach the goal of education for everyone will be determined chiefly by their success in curtailing population growth, the degree of improvement they can make in educational planning and execution, and the amount of money that can be put into the educational enterprise.

Qualitative Improvement of Education

GOALS

Nations recently freed from colonial control usually give initial attention to increasing the amount of educational opportunity, then later focus attention on improving the quality. Such has been the pattern in Southeast Asia. During the 1950s and early 1960s those people in charge of education in the ASEAN region sought to expand the numbers of teachers and schools as rapidly as possible, but in the process the quality of education did not improve. Indeed, it often deteriorated from the level of the 1930s or 1940s when fewer students attended school. However, in the 1970s, all ASEAN members exerted great efforts to improve the level of learning.

Such efforts have been directed toward making the objectives of the instructional program more relevant to the needs of both the society and the individual learner. The most basic major aim is to produce universal literacy and numeracy. A further goal is to raise the level of achievement for each grade level or age level of pupils. Efforts are also directed at diminishing the achievement gap between various groups — between ethnic groups, between language groups, between urban and rural children, between social-class levels, and between boys and girls.

These goals are common to most areas of the world, but the systematic manner in which the ASEAN countries have been attacking the task is worthy of particular note.

CONDITIONS INFLUENCING QUALITATIVE IMPROVEMENT

One significant condition bearing on qualitative improvement has been the discrepancy between the sort of education considered relevant in the first half of the twentieth century and that regarded as relevant in recent years. As earlier chapters have shown, four of the five ASEAN countries (Thailand excepted) were under the control of European colonialists until the early 1940s, and during World War II all were occupied by Japanese military forces. During these eras the central goal of education was to serve the aims of the colonial rulers, which typically meant that schools were fashioned in the image of those in the colonialists' homelands. Only a small elite were schooled in the colonies, and standards of quality as well as the focus of the curriculum were those imported from the ruling nations.

Once independence had been achieved by the ASEAN nations in the late 1940s and 1950s, the indigenous educational leaders expressed a desire to alter the direction of education, making school offerings relevant to the socioeconomic and cultural needs of newly developing, independent societies and well suited to the aspirations of individual citizens. In the 1960s and 1970s, there has been an upsurge in national curriculum development, and educational leaders have appeared more confident and willing to define their own directions and, if they do borrow from the West, to borrow selectively as determined by their own goals and analyses rather than tradition.

Besides tradition and the pressures to increase the quantity of children in schools, another factor that has influenced the quality of education has been the nature of teacher preparation. During colonial times, instructors in many secondary schools and often in primary grades were foreigners from the colonial power. Following independence, the foreigners returned home in most cases, and the indigenous teachers often accepted leadership posts in the new governments, which were short of educational personnel. In consequence, schools lost a significant proportion of their teachers just at a time the new nations were seeking to expand the number of schools. To fill the need for teachers, short courses were set up, or teachers were awarded certificates after completing only a junior-secondary level of schooling. Although the training of teachers has improved over the years since the early 1950s, there are still significant numbers of ones with substandard credentials in the classrooms of nearly all ASEAN countries. Studies of pupils' progress under older teachers who had less adequate preparation have shown that such pupils do not succeed in school as well as ones taught by instructors with more recent and more advanced teacher training. (Moegiadi *et al.,* 1979, pp. 322, 329.) Therefore, the quality of education has been strongly affected by the adequacy of teachers' preparation.

A further influence on quality has been the adequacy of instructional materials, particularly of textbooks. In the larger ASEAN countries, texts have frequently been in short supply so that children have had to share books, or in many schools only the teacher has had a book. Sometimes available materials have been poor in quality, with one major fault being that the language used in textbooks is too complex for the students' reading level. When textbooks have been either unavailable or inappropriate, teachers have commonly adopted a lecture-and-recitation approach to instruction or have copied material onto the chalkboard for pupils to copy into their notebooks.

Quality of learning has also been influenced by the amount of time pupils have spent on their lessons. When the school day is as short as two or three hours, and when inefficient management of the classroom by a teacher reduces the time pupils spend studying, progress in learning suffers.

ACTION BEING TAKEN

Educators in the ASEAN region have been making significant progress in upgrading the quality of learning. To ensure constant, expert attention to matters of quality, each of the nations has established key curriculum-development groups as a permanent part of the education system. Curriculum-development centers have been organized in Malaysia, Thailand, and Indonesia during the 1970s. Curriculum-development groups in the Philippines and Singapore operate within the respective ministries of education.

A basic requirement for systematic upgrading of quality is that accurate information is available about the current quality of schooling and of factors influencing quality. To obtain such information, all five nations have conducted assessments of educational needs. These assessments have ranged in scope from large-scale national surveys, such as those conducted in Indonesia in 1975–78 (Moegiadi *et al*, 1979; Mangindaan, 1978), to small-scale evaluations of one segment, such as vocational education (Atikah, 1977; Nasoetion, 1976). On the basis of data collected from such studies there have been major revisions of educational objectives for the various grade levels in the formal school systems of all countries.

One of the major research findings from the surveys of educational achievement such as those in Indonesia (Moegiadi, 1979; Mangindaan, 1978), Thailand (N.E.C., 1976) and the Philippines (Project Soutele, 1976) is the large gap in achievement between pupils in various regions of the country. Part of this disparity is due to the difference between urban and rural areas. The analyses of factors associated with such differences point to the differences in the quality of teachers (and most countries have problems in ensuring that good teachers go to rural areas), and differences in what is commonly referred to as educational facilities — enough textbooks, school libraries, classroom libraries, audiovisual aids, etc. The educational authorities are aware of these research results and are making every effort to increase good teaching in schools and to improve the provision of educational facilities. But with increase of the number of pupils in schools and with limited resources, this will remain a problem for quite a time to come.

As a further step toward qualitative improvement, each of the nations has trained specialists in the writing of textbooks and instructional modules. Equipment has been imported to outfit science laboratories and vocational-education shops and classrooms. Inexpensive kits for conducting science experiments have been produced within the ASEAN region, featuring materials and activities suited particularly to the Southeast Asian setting.

Significant advances have also been made in devising ways to evaluate pupils' progress and to assess the quality of the educational program. (See Lewy, 1976.)

One of the most encouraging features of recent curriculum development is that some of the methodology used in ASEAN countries is among the best in the world. National educational aims have been systematically analyzed down to the classroom level, where objectives are cast in the form of desired student behaviors that are readily evaluated. Feedback systems to furnish curriculum planners information about which objectives are not being reached by pupils have been implemented so curriculum developers and textbook writers can revise their placement of objectives in the school's learning sequence. An increasing number of instructional programs are experimenting with multimedia approaches, so teachers have more than textbook and lecture–recitation methods of instruction. Learning units or modules are increasingly designed to include discussions, field trips, radio programs, tape recordings, and laboratory experiences when these techniques appear most suitable. Experimentation is going on with mastery-learning programs in which pupils' background preparation for an upcoming learning unit is first assessed, remedial work is immediately provided for pupils with inadequate preparation so they can attempt the new unit with promise of success, and enrichment activities are furnished for the faster learners while their classmates are still completing the basic unit. Although aid in conducting such experimental programs is sometimes obtained from educators in North America and Europe, the major part of the work is carried out by Southeast Asians themselves as the corps of indigenous educational experts with modern planning skills has increased markedly over the past decade or two.

Although not all curriculum projects in the ASEAN region are of uniform high quality, there is evidence that the best programs are having a spillover effect, with the leaders of the programs serving as consultants to less advanced projects. Furthermore, publicity about important projects has attracted visitors from both within and outside the region, so innovative practices are having an impact beyond the immediate programs in which they are found. Publications describing projects in the ASEAN area have been issued by international bodies, such as UNESCO, so educators Southeast Asia have been able to profit from work done there, (*Educational Building and Facilities in the Asian Region,* 1976; Nasoetion, 1976.)

An example of a publicized program that illustrated forward-looking planning is the Malaysian project conducted in a rural district that promises to become industrialized and urban within a few years. In anticipation of this industrialization, educational researchers studied the sorts of educational objectives which will be required for the new situation for the children who are at present in the rural area, and curriculum materials are produced and put into the schools for future needs in order to have a smooth transition. A description of this study has been published as an aid to educators in other countries who face similar prospects of population shifts. (Postlethwaite and King, 1975.)

In summary, the quality and variety of work in curriculum improvement over the past two decades in ASEAN countries has been increasing, with a larger number of the ideas for innovation coming from indigenous educators themselves rather than foreign consultants. The recognition of the roles of educational research and evaluation in the improvement of learning quality and the upsurge of research and evaluation activities in the ASEAN area are notable features of the past decade.

PROSPECTS

The creation of ways of improving school facilities and of increasing the general level of student achievement, while reducing the gap between the lowest achievers and the highest, will likely continue in the future at an accelerating pace. Research and development centers that focus on curriculum improvement are now well established in the ASEAN countries, and their staff members are becoming increasingly expert at their assignments.

There is a question, however, about how widely newer instructional practices will be disseminated in the coming years, given the cost of improved text materials and audiovisual media and the difficulty of upgrading teachers' skills in using the newer approaches. Once more, high population growth rates are the educational planner's adversary. Without gaining control over population increase, ASEAN educators may well find that the experimental programs they have devised to increase learning will remain islands of quality for a minority of schools in an expanding ocean of children and youths. The task of providing any education at all for the growing cohorts of children is a sufficient challenge. Far greater yet is the challenge of providing high-quality education for all.

Achieving a More Effective Structure for Education

In speaking of educational structure, we are referring to such matters as (1) class and school size and organization, (2) formal versus nonformal education, (3) general versus vocational education, (4) the length of primary and secondary schooling, (5) private versus public control, and (6) examination and certification systems. All six of these matters pose problems for ASEAN educators.

CLASS AND SCHOOL SIZE AND ORGANIZATION

The Goals

Class and school size are perennial problems in all countries of the world. The optimal class size is presumably one that permits pupils to learn efficiently and receive attention to their individual needs, and that permits the teacher to maintain control of the group's learning activities. Classes should also be of a size that can be housed efficiently and that the nation can afford to finance. Presumably the school size should be such that pupils can reach the school easily and that a variety of learning opportunities can be offered for the cognitive advancement of each pupil but not so large that the child could feel emotionally or socially lost in it — lost in the sense of lacking a sense of personal worth and identity and lacking close identification and social interaction with teachers and classmates. Ideally, the school should be of such a size to permit effective, economical administration.

Conditions Influencing Class and School Size

From the planners' point of view there are obvious conditions affecting class size, such as the physical dimensions of the classroom, the number of teachers available, the number of pupils in the catchment area, and the amount of funds available for school-building. Typical instructional methods could be said to be important when considering class-size. Although class sizes of 20 to 40 seem to be typical for most countries, it is to be noted that Korea (Lee, 1978) increased the average level of achievement dramatically for all middle-school pupils in the mid 1970s by using a variant of mastery learning as an instructional strategy. And this was with class sizes of 50 to 90 with a median class-size of 70. Lindsey (1974) has shown in several so-called "developed" countries that class size interacts with hours of instruction, the socio-economic status of the pupil, the type of school program and the sex of the pupil. Thus, different class-sizes seem to be optimal under different conditions.

As for school size, the density of population is clearly a conditioning factor. The technique of school mapping (Hallak, 1977) introduced by the International Institute for Educational Planning in Paris is beginning to be applied in several of the Southeast Asian nations where not only is population density taken into account but also such factors as geographical conditions, migration trends, the planning of the location of industry among others are considered. Elementary schools are less specialized than secondary schools and hence primary education – and often lower-secondary education – can have smaller schools than those schools requiring special equipment and very specialized teachers.

School size is also influenced by the numbers of specialized teachers needed and their availability. In a city, a school might be smaller if it can employ part-time teachers for specialized courses. But in remote rural areas the school might need to be larger, since specialized teachers would usually need a full-time job, as they could not find the sorts of nearby supplementary employment in other secondary schools that can be found in cities.

A further contingency is the language pattern in schools. A Tamil-language school in Singapore could be expected to be smaller than a Chinese-language school, since fewer parents send their children to Tamil-language schools.

Other contingencies that affect school size are parents' religious convictions, the space available to erect a building and provide a playground, and the concepts of building design held by architects who plan schools.

The recent surveys in Indonesia have shown that larger classes and larger schools produce higher achievement in their pupils; but that larger classes and larger schools tend to have more highly qualified teachers and better facilities, and it is these features which are important rather than the larger classes or schools *per se.*

Action Being Taken

Two problems of opposite nature found in all four of the largest ASEAN countries are those of overcrowded classes in urban centers and of inefficiently small classes in the sparsely populated hinterlands.

One conceivable solution to overcrowding is to reduce the country's population growth so there will be fewer school-aged children. With such a reduction the class size in existing schools could be lowered. However, the only nation able to effect such a solution over the past two decades has been Singapore. As noted earlier, the other four ASEAN members cannot be expected to reduce their growth rates significantly over the next decade or so. Hence the diminishing-population solution cannot care for their overcrowding problem.

A second solution is to build more schools more rapidly. And though all ASEAN members have made good progress in increasing the numbers of schools, this approach cannot be expected to accomplish much unless population-control programs are more successful in the future than they have been since 1950.

Two other solutions to overcrowding that have been used in ASEAN school systems are those of multiple sessions of children using the same classroom each day or of nonformal modes of education. We shall first consider the multiple-sessions approach, then in a later section discuss nonformal education.

The system of using one classroom for two sessions of pupils has apparently operated with some success in schools which start early in the morning and continue until evening, so that each group of children attends a full session of five or six hours of instruction. However, oftentimes the sessions are shortened to three hours or less. This shortened-class-time arrangement is most often found in schools in which three sessions of pupils are accommodated each day in the same classroom or in which the same teacher must handle more than one session. Research results have supported the common-sense idea that the less time pupils spend on their lessons, the less they learn. Thus, short sessions reduce the amount of learning. In addition, the efficiency of learning declines if the children in afternoon or evening classes are too tired to profit from instruction or if the same teacher who instructs the morning group must also teach for a full afternoon or evening period as well. Studies of multiple sessions in Indonesian schools have shown that pupils in the morning session learn about the same as those in later sessions. (Moegiadi *et al.,* 1978, p. 319.) In effect, multiple sessions can reduce class size, but there may be a danger that if the same teacher is used for all sessions the afternoon or evening sessions may result in less learning than do single-session classes. (Mangindaan, 1978, p. 71.)

The opposite problem — that of unduly small classes — has stimulated educational planners to set up projects for preparing teachers to work with a class in which students of several grade levels are enrolled. This is the problem of the one-teacher or two-teacher school that is found in rural areas in many parts of the world.

As for school size, the people who have planned school buildings have been architects working without much aid from the sort of people who determine what goes on in classrooms, such people as teachers, curriculum specialists, and teaching methodologists. As UNESCO school-building experts have observed:

> The need for designers to question and to understand the uses to which the schools they design are put has never been greater, for Asian education is now at a stage in its development where many significant changes planned in the recent past are in the course of implementation, and changes of a much more wide-ranging nature are on the horizon. (*Educational Building and Facilities in the Asian Region,* 1976, p. 12.)

There is evidence that more of this cooperative planning between architect and educator is in the offing. Clearly also, more research needs to be undertaken within the specific ASEAN settings. The evidence on school size from Indonesia (Moegiadi *et al.,* 1979, p. 314; Mangindaan, 1978, pp. 58 and 103) comes from the first attempts of systematic research into such problems. It is to be expected that the current IEA project on Classroom Environment (IEA, 1978) in which Indonesia and Thailand are participating will furnish more detailed information on the interactions of certain teacher behaviors with class and school size for those countries.

In the meantime, it must be recalled that planners have a difficult

287

time in providing just the number of schools required for the growing number of children in the country, and hence have tended to adopt one or two basic school designs and then replicate them throughout the nation.

Prospects

Without a reduction in the population growth rates in the four largest ASEAN countries there is little hope that all children can find a place in school in the foreseeable future. Class sizes and school sizes can be expected to stay large or grow even larger. We can expect schools to continue using multiple shifts just in order to keep class size within manageable limits. Standardized school building designs will be used.

Finally, it is to be expected that ASEAN educators will experiment increasingly with innovative programs to maximize learning in very large or small classes and schools and, in general, increase research into these problems. It is to be noted that this type of research could well be conducted cooperatively by the ASEAN members.

FORMAL VERSUS NONFORMAL EDUCATION

Before proposing a formal/nonformal goal for ASEAN educational systems we need to define *formal, nonformal* and *informal* education. Although no standard definition for the three terms exists, for present purposes we can offer a somewhat loose distinction among them that many educators would likely accept. By *formal* education we mean planned education in the usual school setting where students meet for a regular period of time each day, are instructed in a classroom or laboratory by a trained teacher, and are evaluated to determine whether they should pass on to a subsequent grade and should ultimately receive a diploma or certificate. By *nonformal* we mean planned organized learning, but not with all the characteristics of the regular school. Nonformal programs may be in settings other than the typical school (such as in the home or in a business location) or in the school but at unusual hours (such as in the evening or on the weekend). Likewise, the instruction may be given by someone other than a trained teacher (such as by an auto mechanic or an expert wood carver or seamstress). In addition, the instructional media may not be textbooks or a teacher lecture but rather radio, television, a correspondence course, or a packet of activities the learner is assigned to complete under his or her own initiative. By *informal* education we mean nonorganized learning opportunities for learners without the formal guidance of a teacher or tutor. Examples of informal-education resources are newspapers, magazines, how-to-do-it booklets purchased in a book store, libraries, museums, and informational radio and television programs.

The Goals

The aim of ASEAN countries in formal-versus-nonformal structures apparently is to achieve a distribution of formal and nonformal programs that best suits the nation's educational aims, the characteristics of learners, efficiency of instruction, the location of facilities, and the pace at which educational planners can provide facilities and personnel. Where there are insufficient places in the formal school system, then nonformal programs are offered whereby pupils can study the same content as they would have done had they been fortunate enough to have a place in the formal school system.

Conditions Warranting the Creation of Nonformal Programs

One way to view nonformal education is to see it as an alternative adopted when conditions prevent the formal school system from doing the job satisfactorily. For example, a nonformal apprenticeship system may be instituted because the school does not have the equipment or the working conditions normally found in a factory or business office or on a farm. Thus students are placed in on-the-job assignments, perhaps supplemented by evening courses in theory or academic subjects related to the occupation for which they are preparing. Or there may not be enough formal schools to accommodate the number of qualified applicants, so correspondence or radio courses may be offered to care for those not enrolled in the regular schools. Teachers who wish to upgrade their qualifications may not be able to enroll in college because the college is too distant from the place they teach, so nonformal opportunities may be offered them in the form of weekend workshops conducted in a nearby town by personnel from the distant college.

Therefore, the lack of any condition normally found in a formal school may be the motivation for setting up nonformal options that compensate for that lack.

Action Being Taken

Interest in nonformal options has been high in ASEAN countries in recent years, so that a variety of programs has been instituted. As indicated in the preceding chapters, one realm in which nonformal education has been playing a strong role is that of vocational training. Another is community living — family planning to control population expansion, nutrition to enhance health, safety practices to reduce injury, consumer education to help buyers make wise purchases. Still others are in the area of religious training and trace their origins into the distant past — the pondok of Malaysia and Southern Thailand, the pesantren of Indonesia, and the Buddhist monastery of Thailand. Nonformal programs are also serving as a substitute for formal education, that is, furnishing opportunities for people unable to take advantage of the established formal school system. This sort of nonformal education provides literacy training for adults, primary education for school dropouts, secondary education by means of radio or correspondence courses for students living in remote areas, and the like. Radio and booklet courses for teacher-upgrading (inservice education) are being undertaken more and more.

An important decision facing educational planners is whether a particular nonformal project is intended to function as a permanent program or only as a temporary measure until enough formal schooling facilities are available. The importance of this decision has been illustrated in several ASEAN nonformal efforts of recent years, including the IMPACT program in the Philippines and its Indonesian equivalent, the PAMONG project described in Chapters 1 and 2. The intent of these projects has been to furnish out-of-school primary education for pupils who dropped out of school before finishing the sixth grade. However, in the tryout of the PAMONG approach in Central Java, developers of the project found that before the plan had been operating for more than two or three years, there were almost no new candidates willing to enter it. Observers of the program speculated that there were two significant causes for this. First, the characteristics which caused many children to drop out of a formal program — such as lack of interest, lack of ability, or lack of diligence — were even greater liabilities when the pupils were expected to learn with self-instructional materials in their own homes. Second, there is considerable observational evidence in ASEAN societies as well as in other parts of the world that nonformal alternatives to the regular school are not as prestigious as the formal school. In colonial times, a diploma or degree from a formal school or college was one of the marks of superiority among the colonial rulers. Today it continues to carry high status value. Hence, if parents are given the choice between having their children in a formal school and a nonformal alternative, they appear to select the formal school. Such apparently was the case with the absence of candidates for the PAMONG project. Rather than accepting the out-of-school self-instructional alternative as a desirable option, parents in the district clearly preferred formal traditional schools. Therefore, it is important to estimate how acceptable a nonformal program that parallels a formal school will be to its potential enrollees. Such preliminary research could easily be undertaken. Planners would appear unwise to invest large sums and to appoint large permanent staffs for nonformal programs that will function primarily as stop-gap measures if such programs parallel formal programs which the populace prefers and expects to have established in the future.

Prospects

In keeping with the trends of the 1970s, future years should witness an increase in the variety of nonformal programs in the ASEAN region. Furthermore, if the growing potential of ASEAN members in the areas of curriculum development and evaluation continues to increase, the quality of the programs should improve as well. Cooperative efforts among the ASEAN countries, such as with the IMPACT and PAMONG projects, should hasten such progress by enabling the five nations to share costs, specialists, and experience rather than each country having to bear the weight of research and development alone. It is hoped that evaluation and research will become integral components of the many nonformal innovations taking place.

GENERAL VERSUS VOCATIONAL EDUCATION

At the outset we need to explain the distinctions made in the following paragraphs among the terms general education, vocational education, and vocational training. *General education* means the sort of studies intended to furnish a good foundation in communication and mathematical skills and in social, scientific, and historical understandings. At the primary level, such studies are often referred to as *basic fundamentals.* At the secondary level, they are usually called *academic* subjects or *college-preparatory* studies. They are "general" in the sense that they do not lead to any particular vocation.

In contrast, the terms *vocational education* and *vocational training* identify studies leading to a particular vocational field (vocational education) and a particular job within that field (vocational training). In other words, the term vocational education usually indicates preparation to suit an individual to a field such as that of business-office work or the machine trades. Whereas, vocational training usually indicates preparation for a specific job within that field. For example, in business-office work an individual may be trained as a bookkeeper or an executive secretary. In the machine trades a person may be trained as a metal-lathe operator or tool maker. One of the problems facing vocational-education planners is that of deciding how specific job-preparation should be. Should the vocational school seek to furnish only the more general vocational-education level, and leave the vocational training to private industry? Or should the vocational school train youths to fill specific jobs? Or what should be the mesh between education in school and education in industry?

The Goals

The task of educational planners is to achieve a proper balance among general education, vocational education, and vocational training and to determine what sorts of institutions are best fitted to perform each of these functions.

Conditions Influencing the General-Versus-Vocational Ratio

The condition that has most significantly affected the ratio in recent years has been the governments' manpower-need projections as found in five-year national-development plans. During the 1960s and 1970s, more than any time in the past, ASEAN governments have sought to make accurate estimates of how many of each type of worker will be needed in the future and then to alter schools and nonformal programs in ways that will produce such workers.

A second condition that usually has run counter to the manpower-prediction condition has been the people's educational preferences, that is, social demand. The great majority of secondary education in all ASEAN countries has been of a general, academic variety intended to lead to the university. This type of schooling still carries greater prestige than vocational schooling, so manpower planners have faced opposition from the general populace in altering the general/vocational ratio of schools. There is evidence (Musa, 1979) that in certain industries, the employers prefer employees recruited from the academic type schools rather than from the vocational schools training persons for those industries.

A third condition is that of cost. Academic classrooms are generally less expensive to equip and maintain than are vocational classrooms.

A fourth condition is teacher supply. As noted earlier, teachers who are prepared as experts in machine-shop operation or business-office management are able to earn higher wages in the business world than in the classroom, so graduates of vocational teacher-education programs often reject teaching posts in favor of jobs in their occupational speciality.

A further influence is the willingness and capability of the industrial and business sectors of the economy to cooperate with vocational-education officials in carrying out an overall vocational education and training program. Active involvement in vocational training by private businesses can relieve the schools of having to establish elaborate facilities which business firms are willing to provide.

Action Being Taken

The most obvious trend of the 1970s in all ASEAN countries has been a movement toward increased vocational education in the schools and the provision of more nonformal-education courses. However, as indicated in the separate country chapters, the manner in which ASEAN governments are pursuing this tack varies somewhat from nation to nation.

Since 1966, Thailand has sought to reduce the sharp distinction between academic and vocational secondary education by changing an increasing number of academic high schools into comprehensive high schools that offer both a college-preparatory track and one or more vocational specialities — agriculture, home economics, technical education, and the like.

Most secondary education in the Philippines is still academic. In the early 1970s, nearly 84 percent of public and almost all private high schools were academic. However, during the 1970s some growth was realized in vocational schools and in training courses for out-of-school youth sponsored by the Department of Labor.

In the mid-1970s, Malaysia was moving noticeably from an almost exclusively academic secondary-school system to one that includes a higher proportion of vocational institutions. For example, the percentage of academic schools declined from 92.5 in 1974 to 85.8 in 1976, because the establishment of more vocational schools brought the percentage of specialized technical-education institutions up from 5.2 in 1974 to 9.6 in 1976.

Singapore has achieved the best record in the ASEAN region in coordinating academic and vocational offerings, particularly with specialized courses in which industry cooperates. In 1974, nearly 25 percent of secondary schools were already of a vocational variety, with some observers predicting that the balance toward which the school system should be moving was 50 percent vocational and 50 percent academic.

Indonesia inherited from the Dutch colonialists a complex scheme of specialized vocational schools in which students entered their speciality at the junior-secondary level. Over the past three decades, the junior-secondary school has been changed into a general-education institution, with specialization not beginning until the upper-secondary level in most instances. However, because so many students have ended their schooling with the primary level and have carried no vocational skills into the world of work, the government in the 1970s instituted some vocational education in the upper-primary grades, seeking to suit the nature of the studies to the community in which the school is located. Rural schools feature agricultural studies; urban schools offer simple trades found in cities.

Prospects

In future years we can expect increased vocational studies in comparison to general academic offerings in all ASEAN countries. We can also expect experimentation with a variety of forms of vocational education and vocational training, both formal and nonformal, with more coordination between government and private business sectors. The chief problems faced by educational planners are those of (1) making accurate predictions of the amounts and kinds of workers needed, (2) determining how specific vocational studies should be in schools (the proper balance between the school's role and that of private industry and on-the-job training), (3) encouraging able students to enter vocational schools rather than remaining in the college-preparatory stream, and (4) deciding at what level of the school system vocational education should be offered for those nations in which a significant dropout rate can be expected in the primary and early secondary grades.

THE LENGTH OF PRIMARY AND SECONDARY SCHOOLING

Prior to the arrival of European colonialists, the schools of Southeast Asia were not organized in a series of grades through which students progressed by annually ascending from the present "grade" or "standard" or "form" to the next higher one until the sequence had been completed and the certificate or diploma awarded. Instead, a youth who entered a Moslem pondok or pesantren or a Buddhist monastery did so at whatever time he seemed ready and stayed as long as he or the guru or monk deemed suitable. But with the establishment of Western-style graded schools, the systems of all ASEAN countries are now predominantly of the grade-hierarchy type. Under these conditions, one of the significant problems facing educational planners is that of deciding what the most desirable length of primary and secondary schooling will be.

The Goals

The best length for schooling depends somewhat on the viewpoint of the person setting the goal. Manpower planners want schooling to be long enough so that the potential worker is physically, intellectually, and emotionally mature and properly trained, yet not so long that the cost of schooling is an undue drain on the country's budget — and also not so long that there is an undue gap between when the worker is needed and when he is available to take the job. Parents in rural areas where children or youths can profitably work in the fields, around the home, or in fishing and hunting activities are prone to want schooling to be rather short so the children are absent from the family work force as little as possible. Pupils who find school boring or oppressively difficult also wish to have it over at an early date. But those who find it interesting, a desirable place for social interaction with peers, and a place to gain satisfaction with increased knowledge and skill are apt to like it to last a long time. Officials concerned with maintaining political-economic stability in a nation which has a high rate of unemployment or underemployment may prefer to keep youths in school for a relatively long time in order to keep them "profitably occupied" rather than idle on the streets or overcrowding the job market.

Conditions Affecting the Length of Schooling

Several of the potent influences on length of schooling are reflected in the description of goals above — level of maturity needed in employees, the needs of the family work force, the profit students feel they gain from school, and the relationship between the number of job openings and job applicants in the labor market.

A further factor is tradition. People often appear to believe that the length of the established, respected school — particularly the school they themselves attended — is the proper length. So it may be difficult to convince them that some different pattern would be more desirable.

An obvious additional condition is the efficiency of the learning system. Children who attend school two hours a day under poorly-trained teachers in crowded classrooms without textbooks are not likely to learn as much as children who attend school one year less but who go five hours a day to well-trained teachers in well equipped classrooms.

Action Being Taken

Over the past decade or so ASEAN educators have been experimenting with several lengths of elementary and secondary schooling and with several ways of dividing the years into types of schools.

From earlier chapters, we may recall that each ASEAN country has adopted a system slightly different from the others and that in recent years all of them have altered length of schools in different ways. In the Philippines, children are scheduled to enter the primary grades around age seven. The typical primary course is six years long, though officially schools are to provide a seven-year elementary education — a regulation that only a few private schools have been able to implement because of a shortage of funds.'

During the past two decades, Thailand has shifted from a 4 + 3-year elementary program to a six-year elementary school and from a 3 + 2 secondary pattern to a 3 + 3 plan. Thus schooling through the secondary level is still normally 12 years long, but a year has been saved from the primary school and added to the upper-secondary level.

Malaysia operates a six-year primary school in which students are automatically promoted from one standard to the next. Secondary education consists of a three-year junior-high school plus a two-year senior high and then a two-year sixth form, a total of 13 years of schooling, with pupils leaving at different stages of the hierarchy to enter the world of work.

Singapore has a six-year primary school after which pupils must pass a school-leaving examination in order to gain entrance to the junior-secondary school which offers a general program (including basic vocational education) the first two years, after which students are streamed into vocational or college-preparatory studies according to their aptitudes, interests, and the needs of the Singapore labor force. Following this 6–2–2 sequence is an additional two-year program in either a preuniversity course or some specialized vocational program, such as one leading to a certificate to teach in the primary school.

Indonesia has operated a 6–3–3 plan for some years. However, in the latter 1970s the Ministry of Education has experimented with a five-year primary school which follows a special modularized-instruction classroom methodology intended to achieve in five years what traditional schools have accomplished in six. Since the data from the experiment will not be available until the early 1980s, the effectiveness of the five-year plan is not yet known.

Prospects

In the future, the ASEAN members will likely be experimenting further with different lengths of schooling. The changes effected in the length of primary, lower-secondary, and upper-secondary levels will be in response to the factors described above under goals and conditions. As nations experience the economic pinch of having to operate more primary schools for larger cohorts of children, they may be expected to shorten primary school to save money — or else they will continue to suffer high dropout rates. As more mature workers are needed for higher-level industrial jobs, the length of prevocational education and job training may well become greater. And in like manner the structure of schooling will mirror other shifts in the broader political and socioeconomic environment in which the schools operate.

PRIVATE VERSUS PUBLIC CONTROL

The terms *public* and *private* by themselves are of no use in explaining the characteristics of ASEAN schools, for schools listed under each of these designations are so varied. In several of the nations, there are "private" religious schools funded by government subsidies and following a curriculum authorized by the government. And in several nations, there are "public" schools that teach a religious curriculum, such as Islamic or Buddhist or Christian beliefs, along with secular subjects, and they collect "private" fees from parents to supplement monies they are supplied from the public coffers.

Therefore, to learn what meaning the terms *private* and *public* carry in a given country or district, we need more information. We need to know the differences between the two types of schools in terms of their sources of funding, who determines the curriculum, their student-admissions policies, and the clientele they serve.

298

The Goal

We would speculate that top officials in all ASEAN ministries of education might well subscribe to this general aim: that the proper ratio of private to public schools is one which best promotes the nation's educational objectives and ensures a high quality of instruction at a reasonable cost, while protecting the welfare of the significant subgroups of the society.

But we are convinced that how this general aim is interpreted in practice can differ markedly from one country to another, depending upon how the following conditions interact in each of the five societies.

Conditions Influencing the Public/Private School Ratio

One powerful force is tradition. All five countries have had large numbers of private schools in the past, ones sponsored by religious or ethnic groups. Most prominent in the Philippines have been Catholic institutions started during Spanish colonial times. In Thailand is the great array of Buddhist monasteries. Indonesia still has thousands of private Islamic schools. And Singapore, along with several of the other ASEAN members, has a background of private institutions sponsored by ethnic groups – Chinese, Indian, Malay, and English. Graduates of these private schools often form a significant force, powerful because of their numbers or their key positions in the nation's political-economic structure. The graduates' allegiance to their school and its mission motivates them to urge the government to offer the school preferred treatment or, at the very least, to tolerate its continuing.

Another factor is the ease with which the government can control the curriculum and staff of the private institutions. If the government feels sure that a private school will not deviate from the political direction of those in office, then the school has a better chance to survive than if it appears to teach ideas considered subversive. It was apparently a fear of subversion that caused the Indonesian government in 1966 to permanently close all Chinese-language schools following the attempted political coup by the Communist Party of late 1965.

Private schools can also save the government cost and bother by helping satisfy social demand for education at a time that the government is

299

too hard pressed to meet the demand from its own resources of funds and personnel.

Finally, private institutions may be valued for the high quality of their educational programs. In each of the ASEAN countries, certain private schools are noted for the high scores their students earn on national examinations or for the key positions in the society they enter after graduation. Where national surveys of educational achievement have been conducted, it would appear that private schools produce higher achievement even after their initial advantages of higher socioeconomic-status pupils and better teachers and facilities have been taken into account. And because children of the society's elite are often sent to such institutions, these schools are looked upon with favor by the elites that influence government policy.

Action Being Taken

In recent years there appear to have been no strong moves by ASEAN governments to alter in a significant way the private/public ratio that obtained in the late 1960s and early 1970s. Apparently this is because the conditions mentioned above are rather stable at present. The governments in power appear able to control the curricula through regulations and the inspectorate system, the larger private-school systems have strong supporters within the government policy-making bodies, and pressure of social demand — particularly at the secondary-school level — is relieved by private foundations and religious bodies sponsoring schools on their own initiative.

We recall from preceding chapters that particularly in the Philippines and in Indonesia private secondary schools serve a large segment of the population — 52 percent of Filipino high schools were private in 1970, while 48 percent of secular Indonesian high schools were private in the late 1970s (13 percent of them with government subsidies and the remaining 35 percent unsubsidized). Among Indonesia's large number of religious schools, primary and secondary, over 95 percent are private, with a substantial proportion receiving some public financial aid.

In Thailand and Singapore, a large amount of vocational education is offered under private auspices. For example, in the Thai informal vocational education sector under the control of the Ministry of Education there were over 100,000 students enrolled in private vocational schools while only slightly more than that in publicly supported programs in 1977.

In short, private schools are a highly significant part of education in the ASEAN region.

Prospects

There is little reason to believe that the pattern of private/public schools in the region will change in any significant way in the coming years unless the conditions described earlier are markedly altered. But if certain of these conditions should change significantly, we believe the effect on the private/public ratio is predictable. For example, if the governments cannot keep up with a rising popular demand for secondary schooling, then an increase in private secondary schools can be expected. If a sudden and widespread increase in Islamic fervor were infused into Malaysian, Indonesian, Southern Thai, and Southern Filipino societies as a result of recent events in the Middle East, then we might expect an increase in private Moslem schools. But if the doctrine advocated by a private system of schools appears to threaten the stability of a government in power, the restriction of the schools' activities or abolition of the schools would occur.

EXAMINATION AND CERTIFICATION SYSTEMS

Just as the graded school system was an importation into Southeast Asia from the West, so were certificates and diplomas. And today these evidences of academic achievement are important, widely adopted elements of ASEAN education systems.

The Goals

From the viewpoint of the society or government, a certificate symbolizes a level of expertise and as such qualifies its holder to enter a given line of work or to advance to a higher step in an educational or professional system.

From the viewpoint of the individual in the society, the certificate also symbolizes expertise and serves as the ticket of admission to valued occupations or higher educational opportunities. In ASEAN societies, as in other regions, diplomas and academic degrees in recent decades have increasingly replaced hereditary family titles as status symbols. This trend is in keeping with the modernization attitudes which accord more credit to what an individual has accomplished himself than to his family origins. However, the trend has also contributed to accusations that too many people seek the symbol itself – the certificate or degree – rather than the competence which the certificate is intended to represent. As a result, some educational institutions in Southeast Asia as well as in other parts of the world are charged with offering "cheap diplomas" that are awarded more on the students' desires of financial willingness than on merit. In addition, students are indicted for cheating on examinations, for not applying themselves consistently to their studies, and for falsifying records in order to get "the name without the game".

In effect, what the goals of certification and examination systems are depends upon whose interests one has in mind.

Conditions Influencing the Examination and Certification Systems

One of the key factors determining the nature of such systems is that of supply and demand. As the supply of a particular sort of expertise in a society is short of the demand, certification standards are relaxed. As the supply exceeds the demand, the standards are likely to be tightened. For example, Skolnik (1976, p. 60) has written that in Singapore the average rate of failures on the Primary School Leaving Examination in recent years has been about 50 percent. "The percentage of failures, however, is mostly a reflection of the number of students government is prepared to place in Secondary One (the initial class of the secondary school) and not a function of clearly defined and publicly stated standards of achievement necessary for promotion."

A second condition is social demand. If great political pressures are brought against the government by significant numbers of families that cherish diplomas, opportunities for earning diplomas will expand or else requirements for attaining diplomas will be reduced.

A counter force is the tendency for people who already hold a certificate or degree to want to maintain or stiffen the standards so only a restricted number of people can obtain certification. The tightening of standards can be motivated either by a sincere desire to improve the quality of education or occupational performance or by the less noble intention of enhancing one's own status by reducing future candidates' chances of certification.

Action Being Taken

Data from Chapters 2 through 6 lead to several generalizations about development in the ASEAN region.

First, there has been a trend toward instituting automatic- or social-promotion systems in primary schools so that children do not repeat a grade because of low academic performance, but they progress up through the grades after spending one year at each level. Such automatic-promotion practices were instituted in Indonesia, the Philippines, and Malaysia in the 1970s. However, recently Indonesian officials have expressed doubt about the wisdom of this move and have reintroduced promotion on the basis of performance so that there are once more repeaters at each level of the school system. However, a recent report of achievement in Grade 9 (Mangindaan, 1978, p. 49) has recommended strongly in favor of automatic promotion.

Second, all of the ASEAN school systems conduct examinations at or near the close of the primary and secondary schools, and certificates of completion usually are awarded on the basis of the examinations. One important function of the examinations is to determine who will advance to the next higher level in the educational hierarchy and which specialized track each student will enter.

Over the past two decades there has been some debate and confusion in the larger nations about whether it is better to have examinations written and corrected by a central authority or by regional authorities or local schools. Malaysia has held with the central-authority approach, while Indonesia in the 1970s turned the job over to the schools, using the central ministry in the role of giving advice about evaluation rather than preparing the tests itself. The Philippines has depended primarily on individual teachers' evaluations of pupils, with an occasional national assessment of pupil achievement made to reflect general trends throughout the country. In the British tradition, both Singapore and Malaysia at the secondary level use the "O level" (after fifth form) and "A level" (after sixth form) types of tests modeled on the overseas Cambridge examination plan. These tests are essentially screening devices used to determine who is qualified for certain further educational opportunities. When Indonesia still used national achievement examinations at the close of junior and senior secondary schools, the scores students earned on the tests were used for determining entrance to higher levels of the school system. But since schools have prepared their own examinations, upper-secondary and tertiary institutions have not trusted the schools' scores and have tended to give their own entrance examinations.

A significant trend in examination procedures throughout the ASEAN region has been the technical improvement of tests and better methods for assessing student progress in areas that are not readily measured by tests. More education systems are using computers to store good test items for easy retrieval (item banks), to score objective test papers, to summarize statistical results, and to feed back information on good and poor test items to the creators of examinations.

In summary, while changes in ways of evaluating pupils' progress have been effected in recent years, the awarding of certificates or diplomas at each level of the school system has continued basically unchanged, with the certificates continuing to function as important determinants of students' educational and occupational futures and of their social status.

Prospects

There seems to be no reason to expect the certification system to change basically in the coming years, other than to have standards tighten or slacken occasionally in response to the conditions described above. Diplomas and degrees appear to serve useful purposes in ASEAN societies, particularly within the modernization programs represented by national-development plans. However, we can look forward to improved methods of evaluating student achievement as a growing corps of technically skilled evaluators is taking over the leadership in this area in the ministries of all five nations and on examination boards of private school systems. Better teacher education in evaluation techniques and the increased use of computers for test construction, test correction, and item banking can upgrade the accuracy of judging pupil progress. Likewise, more frequent and accurate national assessments of the education systems can be expected in the next two decades so that the quality of schools of different types and in different districts can be appraised and improved.

Increasing Administrative Efficiency

Our speculation about administrative prospects will likely make better sense if we first explain a set of tacit assumptions underlying the use of the concept of educational administration in earlier chapters. We have assumed that *administrative structure* refers to the elements of the educational system and to the channels of power and communication that connect the elements. Examples of elements are the central ministry of education, provincial education offices, and individual schools. Each of these elements is also an administrative structure in itself with its own subunits and their lines of power and communication. For instance, within the ministry there are different bureaus or offices, and within the school there are classrooms and perhaps different academic departments or offices.

We identify channels of power in an administrative organization by answering the question "Who is in charge of whom?" or "Who causes whom to do what?" We identify channels of communication by answering the question "Who tells what to whom?" Usually the channels of communication are the same as those of power.

As illustrated in the chapters on separate countries, a diagram or flow-chart of an administrative organization pictures the elements of the system as small boxes connected by lines. Typically the boxes near the top of the diagram display elements that exert power over those farther down. The minister of education is near the top, the teachers near the bottom. The lines connecting the boxes are intended to indicate the channels through which power is exerted and through which messages are to flow.

305

Each element in the structure is assigned a set of tasks to perform for the good of the system. If the system is going to run properly, it is important not only for each element to perform its assignments well, but the jobs carried out by one element must be coordinated with those carried out by other elements to which it is connected.

So far we have been talking about administrative elements as if they were automatons that performed duties without human intervention. But obviously the elements are staffed by people, and how efficiently an element operates depends on the talent and diligence of the people on the staff.

THE GOAL

The central aim of administration is to promote effective learning in the schools and in nonformal programs. Administrative tasks include setting guidelines for the schools, monitoring how well schools do their instructional job, supplying goods and services to schools, identifying shortcomings and correcting them, and applying sanctions (rewards and punishments) that encourage staff members to behave with wisdom and perseverance. The measure of administrative efficiency is how well these tasks are carried out.

CONDITIONS INFLUENCING ADMINISTRATIVE EFFICIENCY

Although a host of variables affect how well the administrative system functions, we shall limit our attention to three we believe have been most important in the ASEAN region: (1) the size and complexity of the educational enterprise, (2) the availability of skilled, dedicated personnel, and (3) the efficiency of the information-supply system.

Even casual observation of ASEAN educational systems shows that Singapore's schools are administered far more efficiently than those of such large nations as Thailand and Indonesia. It is clear that the more schools and the more difficult the geography of a nation, the more the administrative problems to be solved. In the mid-1970s, while Singapore enrolled one-third of a million pupils in primary schools, Thailand was enrolling 18 times more (6 million) and Indonesia 60 times more (over

13 million). Thus, a chief cause for the greater efficiency of Singapore's administration was apparently the difference in the size and complexity of the school systems of these nations.

The factor of the availability of skilled, dedicated personnel was particularly important in determining administrative efficiency as the former colonial officials left ASEAN school systems and local educators took over the roles the officials had performed. To compound the problem, this transition occurred at the same time ASEAN countries were seeking to expand educational opportunities at an unprecedented rate. Inevitably the tasks of both teaching and administering passed into the hands of people who frequently were not well prepared for their jobs. In many cases this led to unfortunate consequences. Not only did they perform their assignments ineffectively, but often they sought to mask their lack of skill and knowledge behind a facade of officiousness and pomposity. In any large establishment there is always the danger of the petty bureaucrat who confuses his assignment with his own needs. Rather than seeking to serve the constituents as quickly and pleasantly as possible — with the constituents in this case being the schools — the inadequate administrator seeks service and honor himself. To show his importance, he makes those below him in the hierarchy wait for answers to questions, he denies them services, and he requires agreement with his opinions, even when the opinions are in error. Hence, an important element in the operation of ASEAN administrative affairs has been the skill and the attitudes of administrative personnel.

The third factor of particular import is that of the information-supply system. As already mentioned, the lines connecting boxes on an administrative flow chart are usually intended to represent channels for both the execution of power and the flow of information. If the flow of messages from the upper reaches of the system down into the districts and individual schools is inaccurate or slow, then school personnel do not know what the top officials want done or how to do it. Furthermore, poor communication from the top means schools lack supplies and teachers' pay is delayed, resulting in problems of morale and teaching effectiveness. If data at the school level are not collected accurately and transmitted promptly to officials in the upper strata of the system, educational planners cannot formulate sound programs to improve the quantity and quality of schooling. Bad data make for bad planning. Too often in the past, inadequacies in the information-supply system, both downwards and upwards, have contributed to inefficiency in the administration of ASEAN schools when planning has depended on coordinating activities of a central authority with those of individual schools.

ACTION BEING TAKEN

If need be, individual schools can run themselves without an administrative network linking them together. This has been amply demonstrated by the widespread array of private schools — mostly Moslem pondoks and Buddhist monasteries — that have evolved over the centuries in Southeast Asia. However, from the viewpoint of a developing nation in the process of modernization, such an individualistic, laissez-faire arrangement has three noteworthy disadvantages. First, it cannot assure that all schools are pursuing the common goals to which the nation is dedicated. Second, in a society that promises equal opportunities for education to all regions, a laissez-faire policy does not ensure that each region will indeed receive proper attention, for the existence and quality of schools depends entirely on the initiative of local people. Third, it does not make efficient use of talent and facilities that are in limited supply. A series of science-teaching units created by a clever instructor in one school is not made available to other schools. Each school cannot afford to publish its own textbooks, nor can each school keep abreast of improvements in the profession.

An obvious approach to counteract these disadvantages is to connect all schools into an administrative system that is directed from a central authority. This is the approach adopted by all five of the ASEAN countries. Not only do all public schools fall within the purview and authority of a central ministry of education (and of parallel ministries, such as the ministry of religion in Indonesia), but as noted earlier, even private institutions are bound by certain regulations emanating from the central office.

Centralization is obviously a mixed blessing. In addition to the advantages suggested above, it can bring the sorts of disadvantages that currently are posing problems in the ASEAN region. Centralized administration is less responsive to local needs and far slower to respond than is locally placed authority. Before local school personnel can receive equipment or act to solve a problem, requests must be sent up through the communication channels to the level of the hierarchy authorized to make the particular decision or provide the requested facilities. As it passes up or down the network, the message is often delayed for long periods, stalled in a pile of papers on a clerk's or official's desk. Such delays produce frustration, inefficiency, and loss of confidence in the system at the local school level. The four largest ASEAN members — Indonesia, Malaysia, the Philippines, and Thailand — have all suffered such administrative problems. Consequently, in each of the nations some measure of decentralization has taken place, motivated in some cases by conscious intent of the top authorities and in other cases by their self-admitted ineptitude. By *ineptitude* we mean that the centralized authority recognizes that it cannot manage a task itself, so it delegates the task to local officials to help ensure the task will be done at all, even though somewhat inefficiently. The national achievement examinations in Indonesia during the early 1960s are a case in point. At this time, the country's economic system was deteriorating so that transportation among the islands was increasingly untrustworthy and funds for publishing and distributing the nationwide achievement tests were in short supply. To make the best of this bad situation, the Ministry delegated to the provinces and their subdistricts the preparation of achievement tests, even though it was recognized that the quality of tests would now vary from district to district.

However, increasingly in recent years ASEAN educational leaders have been delegating more responsibility to provincial offices and local schools out of "conscious intent", that is, out of the conviction that the central office can do the task but that local officials can likely do it better. One disadvantage of a highly centralized system is that it discourages local initiative. It is a common observation that when villagers cooperate to build and support their own school, they have a greater commitment to its fate than when the central authority builds the school and maintains complete control over its operation. Hence, part of the decentralization move in recent years has been intended to revitalize local initiative, which both saves money and encourages bright local residents to create ways of solving problems, ways suited to local conditions.

One requirement for efficient decentralization is a training program for personnel who will staff district offices and local schools. All five ASEAN countries, often through such regional bodies as SEAMEO, have been exerting strong training efforts ranging from short-term workshops to degree programs in colleges at home and overseas. Thus, more highly skilled personnel have become available both in central ministry bureaus and in provincial education offices. As time passes, the less well prepared officials who were pressed into responsible jobs by the departure of colonialist personnel in the 1940s and 1950s are retiring, replaced by younger people with recent advanced professional training. More specialized departments and institutions, such as the Ministry of Education Staff Training Institution (MESTI) which opened in Malaysia in 1979, are being added. MESTI was established to train school administrators and professionals. Initially, the focus will be on headmasters and other administrative assistants. Thus the corps of capable personnel for the administrative structure is expanding.

Progress has also been made in collecting data from schools (enrollments, teacher supply, class size, test results, dropout and repeater rates, and the like), in transmitting the data to the central authority, in analyzing the data, and in applying it to plans for improving the schools' operations. The increasing use of electronic computers has contributed to this progress. More systematic evaluation is also beginning to be built in to the school building programs. Recently in Indonesia (Suharno, 1977) a formative evaluation was undertaken of the time-discrepancies in the building construction program of the Ministry of Education.

One result of improved evaluation and data-collection techniques has been that administrators know more precisely the magnitude of their problems and where the most serious problems lie. Administrators have always known the types of problems schools experience, for the types are recognized by observations of schools and complaints from teachers, headmasters, inspectors, and parents. But with accurate data-gathering and analysis, greater wisdom can be applied to deciding which solutions to attempt, where, when, and in what amount.

In summary, advances have been made in recent years in improving the efficiency of the administration of ASEAN educational systems through the improvement of skills among the personnel and the application of more advanced technology, both in terms of hardware (electronic computers) and such techniques as systems analysis.

PROSPECTS

In terms of the centralization–decentralization issue, we would expect in the future more decentralization by conscious intent as a greater number of capable administrators, evaluators, and planners are educated within the ASEAN region. In the past, the planning of curricula, the location of schools, teacher education, and the like have been located primarily in the central ministry, unless the inability of the ministry to perform these functions adequately has resulted in the task falling to local schools or regional authorities by default. However, such experiments as the regional research-and-planning centers in Indonesia's East Java and West Sumatran provinces suggest that more responsibility in the future will be delegated to districts so that needs unique to districts can be met more adequately. We can expect such decentralization moves in the future to stop or even reverse themselves under two conditions – if central authorities suspect regional personnel are deviating from the national government's political tack or if central authorities decide that regional personnel lack the professional skill or dedication to carry through the planning-and-execution functions satisfactorily.

Another development we would expect in the administrative sphere is the increased application of technological aids, such as computers and document-publishing techniques (photocopying, offset printing), and of administrative theory and practices from Western educational systems. But, it must be noted that some members of ASEAN societies have so resented intrusions of Western culture (foreign elements) into their own that they have blindly rejected proposed administrative innovations from the West, ignoring advantages these innovations might bring in terms of greater administrative efficiency. We would speculate that over the coming decades more research on matters of which adaptations of imported practices are most suitable to the ASEAN scene will come out of the five nations as the educational research capabilities in the region continue to grow.

Improving the Teacher-Supply System

THE GOALS

The obvious intent of the teacher-supply system is to ensure that all of the nation's classrooms and nonformal education programs are uninterruptedly staffed by highly skilled instructors. Three subgoals that contribute to this general aim are concerned with the recruitment, training, and placement steps of the teacher-supply system. (1) A large enough quantity of apt and motivated candidates will apply for teacher-education programs to ensure that the products of teacher education will be skilled, diligent instructors. (2) Teacher-education programs will efficiently equip candidates with up-to-date knowledge of subject-matter fields and teaching methodology that enables them to function as efficient guides of pupils' learning. (3) The job placement system for teacher-education graduates will ensure that all of the nation's classrooms are staffed by skilled instructors.

CONDITIONS INFLUENCING THE TEACHER-SUPPLY SYSTEM

The most important factor affecting the recruitment of apt candidates into teacher education is apparently that of the status or attractiveness of the teaching profession. In Southeast Asia, there is a long tradition of respect for the teacher or guru or monk. And during colonial times, the wages and prestige of teaching were high, since the occupation within the colonial structure paid well compared with most occupations that the indigenous people followed. However, with independence, more attractive occupations in government service, business, and industry have become available, and teaching has declined, particularly teaching primary grades at low salary in rural areas. Among types of secondary and tertiary schools, those preparing teachers are among the less prestigious today, and as such they do not attract the brightest, most ambitious young people.

Assessments of teacher-education programs in ASEAN nations have shown that many programs are not of high quality. For example, in the Philippines a large proportion of the graduates of the great number of private teacher-training schools fail the government examination for teachers. In some programs, the theory taught in the college is not closely linked to the practice of teaching in schools, a fault often due to the lack of skill and experience of the teachers-college staff members in applying the theory wisely to elementary and secondary classrooms. Furthermore, effective reading materials in teacher education printed in the national language of the nation are often in short supply. Each of these conditions has contributed to the low quality of certain teacher-training institutions. There is also a problem in ensuring that the content of teacher upgrading (teacher inservice education) courses is relevant for the practical teaching the teachers must undertake in their schools. Despite the good work of curriculum centers in revising or producing new curriculum materials, it is difficult to ensure that those responsible for the training in upgrading courses teach the new material. Typically, this is because the two groups — curriculum developers and inservice teacher trainers — come under different administrative authorities. However, the Curriculum Development Centre in Malaysia appears to be developing ways of dealing with the problem, mainly because a third of the budget for teacher upgrading comes under their jurisdiction.

In terms of teacher placement, three conditions are of special import. One is the placement of the teacher-education program in relation to the schools in which new teachers are needed. In general, the closer the teacher-education institution to the needy schools, the more likely graduates are aware of the job openings and are willing to take the jobs. A second condition is attractiveness of the setting in which the needy schools are located. A general problem throughout developing nations has been that of convincing youths educated in cities to return to the villages to teach in rural schools. Thailand, for instance, currently experiences an oversupply of teachers in large cities and a serious shortage in rural districts. A third condition is related to the recruitment issue described above. It is the motivation of youths in their original choice of teacher-training as a mode of education to pursue. For many youths, teacher training is a second or third choice for vocational preparation. They fail to meet the academic or financial requirements to enter a more attractive educational program, so they take teacher-training as a less desirable alternative, one which will lead to at least some type of diploma. When they graduate, their desire is not to become a teacher, but to use their diploma as a means for entering a more desirable occupation. Hence, they do not become placed as teachers because their original motive for entering teacher-education was improper.

In addition to the foregoing conditions, one overriding factor has been the rate at which new teachers have been needed. In periods of rapid expansion of schools, emergency teacher-education programs staffed by less capable instructors are not likely to turn out the most effective teachers. Such has been the case at certain periods in the growth of education in the ASEAN region.

ACTION BEING TAKEN

The most notable advance in ASEAN teacher education over the past two decades has been the increase in the amount of schooling teacher-education candidates receive in order to become officially qualified for their jobs. In most of the countries, a year or so of "normal classes" after primary school was sufficient to qualify as a primary-grade teacher during the latter 1940s and throughout the 1950s. Today, a special three- or four-year course at the upper-secondary-school level is required for a primary-school credential. In like manner, requirements for secondary-school teaching have advanced, requiring from two to four years of post-secondary teachers college study.

A second notable feature has been the increase in the variety and amount of inservice education for teachers. In the past, completion of a preservice course was considered enough to produce a "finished teacher". But today, preservice education in ASEAN countries is viewed as only the starting point. A continuing series of inservice experiences is seen as necessary to enhance teachers' skills and keep them up-to-date with recent improvements in teaching methods and materials. As a result, each ASEAN country has been sponsoring more active inservice programs, as illustrated by the examples in Chapters 2 through 6. The innovations in inservice teacher training through radio and booklet courses are worthy of note. They have built in formative evaluation, and within one to two years they should be operating reasonably efficiently.

The quality of teacher education has also been receiving marked attention in each nation. Efforts are being made to improve textbooks in the national language, to employ such technology as microteaching and simulation activities, and to increase the quality of practice-teaching experiences.

In several countries, salaries and fringe benefits for teachers have been increased in an effort to make the profession more attractive, so better candidates will enter teacher-training programs and graduates will

314

be willing to adopt the profession and remain in it. However, the low status of teaching, particularly the role of the teacher in remote rural schools, is a continuing problem. This remains true even after some ministries have added extra stipends to the wages of teachers willing to take posts in the hinterlands.

To solve the problem of teacher-training graduates not being willing to enter the profession, some nations have required one or two years of teaching service after graduation for each year of training the individual received at government expense. However, administering such a requirement has proved either difficult or impossible in the larger nations, so the regulation remains on the books but is seldom implemented.

An encouraging facet of the teacher-education scene is the growing amount of research and evaluation effort being directed at teacher-preparation problems in ministries of education and institutions of higher education. Over the past decade these activities, which include cooperative intercountry projects under SEAMEO and UNESCO, have contributed to improving teacher quality. Surveys of educational achievement (Mangindaan, 1978; Moegiadi *et al.*, 1979) have produced interesting findings, e.g. that women teachers produce slightly better achievement with their pupils than men teachers, that more experienced teachers tend to produce better results, that teachers with inservice training produce better results than those without such training, and that schools where the teachers hold regular staff meetings (an indicator of school efficiency?) produce higher achievement than schools which do not have staff meetings. These results need to be replicated and other surveys are currently being planned. However, as in all countries of the world, too little is known about teaching effectiveness in terms of what particular teaching behaviors and activities are most important for engendering high achievement and positive attitudes towards learning in the ASEAN region, and this is an area which will require a great deal of research within each of the nations.

PROSPECTS

We estimate that the trends of the 1970s will continue into the future. Higher standards of education will be held than in the past for teachers becoming certified, and an increasing quantity and variety of inservice programs will be developed both to upgrade poorly qualified teachers and to improve the skills of fully certified teachers currently in the classroom.

The quantities of teachers graduated from different countries' teacher-training programs will reflect the nations' differential staffing problems. For example, with Singapore's control of population growth over the 1960s and 1970s, the Institute of Education which is responsible for teacher education reduced its quantity of graduates. If population growth in Singapore continues at a low rate, a relatively steady, low rate of teacher-education graduates may be expected as well. Under such conditions, greater emphasis on improving the quality of graduates through more selective recruiting of candidates and more effective teacher-training methodology should be possible. The largest nation, Indonesia, can likely be expected to continue its efforts to produce large numbers of teachers through the established teacher-education secondary schools (for primary school teachers) and post-secondary colleges (for secondary teachers) as well as through emergency, shorter-term programs, such as the post-secondary course to graduate junior-high teachers. More effort can be expected in experimenting with different forms of inservice teacher education to improve the quality of teaching and of updating teachers for new and revised curricula. The types of approaches and accompanying evaluation could well be coordinated through agencies such as SEAMEO.

The same unevenness in teacher supply from the past will apparently continue in the future — a shortage of primary teachers in rural areas and a sufficiency or even oversupply in the cities, and a shortage of science—mathematics teachers at the secondary level and a sufficiency or over-supply in the social sciences. To solve these problems, the nations will likely offer more of the special incentives that some countries have tried in the past to attract teachers into needy areas — scholarships for teacher training and higher pay and fringe benefits (such as housing or a rice or clothing allotment) for people located in schools in remote regions.

Further research aimed at improving the use of new media, such as radio broadcasts and modularized self-instructional materials, and at bridging the gap between theory and practice in teaching, should increase significantly over the coming decades as the corps of well prepared personnel in teacher-education systems is enlarged. It is of interest to note that Indonesia and Thailand have already begun, in a coordinated way, research on the problem of teacher effectiveness and on ways of improving it in their involvement in the IEA "Classroom Environment: Teaching for Learning" project.

Intercountry Cooperation

The intercountry cooperation among ASEAN members continues to expand. As noted in Chapter 1, the main vehicle through which the direct cooperation takes place is the Southeast Asian Ministers of Education Organization (SEAMEO). The active members of SEAMEO at the end of the 1970s have been the five countries whose educational systems have been described in this book. Three others, referred to as "inactive members", are Cambodia, Laos, and Vietnam. (*Director's Annual Report,* 1977.)

Of the various institutions within SEAMEO there are three which are directly connected to schooling in the ASEAN region. These are the Regional Centre for Science and Mathematics (RECSAM) in Malaysia, the Regional Language Centre (RELC) based in Singapore, and the Centre for Innovation and Technology (INNOTECH) now based in the Philippines. In addition, the SEAMEO Nonformal Education Programme (SNEP) is now well under way.

RECSAM moved into its new buildings in Penang at the end of 1977. It continues to run its short training courses and regional workshops in science and mathematics for primary and secondary-school personnel from the five Southeast Asian countries. These training opportunities are primarily in the areas of curriculum development, teaching methods, and the production of teaching modules. A certain amount of research is also sponsored by RECSAM, such as in 9-to-13-year-old pupils' development of the concepts of volume, heaviness, speed, and movement of objects. RECSAM has recently become an Associated Centre of UNESCO's Asian Programme of Educational Innovation for Development (APEID) based in Bangkok, hence widening its network of cooperation. It also has established working relationships with national curriculum development centers in the region in order to consolidate regional cooperation in science and mathematics education.

RELC continues its training program of advanced courses at the postgraduate level in language education. It also conducts special intensive inservice courses for senior teachers of English and continues to offer consultancy services. Distinguished scholars from all over the world are invited to RELC regional seminars. Many of the professional staff members of RELC conduct their own research and development projects. As an institution, RELC currently is carrying out three major projects — English for special purposes, the teaching of French and other foreign languages, and the study of sociocultural factors in the acquisition of communicative competence relevant to the improvement of the teaching of national and official languages. RELC's publications programme is impressive, including an anthology series, a monograph series, occasional papers, and the RELC Journal.

INNOTECH continues its training programs of varying durations whereby it aims at accelerating educational change in the five countries "by developing a 'critical mass' of trained innovative thinkers and dynamic change agents". (*Director's Annual Report,* 1977, p. 69.) The general themes of the programs are concerned with educational planning, innovation, technology, cost-effectiveness analysis, and statistical methods. In the six-month program each participant conducts his own miniresearch project.

The research division of INNOTECH has undertaken four important programs:

IMPACT aims at providing a nonformal version of elementary schooling to all children who have dropped out of school in rural areas. This project is now being extended to new sites in both the Philippines and Indonesia. One purpose in the extension exercise is to make such schemes as self-financing as possible. This project should prove very important to Southeast Asia.

RIT aims at saving on per-pupil cost by reducing the time it takes a child to learn, so that the time saved can be used to provide learning opportunities to children at present denied them. This project is being conducted initially in Thailand.

NTR attempts to develop models for training teachers to prepare them for nontraditional roles in innovative educational settings. All five countries have indicated their interest in the NTR program.

CB-BLP (Community-Based Basic Learning Package) aims at reaching the out-of-school youth and adults with learning objectives relevant to community living. The Philippines, Indonesia, and Thailand will be participating in the project.

In order to disseminate information about its activities, INNOTECH also publishes a newsletter, journal, and technical reports.

The SEAMEO Programme in Nonformal Education (SNEP) provides an integrated plan for nonformal education in rural development, literacy, occupational training, and the use of mass media. The activities consist of action-oriented training and research programs connected with ongoing development projects, personnel exchanges, and clearing-house and information services. The overall objective is to improve the quality of life for the rural and urban underprivileged.

The typical funding sources for SEAMEO are reflected in the 1977 budget. In that year, SEAMEO operations cost over eight million U.S. dollars. Most of this money came from the member countries and the United States, Canadian, Netherlands, and Japanese governments. Smaller grants were furnished by bilateral agencies and foundations.

The Association of South East Asian Nations (ASEAN) has been far more active in the political and economic spheres than in education. However, in the late 1970s the association allocated funds for cooperation in educational programs and plans were being formulated in 1979 for specific activities. But the prospects for useful projects in the decade of the 1980s were at that time still unclear.

All five of the Southeast Asian nations are members of UNESCO and as such participate in all programs directed by the UNESCO Regional Office for Asia based in Bangkok. The regional office conducts training courses in country locations and by correspondence. The Office's projects and consultancies in curriculum development and in evaluation are excellent by UNESCO standards and indeed serve as a model for the rest of the world.

Finally, the major education research and development bodies of Indonesia and Thailand are members of the International Association for the Evaluation of Educational Achievement (IEA), an organization that includes 35 nations that engage in collaborative educational research. Malaysia at the end of the 1970s was also contemplating joining the association. The association sponsors a variety of research projects, such as national assessments of educational achievement, studies of teacher behavior and classroom management, and the collection of test items to

319

be located in an international item bank for use by member nations. Each project is of direct use to the nations in improving their educational efforts. In addition to conducting research programs, IEA also provides training sessions for personnel from member countries.

What, then, are the prospects for future collaboration among ASEAN educational systems? In light of the problems for the future described earlier in this chapter, there can be little doubt that the need for cooperation in both research and development is great indeed. When the ASEAN members have so many problems in common and the pool of experts and amount of funds in any one country are so limited, it would appear to make sense for them to increase cooperative efforts markedly in the decades to come. However, in view of the very limited level of collaboration and of funding of regional programs in the 1970s, the prospects for large-scale regional developments in the near future are not bright. The SEAMEO, UNESCO, and IEA activities of the 1970s were admirable and in the right direction, but more such cooperation appears warranted. In comparison to the magnitude of the countries' educational problems, the cooperative research efforts of the past have been very weak. It would seem that funding will need to be increased dramatically and that more high-powered projects with highly competent personnel will be required if significant progress is to be made toward solving the problems common to the ASEAN members. To ensure improved education for children in both formal and nonformal programs, there needs to be a stronger commitment on the part of the five ministries of education to cooperative research and development in education.

Thus, increased regional coordination in all sorts of educational efforts promises to enhance the five ASEAN countries' efficiency in furnishing a high quality of relevant schooling for the entire populace.

Postscript

As ASEAN educators turn now to the future, their endeavors would appear to require not only cleverness and sound professional training, but also the virtues Prof. Hatta proposed years ago — character and a strong nature, patience and a steadfast heart.

The Future

References

ADAMS, R. S. (1978) *Educational Planning: Towards a Qualitative Perspective,* International Institute for Educational Planning (UNESCO), Paris.
ATIKAH, S. (1977) "Evaluation of Home Technology (SMTK) Curriculum" in *Report of Intensive Course on Educational Evaluation,* pp. 27–32, BPPPK, Department of Education and Culture, Jakarta.
HALLAK, JACQUES (1977) *Planning the Location of Schools: An Instrument of Educational Policy,* International Institute for Educational Planning (UNESCO), Paris.
IEA and Its Activities (1978) Association for International Evaluation of Educational Achievement, Stockholm.
LEE, YUNG DUG (1976) *KEDI Instructional Strategies Project,* seminar paper, International Institute for Educational Planning (UNESCO), Paris.
LEWY, A. (1977) *Handbook of Curriculum Evaluation,* Longmans, New York.
LINDSEY, J. K. (1974) A Reanalysis of Class-Size and Achievement as Interacting with Four Other Critical Variables in the IEA Mathematics Study, *Comparative Education Review,* 18, No. 2, June, pp. 314–326.
MANGINDAAN, C.; SEMBIRING, R.; and LIVINGSTONE, I. (1978) *National Assessment of the Quality of Indonesian Education: Survey of Achievement in Grade 9,* BPPPK, Department of Education and Culture, Jakarta.
MOEGIADI; MANGINDAAN, C. and ELLEY, W. B. (1979) Evaluation of Achievement in the Indonesian Education System, *Evaluation in Education: International Progress* (B. H. CHOPPIN and T. N. POSTLETHWAITE, eds.), Vol. 2, No. 4.
MUSA, I. *et al.* (1979) *The Value of Technical Education for Modern Factories and Their Workers,* (mimeograph) BPPPK, Department of Education and Culture, Jakarta.
NASOETION, N.; DJALIL, A.; MUSA, I.; SOELISTYON, S.; CHOPPIN, B. H.; and POSTLETHWAITE, T. N. (1976) *The Development of Educational Evaluation Models in Indonesia,* International Institute for Educational Planning (UNESCO), Paris.
National Education Commission (1976) *Factors Affecting the Scholastic Achievement of Primary School Pupils,* Thailand National Education Commission, Bangkok.
POSTLETHWAITE, T. N., and KING, K. (1975) *Curriculum Development for Basic Education in Rural Areas,* Seminar Paper 18, International Institute for Educational Planning (UNESCO), Paris.
Project Soutele (1976, 1977) *Report on the Survey of Outcomes of Elementary Education,* Mahati, Rizal: Philippine Department of Education and Culture – EDPITAF, Vols. I–IV.
RELC *Director's Annual Report* Regional Language Centre, Singapore.
SKOLNIK, RICHARD L. (1976) *The Nation-wide Learning System of Singapore,* Institute of Southeast Asian Studies, Singapore.
Southeast Asian Ministers of Education Secretariat (1977) *Director's Annual Report,* Southeast Asian Ministers of Education, Singapore.
SUHARNO (1977) "A Plan and Its Implementation" in *Report of Intensive Course on Educational Evaluation,* pp. 71–78, BPPPK, Department of Education and Culture, Jakarta.

321

Schooling in the ASEAN Region

UNESCO (1976) *Education Building and Facilities in the Asian Region*, UNESCO Regional Office for Education in Asia, Bangkok.

UNESCO (1974) *Population Dynamics and Educational Development*, UNESCO Regional Office for Education in Asia, Bangkok.

Index

Abangan 19
Ability grouping 217–220
Academic curricula 8–9, 64–68,
    72–76, 109, 111–112, 114–115,
    126–128, 133, 158, 165, 200, 233,
    238, 255, 292–294
Administration, educational 14–16,
    67–69, 80–83, 86–89, 110–113,
    118–125, 139, 140, 151–157,
    162–164, 181–182, 194, 208,
    211–213, 231–232, 236–241,
    244–251, 258, 268–269, 284–288,
    305–310
Aims, educational 3–13, 54–56, 66,
    69, 72, 76, 80, 86, 104, 107–110,
    112, 129, 139–140, 157–158,
    160–161, 164, 168, 173–174,
    251–254, 260–271, 277–278,
    281–282, 284, 290, 292–293,
    295–296, 299, 301–302, 306, 308,
    311–312
Ajengan 60
APEID – Asian Programme for Edu-
    cational Innovation for Development
    317
Apprenticeship 32, 34, 161, 210, 264,
    289
Arabic language 11, 20, 60, 147, 188
Arabs 18, 27, 185
ASEAN xi–xiii, xvii, 1–46, 48, 184,
    208, 211, 216, 220, 273–322
Asrama 60–61
Assessment, educational. See Evaluation,
    educational

Association for Southeast Asian Nations.
    See ASEAN
Aziz, A. A. xiv, 98

Bahasa Malaysia. See Malaysian language
Beeby, C. E. 83, 95
BIOTROP – Research Training and Post-
    graduate Study in Tropical Biology
    43
Birth control. See Family planning
Birth rate xii, 16, 92, 199, 224–225
British colonialism 1, 49, 99–100,
    105–107, 184–197, 212, 214
British Council 88
Buddhism 10, 19, 24, 53, 60, 99, 223,
    228–229, 231, 295, 298, 308
Buildings, school 56, 69–72, 110,
    173, 198–199, 276, 285–287, 310
Burpakdi, C. xv, 41, 223, 225, 272
Burma 222, 224
Business education 8, 33–34, 175,
    232, 242, 256, 292

Cambodia 19, 222, 224, 226, 317
Catholics 20, 24, 53, 64, 106, 145,
    147, 151–152, 163, 189, 299
Certification 301–305
Character education. See Citizenship
    education
Chew, Tow Yow xv, 98
China 58–59, 106, 147, 185, 193–
    194, 196, 214, 225

Index

Chinese language 20, 23, 25, 126–128, 135, 188, 193–195, 197, 200, 202–208, 214, 216–218, 285
Chinese, Southeast Asian 4–5, 9, 12, 18–19, 21–22, 24–27, 65–66, 99–101, 105–106, 185–186, 189–197, 225–226, 228
Christians 5, 10, 19–20, 24, 52–53, 106, 145, 147, 151–152, 163, 189, 226, 298–299
Chulalongkorn, King 231–232
Citizenship education 4–5, 40, 110, 126–128, 137, 164, 166–167, 197, 219, 252–253, 261–263, 265–266
Class size 100, 142, 159, 207, 284–288
Classical curricula 9
Colonialism 1, 10–12, 18, 26–28, 30, 48–49, 57, 64–66, 81, 105–107, 145–146, 150–154, 184–197, 212, 227, 279, 291, 299, 310, 312
Communication arts. See Language arts
Communism xiii, 39–40, 52–53, 58–59, 184, 196, 299
Comprehensive schools 255, 294
Confucianists 19
Correspondence courses 161, 259, 289–290, 319
Cortes, J. R. xv, 145, 177
Cultural integration 201–208, 219–220, 227–229
Curricula 14, 56, 65, 68–69, 83–86, 106, 108, 110, 112, 115, 118, 125–132, 136–137, 139–140, 151–152, 158, 164–168, 175, 188, 197–198, 201, 209–211, 213–214, 220, 231, 251–256, 258, 266, 269–270, 277, 279, 281–283, 287, 299–300, 311, 316, 319

Development-school project 83–84
Dropouts, school 29–30, 77–80, 101, 114, 142, 159, 169, 209, 216–217, 275–276, 290, 295, 298, 310
Dutch colonialism 1, 23, 26–27, 30, 49, 51, 57–58, 64–66, 81
Dutch language 27, 65–66

Economic factors 1, 7–8, 10, 12–14, 30–37, 48, 53–56, 58–59, 93–94, 98, 100, 140–141, 148–150, 157, 171, 173–176, 182, 184–187, 206, 219, 223, 225–229, 254, 263, 265, 271, 274–280, 296, 298–300, 314–315, 319–320
Economic plans. See National development plans
English language 20, 23–25, 101, 105, 120, 126–128, 133–135, 137, 140, 152–153, 166, 185–186, 188–192, 195, 197, 200, 202–208, 214, 216–220, 231, 299
Ethnic influences xiii, 4–5, 9, 12, 14, 17–26, 42, 101–106, 110, 140–141, 147–148, 188–208, 220, 225–226, 279, 299
Evaluation, education 83–86, 112, 127, 132–135, 138, 153–154, 157, 160, 163–164, 167–169, 171, 209–210, 215–219, 251, 256–257, 269, 278, 281–292, 299, 301–305, 310, 314, 319
Examinations 14, 132–135, 171, 198, 201, 209–210, 215–219, 256–259, 268, 297, 299, 301–305, 309, 312

Family planning 55, 81, 92, 199, 212, 290
Feudalism 10–12, 26, 28, 30
Finance, educational 12–14, 29, 35–37, 56, 71, 78, 93–94, 112, 120–122, 139, 163, 171, 175–176, 194, 197, 225, 232, 246–251, 274–280, 293, 296, 299, 313, 319
Ford Foundation 88

General education 292
Geographical influences 9, 14–17, 48–50, 98–99, 146–147, 181, 224, 268, 276, 281, 306
Goals, educational. See Aims, educational
Goh, Keng Swee xv, 208, 217, 219, 227
Goh, Kim Leong xv, 181

Goh report   xv, 208, 217, 219, 227

Haji   188
Hatta, M.   57, 120, 273, 320
Hinduism   10–11, 19, 24, 53, 60, 99, 226
Humanities   8–9

IEA – International Association for the Evaluation of Educational Achievement   319–320
Illiteracy   55, 69, 80–81, 101–102, 118, 148, 150, 161, 174, 206, 216–218, 234–235, 241, 260–261, 278–279, 290
IMPACT   44, 176, 290–291, 318
Indian minorities   4–5, 9, 12, 18–19, 101, 105–106, 185–189, 190–191, 193, 226, 299
Individual differences, student   141, 216–219, 283
Indonesia   xi–xiii, 1, 5, 7–10, 12–14, 18–19, 21–28, 32, 37, 39–40, 43–45, 47–96, 138, 185, 187, 191, 213, 274–281, 285, 287, 290, 294, 297, 299–301, 303–304, 306–311, 316–319
Indonesian language   5, 51–52, 66
Informal education   288–289
INNOTECH – Centre for Innovation and Technology   43–44, 317–319
Inspectorate, school   122, 124–125
Islam   11, 19, 24, 27, 39, 52–53, 59–64, 87, 99, 101, 105–106, 119, 126–128, 147, 163, 187–188, 226, 298, 301, 308

Japanese   52, 65–66, 147, 150, 154, 186, 196, 279

Kampuchea. *See* Cambodia
Karachi Plan   13
Kiyai   60
Koran schools   59–60, 62, 187–188, 191, 214

Langgar   59–60, 62
Language arts   165–167
Language instruction   4–5, 23–24, 165–166, 189–197, 200–207, 210–211, 213–214, 217–220
Laos   222, 224–226, 317
Lee, Kuan Yew   186, 217
Libraries   137, 142
Literacy. *See* Illiteracy

Machmud, D.   xiv, 48
Madrasah   60–64, 69, 147
Malay language   5, 23, 51, 64, 66, 101, 105, 188, 191–192, 195, 197, 200, 202–208, 214, 216–217, 219
Malays   4–5, 9, 12, 18–19, 25, 36, 99, 101, 105, 147, 185–186, 189, 191–192, 225–226, 299
Malaysia   xi, xiii, 1, 4–5, 9, 11, 12, 15, 18–26, 28, 32, 36–37, 39–41, 43, 97–143, 185, 191–192, 213, 219, 224, 274–275, 291, 293, 290, 294, 297, 301, 303–304, 317, 310
Malaysian language   22–23, 101, 108, 126–128, 133–135, 137, 140–141
Manpower production   4–5, 7–9, 30–35, 109–110, 117, 120, 141, 148–149, 157, 164, 171, 173, 175, 182, 208–211, 213, 219, 227, 231, 235, 255, 264, 267, 269, 293, 295
MARA – Malay and Rural Development Agency   113, 117
Marcos, F. E.   157, 163
Mahakhan, P.   xv, 41, 223
Mastery learning   282, 285
Mathematics education   139, 165–166, 172, 213, 252, 316–317
Microteaching   138
Mobile schools   161, 242, 244, 247
Modernization   141, 149, 191–192, 234, 264, 302, 304, 308
Modules, instructional   83–84, 161, 277, 281, 297, 316
Moleong, L.   xiv, 48
Monroe Survey   153–154, 159, 192
Moral education. *See* Citizenship education
Mosbergen, R. W.   xv, 181

Index

Moslems 10, 19, 39, 105–106, 147, 163, 187–188. *See also* Islam
Multiple sessions 286, 288

Nasoetion, N. xiv, 48
National-development plans 1–2, 4–6, 9, 30–35, 42, 53–56, 69–92, 102, 104, 107–109, 120–123, 130–131, 149–150, 158, 164, 173, 183–184, 186–187, 195–198, 223, 233–244, 259–272, 275, 293, 304, 308
Netherlands East Indies 49, 57
Nonformal education 4, 80–83, 115–118, 150, 160–161, 174, 176, 209–211, 239–244, 264, 277, 286, 288–289, 293–295, 306, 312, 318, 320

Objectives, educational. *See* Aims, educational

Pakistanis 19, 226
PAMONG 44–45, 82, 92–93, 290–291
Pangemanan, F. xiv, 48
Pesantren 59–63, 290, 295
Philippines xi, 1, 5, 9, 15, 20–24, 28, 36–37, 41, 43–44, 144–179, 274, 281, 290–291, 294, 297, 299–301, 303–304, 312, 317–319
Pilipino language 5, 9, 24, 166
Political factors xiii, 1, 4, 10, 14, 38–42, 48, 99–100, 105, 150–152, 157, 184, 194–198, 211–212, 219, 223, 233, 236, 254, 263, 271, 296, 298–300, 311, 319
Pondok 59–63, 188, 226, 290, 295
Population: distribution, 14, 50–51, 100–101, 146, 181, 192, 227; growth rate, xii, 29, 76–77, 92–93, 100, 146, 175, 181, 183, 199, 215, 224, 274–280, 283, 286, 288, 290; size, xii, 14, 50–51, 76–77, 146, 181, 211, 224–225, 227, 274–280
Portuguese colonialism 57, 64, 99

Postlethwaite, T. N. xiii–xiv, 1, 84, 95, 273, 283, 321
Private schools 81, 112, 155–156, 158, 161–162, 169–170, 189, 190, 193–196, 199, 205, 226, 232, 239, 242, 246–247, 294, 298–301, 308
Promotion systems 14, 108–109, 167–169, 216, 303
Protestant Christian 20, 24, 106, 147, 163, 189

Quality of education xiii, 29–30, 56, 93, 139, 141, 155, 165, 170–172, 175, 278–284, 316
Quantity of education xiii, 28–29, 138–139, 141, 155, 170–172, 174

Racial influences. *See* Ethnic influences
Radio, educational 82, 90, 102, 142, 210, 220, 241–242, 277, 282, 289–290, 314, 316
Raffles, T. S. 184–185, 188
RECSAM – Regional Centre for Science and Mathematics 43–44, 317
RELC – Regional Language Centre 43, 317–318
Religious factors 9–10, 12, 14, 17, 19–26, 42, 52–53, 147–148, 151–152, 163, 185, 226, 228–229, 231, 239, 270, 290, 298–300, 308
Remediation 112, 138, 282
Repeater rates 77, 79–80, 153, 169, 303, 310
Research and development, educational 83–86, 93, 110, 120, 125–126, 215, 270, 283, 288, 292, 315–320

Sabah 98–100, 113–114, 136, 138, 141
Santri 60–61
Sarawak 98–100, 105, 113–114, 136, 138, 141
School size 284–288
Schooling: compulsory, 12–13, 28, 66–67, 112, 115, 232–234, 253, 267; structure and process, 3, 14–42;

universal, 11, 13, 14, 28, 50–51,
66–67, 69–70, 108, 154, 158, 186,
195, 198–199, 201, 211, 274–278
Science education   8, 70, 110,
112–113, 126–128, 133, 135, 137,
139, 141, 165–167, 172, 213, 231,
252, 261, 281, 308, 316–317
SEAMEO – Southeast Asian Ministers of
Education Organization   2, 13,
42–45, 220, 309, 315–320
SEARCA – Graduate Study and
Research in Agriculture   43
Sex factors   198, 205–206, 232, 279,
285
Sheikh   188
Singapore   xi, xii, 1, 4, 7, 9, 15, 18–26,
28, 32, 35–37, 39, 41, 43, 99–100,
135, 180–221, 268, 274–275,
285–286, 294, 297, 299–302, 304,
306–307, 316–318
SNEP – SEAMEO Nonformal Education
Programme   317, 319
Social class   10–14, 26–30, 51, 65,
109–110, 150, 174, 188–195, 200,
223, 227–228, 231, 234, 265–266,
268, 271, 279, 299
Social demand   4, 6–13, 36, 155, 158,
175, 235, 293, 299, 302–303
Social promotion   303
Social sciences   8, 40, 126–128, 133
Social studies   24, 126–128, 133,
165–167
Social welfare   1, 4, 6, 173
Soedijarto   xiv, 48
Spanish colonialism   1, 20, 57, 64,
145–147, 150–152, 169–170
Spanish language   151–152
Sports   197, 220
Streaming. *See* Ability grouping
Suharto   53, 59, 70, 81, 86–87
Sukarno   53, 55, 57–59
Supervision   250–251
Suryadi, A.   xiv, 48
Swanson survey   159
Syed   188

Tagalog   5, 18, 145, 148, 153
Tamil   22–23, 101, 106, 126–128,

135, 185, 188, 190, 192, 195, 200,
202–208, 214, 216, 218, 285
Tangyong, A. F.   xiv, 48
Taoists   20
Teacher education   xi, 16–17, 24, 33,
50, 54, 56, 89–92, 110, 119–122,
125, 127, 131–132, 151, 153, 165,
167, 169–172, 175, 190–191, 194,
196, 200–201, 206–207, 214–216,
220, 246–247, 251, 257–259, 276–
277, 279–280, 293, 305, 311–317
Technical education. *See* Vocational
education
Television, educational   142, 210, 215,
220, 241–242, 289
Textbooks   23–24, 30, 56, 70, 78,
106, 130, 142, 152, 164–165, 174,
194, 213, 236, 246, 251, 269, 280,
282, 296, 314
Thai language   5
Thailand   xi, xiii, 1, 5, 9–11, 15–16,
20, 24, 28–29, 36, 39, 41, 43,
223–279, 281, 287, 290, 294, 297,
299–301, 306, 313, 316–319
Thanarat, Sarit   233–234
Thomas, R. M.   xiv, 1, 8, 65, 96, 181,
273
TROPMED – Centre for Tropical
Medicine   43

Ulama   60
Underemployment   16, 31, 104, 140,
227, 264–265, 296
Unemployment   16–17, 31, 103–104,
157–158, 173, 175, 196, 264–265,
296
UNESCO – United Nations Educational,
Scientific, and Cultural Organization
45, 88, 282, 287, 315, 317, 319–320
UNICEF – United Nations International
Children's Emergency Fund   45
United States colonialism   1, 20,
145–147, 150, 152–154, 157,
162, 170, 177
Urbanization   16–17, 51, 100, 141,
147, 182, 279, 281, 286
USAID – United States Agency for
International Development   45, 88

Ustaz   188

Vietnam   19, 225–226, 319
Vocational education   8–9, 32–35, 55,
  64–68, 72–76, 80–83, 103,
  109–115, 121–122, 126–128, 135,
  141, 152, 158, 161, 165–166, 172,
  174, 187, 201, 208–211, 213, 218,
  223, 232–234, 238–244, 247,

255–256, 264, 275, 278, 289–290,
  292–295, 297, 300–301
Vocational training   292

Wachirawut, King   232
Wong, F. H. K.   xi
Work force   xiii, 14, 30–35, 103–104,
  149, 184
World Bank   91